D1592338

Fundraising and Institutional Advancement

In this timely textbook, authors Drezner and Huehls take the interdisciplinary, complex nature of the study of philanthropy and fundraising and apply it to the field of higher education. Covering issues of increasing importance to institutions—including donor cultivation, growth of fundraising at community colleges and minority institutions, engagement of young alumni, volunteerism, and the competing roles of stakeholders—this book helps readers apply theory to the practice of advancement in post-secondary education.

Special features:
- Coverage of historical and theoretical underpinnings and insights from related literature and research
- Discussion of new donor populations including women, communities of color, the LGBTQ population, students, and young alumni
- On-the-ground case studies bring theories into focus by creating a bridge to experience and action
- Practical implications for the design of fundraising campaigns and strategies
- Guiding questions that encourage students to think beyond the current literature and practice

This textbook bridges research, theory, and practice to help higher education administrators and institutions effectively negotiate the fundraising terrain and advance their institutions.

Noah D. Drezner is Associate Professor of Higher Education in the Department of Organization and Leadership at Teachers College, Columbia University. Dr. Drezner's book *Expanding the Donor Base in Higher Education: Engaging non-traditional donors* (Routledge, 2013) was awarded the 2014 Skystone Partners Prize for Research on Fundraising and Philanthropy from the Association of Fundraising Professionals (AFP).

Frances Huehls is Associate Librarian for the Joseph and Matthew Payton Philanthropic Studies Library at Indiana University-Purdue University Indianapolis and Associate Professor of Philanthropic Studies at the Indiana University Lilly Family School of Philanthropy.

Core Concepts in Higher Education

Series Editors: Edward P. St. John and Marybeth Gasman

Fundraising and Institutional Advancement

Theory, Practice, and New Paradigms

Noah D. Drezner and Frances Huehls

Routledge
Taylor & Francis Group

NEW YORK AND LONDON

First published 2015
by Routledge
711 Third Avenue, New York, NY 10017

and by Routledge
2 Park Square, Milton Park, Abingdon, Oxon, OX14 4RN

Routledge is an imprint of the Taylor & Francis Group, an informa business

Library of Congress Cataloging-in-Publication Data

Drezner, Noah D.
  Fundraising and institutional advancement : theory, practice, and new paradigms / Noah D.
Drezner and Frances Huehls.
    pages cm. — (Core concepts in higher education)
  Includes bibliographical references and index.
1. Educational fund raising—United States.   2. Universities and colleges—United States—Finance.
3. Universities and colleges—Public relations—United States.   4. College publicity—United States.
I. Huehls, Frances.   II. Title.
  LB2336.D74 2014
  379.1'3—dc23
  2014012396

ISBN: 978-0-415-51733-1 (hbk)
ISBN: 978-0-415-51734-8 (pbk)
ISBN: 978-0-203-12385-0 (ebk)

Typeset in Minion Pro
by Apex CoVantage, LLC

Printed and bound in the United States of America by Publishers Graphics,
LLC on sustainably sourced paper.

CONTENTS

SERIES INTRODUCTION

It is a pleasure to introduce a new book—*Fundraising and Institutional Advancement in Higher Education: Theory, Practice, and New Paradigms*—written by Noah Drezner and Fran Huehls. For far too long, researchers in higher education as well as those teaching in higher education programs have almost completely ignored the subject of fundraising and philanthropy, claiming that it is not central to the study of American higher education. These scholars are dead wrong. More than almost any other topic, fundraising and philanthropy are absolutely essential to higher education, and this importance is growing. Without the act of fundraising and philanthropic giving on the part of individuals, foundations, and corporations—like it or not—colleges and universities cannot survive. It is time to make the study of fundraising and philanthropy a core tenet of higher education programs throughout the nation.

When Ed St. John and I wanted to commission a book for our Core Concepts series, the only people that we could envision writing it were Noah Drezner and Fran Huehls. Noah has single-handedly written more about fundraising and philanthropy in higher education than any young scholar at this point. He has approached the subject using various lenses, including traditional approaches, diversity-focused approaches, and multiple methodologies. Fran Huehls is the premier librarian in the United States around issues of fundraising and philanthropy. She leads the library team at the Indiana University Lilly Family School of Philanthropy and compiles the largest list of resources on fundraising and philanthropy in the nation.

These two scholars have produced a book that gives even a novice in the fundraising and philanthropy area a well-rounded understanding of the topics. Drezner and Huehls provide both a theoretical understanding (which is a huge service, as the area is undertheorized) and practical understanding of the topics.

The book is useful to presidents, deans, philanthropists, donors, fundraisers, and those students and faculty members interested in exploring the topic and furthering our knowledge in this area.

I am thrilled to have *Fundraising and Institutional Advancement in Higher Education: Theory, Practice, and New Paradigms* in the Core Concepts series.

Marybeth Gasman
University of Pennsylvania
Series Editor

ACKNOWLEDGEMENTS

As I began to conceptualize this book and how I would frame the research on institutional advancement and the theories that are used to make sense of it, I immediately thought of Frances Huehls as the best possible partner for this project. Fran is simply the world's foremost philanthropic studies librarian and a great writing partner. Fran has written numerous literature reviews for the former *International Journal of Educational Advancement* and is at the core of the Philanthropic Studies Index, an important tool to locate information in our field. While this book in many ways was a daunting task, Fran's knowledge of the field and friendship made it a pleasure in many ways.

As a scholar and in my life beyond academe I am very fortunate to have so many people supporting me. I have a number of students that I work with formally and informally at the University of Maryland that inspire me as a faculty member in and out of the classroom. I am blessed to have had amazing colleagues in my time at the University of Maryland's higher education, student affairs, and international education policy program and the Center on Philanthropy and Nonprofit Leadership. And, as I begin my time at Teachers College, Columbia University, I already know how lucky I am to have Anna Neumann and Corbin Campbell as my colleagues and friends.

My work would never be what it is without its scholarly foundation. Thank you to my mentor and close friend, Marybeth Gasman—who just happens to be the series editor for this book.

Finally, I am so lucky to have family and friends who support me daily—even in the smallest ways. Thank you to my father, David, for his continued support in all that I do. Life is a journey, and up until just a few years ago, I felt like one aspect of my journey was solo, and then I met Oren Pizmony-Levy. My journey is no longer solo. Oren, thank you for making me feel like the luckiest man in the world. You make my scholarship stronger and my day-to-day life not only happier but also filled with love and new adventure.

Finally, while writing this book, I lost a person who was always there for me—even when there was a distance. My aunt, Judith Lippard, had always been there for me as an avid supporter in all that I did and to help me through the hard points in my life; I dedicate this book in her memory.

—**Noah D. Drezner**

Explaining the role of theory to students of research methodology has been one of my greatest challenges. There have been many times when I wanted to be able to hand them a text and say, "Here, this is where you can start." I am grateful to the series editors, Edward St. John and Marybeth Gasman, and to Routledge for making that possible and to my coauthor, Noah, for asking me along on this journey.

The inspiration and support of many were what kept the momentum going. To my last seminar—Amy Blackford, Liz Farris, Kim Kiser, Sonja Merrild, Robbie Morse, and Amy Conrad Warner—I give thanks for the chance to test-drive ideas for the book on thoughtful students. My librarian colleagues—particularly Meagan Lacy, Kathleen Hanna, Todd Daniels-Howell, and Brenda Burk—have been sympathetic and supportive through the research and writing process. A special thanks to Barb Duffy for reading and commenting on early chapter drafts. A book is truly the work of many hands.

The first person I knew in the field of philanthropic studies was Janet S. Huettner, the first bibliographer for the Center on Philanthropy at Indiana University. Her commitment to building a world-class library collection was matched only by her exuberant love of teaching. This book is also dedicated to her memory.

—**Frances Huehls**

PREFACE

As a subsector within the taxonomy of nonprofit organizations, higher education holds much in common with the rest of the nonprofit sector. The sector itself represents a diverse group of organizations whose missions run the gamut from arts organizations to human service organizations and sports clubs. Like other nonprofit organization subsectors, higher education represents organizational diversity in terms of public, private, and commercial forms. Despite all of these differences, nonprofit organizations share commonalities in areas of practice such as fundraising, marketing, governance, and leadership. This common ground shared by higher education with other nonprofit and philanthropic organizations extends to the multidisciplinary nature of both fields.

The nonprofit sector and philanthropy are studied across multiple academic disciplines, within the social sciences, humanities, and even the natural sciences. The interdisciplinary nature of the study of philanthropy is both a benefit and a hindrance to scholars and practitioners. Research appears in journals geared toward many different disciplines and professional and applied fields, and it is difficult for scholars, practitioners, and students to gain a full understanding of the many theoretical frameworks through which philanthropy and prosocial behaviors can be understood. Scholars publish their work in the academic journals of many fields and disciplines, including anthropology, biology, business, economics, education, history, marketing, political science, public policy, religion, social psychology, and sociology. David Horton Smith recognized that scholars, students, and practitioners could benefit from a systematic survey of the different theoretical approaches currently found in the academic and practitioner literature. In the first *Annual Review of Sociology* (1975), Smith challenged the field, stating that "scholars concerned about VA [voluntary action] research should consciously seek out cross-disciplinary inputs, both in terms of literature and other scholarly consultation/ collaboration/ communication" (p. 265).

In the years since Smith's recommendation, there has been progress in theory development for nonprofit and philanthropic studies. We can now point to a growing body of literature that reflects this growth. The first genre of literature is edited handbooks. Two editions of *The Nonprofit Sector: A Research Handbook* (Powell, 1987; Powell & Steinberg, 2006) presented and then built upon economic theory and theories of governance. Both editions of the handbook included chapters on higher education. The first, written by David C. Levy, focused on comparing private versus public education institutions. The second, written by Patricia Gumport and Stuart Snydman, examined the growth and diversification of higher education (public/private/commercial). Their goal was to relate nonprofit theory to the growth of the field overall, but they did not touch on theory of functions common to both higher education and nonprofit organizations overall—such as fundraising, marketing, and governance. An additional two-volume compilation on leadership, edited by Kathryn Agard (2011), includes five chapters on various theories of leadership.

The second genre of resources for studying theory is monographs containing sections of chapters or individual chapters that are specifically about theory. These include works such as *Improving Leadership in Nonprofit Organizations* (Kravis-deRoulet Leadership Conference, 2004), *Nonprofit Organizations: Theory, Management, Policy* (Anheier, 2005), and *Comparative Corporate Governance of Non-Profit Organizations* (Hopt & Von Hippel, 2010).

Finally, there are journals specific to the field of nonprofit/philanthropic studies that publish papers that are specifically about development of theory. The four that are most prominent are the *Nonprofit and Voluntary Sector Quarterly* (Publication of ARNOVA: The Association for Research on Nonprofit Organizations and Voluntary Action), *Nonprofit Management and Leadership* (Mandel Center for Nonprofit Organizations), *Voluntas* (International Society for Third-Sector Research), and the *International Journal of Nonprofit and Voluntary Sector Marketing*.

Resources that bridge the gap between higher education and nonprofit/philanthropic studies are very limited. Although Smart's *Higher Education: Handbook of Theory and Research* (2007) does address many areas of practice, it does not include the interface activities that are common to both fields. Kotler and Fox's (1995) work on strategic marketing for educational institutions is also a bridge but is limited in its scope. From 2000 to 2003, the *CASE International Journal of Educational Advancement* (Henry Stewart) and then, from 2004 to 2011, the *International Journal of Educational Advancement* (Palgrave Macmillan) published papers that bridged the two fields of study. However, that journal was closed in 2011. Beyond journals, a major body of literature, much of it unpublished, is dissertations. To illustrate this untapped resource, we have included a chart of dissertations covering a twenty-year period (1993–2013) as an appendix.

The literature of higher education points to weak use of theory and the desirability of grounding all research within a theoretical framework. The majority of this writing is directed toward graduate students and the dissertation literature review. Demonstrating understanding of theory and methodology is considered by many to be as critical to the dissertation literature review as thoroughly covering the topic (for example, Boote & Beile, 2005; Maxwell, 2006; Merriam, 2009; Randolph, 2009; Rocco & Plakhotnik, 2009).

Maxwell (2006) points out that the search for theory needs to go beyond the immediate topic, because relevant theory may be found in other fields and disciplines. Aside from needing to incorporate enough theory in a dissertation manuscript to obtain the needed signatures, why bother with theory? Is theory relevant for practitioners?

THE ARGUMENT FOR THEORY—WHAT IT IS AND WHY WE NEED IT

A basic definition of theory is that it is an explanation of how and why things happen (Best, 2003). It helps us develop explanations about how the real world appears (Bell, 2009) and can move us from a stance of being dead sure about something to a more objective view or a place where we will consider other viewpoints (Best, 2003; Nixon, 2004). To apply theory we need to learn how to think from multiple perspectives such as relationships and how society is organized (Best, 2003).

Understanding and relating to theory can be difficult when we are not able to connect it to our personal experience, when it seems irrelevant to our research findings, or when it seems to stand apart from action (Best, 2003; Nealon & Giroux, 2012). Part of this disconnection is the result of theory being defined within a specific context or because there are assumptions built into it that do not mesh with our situation. These assumptions may have to do with what we know (epistemology) and with how we perceive reality (ontology). Theory may also be historically located and reflect the era in which it was developed and even prescribe how we should live and behave (Best, 2003).

Despite what might seem like limitations, theory helps us to analyze what we are seeing and experiencing. It enables us to understand the meaning and intent of our actions—our own and others—and the possible outcomes and consequences of those actions. Theory helps us to evaluate by providing alternative choices and options. It can help us see that options we saw as black and white may not actually be mutually exclusive. Finally, theory provides the tools and common language to explain our position to others, which can be particularly important for developing practice (Nixon, 2004).

Nixon provided a scaffold for translating the use of theory from research to practice. He argued that there is an interplay between theory, thoughtfulness (which we interpret as reflective thinking), and practice. Theory is shaped by practice—through real-world experiences and shared understandings we develop theories about to try to understand. Reflective thinking creates the bridge between scholar and practitioner. He used the political theory of Hannah Arendt to explain this connection, saying:

> *Arendt saw thoughtfulness as a common human resource. Thinking, she maintained, is not the privileged preserve of professional thinkers, but the common heritage of all thinking human beings. Crucially, she argued, it is a deliberative process whereby we move backwards and forwards between a consideration of ends and means in order to decide upon the best possible course of action.*
>
> (Nixon, 2004, p. 32)

Thinking, particularly reflective thinking that involves suspension of judgment, is difficult. But Dewey (1910) told us that thinking and the thoughtful consideration of theory is a form of freedom. By allowing theory to guide our thinking, we can move beyond the ignorance of the gaps in our knowledge, beyond biases and mere reaction, to achieve higher levels of scholarship and practice. Theory gives us a mental surface against which to push and test our ideas and a common body of experience against which to weigh our findings.

PURPOSE AND STRUCTURE OF THE BOOK

The purpose of this book is to provide a coherent starting point for students, researchers, and practitioners to meaningfully incorporate theory into their work. Our intent is to provide a bridge from the theoretical literature of the nonprofit/philanthropic world to higher education research and practice. The published research that is used to illustrate and illuminate theory is also intended to suggest paths to finding additional research and theory. The development of theory for the nonprofit sector is ongoing. Consequently, students and others need routes to follow rather than canons to accept as the last word on theory.

The body of the text is composed of six chapters, representing areas held in common by higher education institutions and the nonprofit sector overall. *Fundraising: Theories of Motivation for Giving* examines a range of theories about why people give, such as altruism, identification theories, relationship development, and social exchange. The chapter *Grounding Institutional Marketing in Theory* complements the frameworks presented on fundraising with an emphasis on the theories that guide institutional relationship development and branding. Because of the close relationship between these two areas, we recommend that these two chapters be read as a unit. The third chapter, *Boards of Trustees and Philanthropy*, incorporates a growing body of theory development in the nonprofit literature. The major frameworks discussed are agency and its subsidiary theories, resource management theories, institutional theory, and integrated approaches. *Leadership for Philanthropy* goes beyond transactional versus transformational paradigms to examine research on servant, authentic, shared, and leader-member exchange theories. *Youth and Student Volunteerism and Philanthropy* presents theoretical frameworks surrounding social participation and about how and why young people become engaged in giving and volunteering. Each of these five chapters utilizes published research studies to illustrate application of theory and suggests directions of additional inquiry that are needed. The chapters conclude with a case study, discussion questions, and exercises designed to deepen the understanding of the theories presented. We hope that the case studies will bring the theories into focus by creating a bridge to experience and action.

The sixth chapter, *Social Identity and Philanthropy*, presents avenues of inquiry that have not been much pursued by either higher education or nonprofit/philanthropy research. Here, we explore frontiers for theory development based on social identities including ability, race, gender, and sexual orientation. Although there is a rich base of theory to work with, to date there has been little work that applies these concepts to giving and volunteering behaviors of marginalized populations. We conclude with thoughts on how to move forward a research agenda that embraces the use and development of theory in all of these areas.

1

FUNDRAISING

Theories of Motivation for Giving

Advancement offices at colleges and universities are tasked with motivating alumni and friends of the institution to give voluntary support. The questions of why donors give freely and how to encourage them to make annual and major financial contributions are the basis of building good fundraising strategy. What motivates alumni and other donors to make financial contributions to their alma mater has been a topic of a lot of research stemming from multiple disciplinary perspectives. In this chapter we explore the literature that grounds the study of philanthropy and philanthropic behavior in theory.

We present the theoretical frameworks that guide most of the research on philanthropy and fundraising. Scholars from the disciplines of economics, psychology, and sociology have all contributed to our understanding of philanthropic motivations. In this chapter we explore different perspectives of the public- and private-good models and the psychological and sociological paradigms that scholars have put forward to explain why people give.

As we begin this literature review, it is important to note that most of the theories that currently exist to explain philanthropic motivations were created using research that almost exclusively looked at the giving of wealthy White men. Therefore, most of the literature that is reviewed in this chapter does not take into account the diverse cultural approaches enacted in communities of color and often among women. Where possible, we have included theoretical approaches that engage populations other than wealthy White men.

MOTIVATIONS

Myriad reasons exist for people giving of themselves and their wealth through volunteerism and philanthropy. There is a debate if there is such a thing as true altruism. Most scholars find that philanthropic gifts and prosocial behaviors are motivated by a blend of altruism and self-interested motives, or impure altruism. Forms of impure altruism vary, with donors thinking of themselves and their self-serving interests obviously varying. Some gifts are given out of a motivation to receive recognition, whether it is for access to networking opportunities, to receive tax deductions, or to see their name etched into building or on an endowed professorship. In its extreme forms, these self-interested types of giving are forms of egoism.

Mutual benefit is a more nuanced motivation for giving. Within a philanthropic and volunteerism context, mutual benefit is when the donor or volunteer receives either some level of intrinsic or extrinsic gain from their action to assist others, while the recipient of the donation of time or wealth benefits as well. Even donors whose giving is considered highly altruistic and recipient-oriented—for example, the 2009 anonymous donor who gave $70 million to 12 institutions led by female presidents with the caveat of total anonymity, not just to the public, as is typical for anonymous gifts, but to the entire institution, including the president—likely still derive some personal benefit in the form of a sense of self-worth or, as Andreoni (1989) called it, a "warm glow." There are many forms of benefit that donors receive in recognition of their financial contributions, including a listing in the annual report, naming of an endowed scholarship, entrance to an exclusive event, a small thank-you gift, or the tax deduction.

Within the context of volunteerism, Clary and Snyder (1990) found, like with financial giving, that volunteers are motivated by a combination of altruism and personal benefit. The personal benefit that volunteers often receive is a form of personal growth— for example, joining a group of colleagues or aspirational peers, learning or enhancing a skill, or even assuaging some form of guilt. As with monetary gifts, the level of egoism and altruistic intentions vary among individuals and situations.

PUBLIC-GOOD/PURE ALTRUISM MODEL

One of the most frequently given reasons explaining why a person engages in different forms of prosocial behavior is out of a want to help others (Piliavin & Charng, 1990). This is the concept of altruism. Roberts (1984), using an economic lens, defines altruism as "the case where the level of consumption of one individual enters the utility function of the other" (p. 137). In other words, altruism exists when the donor or volunteer disregards his or her own self-interest in order to help others. This idea of selflessness has been studied widely in many academic disciplines including economics (Bergstrom, Blume, & Varian, 1986; Ribar & Wilhelm, 2002; Roberts, 1984; Sugden, 1982; Warr, 1982, 1983), sociology (Piliavin & Charng, 1990; Simmons, 1991; Wilson, 1975), and social psychology (Berger & Smith, 1997; Ling et al., 2005; Weyant & Smith, 1987).

Many economists argue that philanthropic giving lies within the **public-good model**. The economic principle of public good assumes that a need, or good, that is consumed by an individual does not reduce the good for others. In other words, a public good does not lie within a zero-sum game. Economists argue that a philanthropic donor gives of him or herself out of an altruistic concern to maximize the public good among others.

The concept of public good and pure altruism only allows for giving to offset a direct need rather than supplement a need. In other words, an increase in one person's (or the government's) contribution results in a decrease of other people's (or the government's) contributions (Sugden, 1982; Vesterlund, 2004). The economic concept of crowding out, in its simplest form, explains that the reduction of private investment in a public good occurs because of an increase in government spending on that good. Using this concept, Roberts (1984) and Warr (1982) found that, theoretically, government contributions to nongovernmental organizations (NGOs) and other nonprofits supporting public goods would "crowd out" private contributions dollar for dollar. Neil Levy (2006), in his essay on philanthropic giving in Australia, contends that philanthropy has the ability to crowd out the government's responsibility to its citizens.

PRIVATE-GOOD MODEL

Identification Model

Many studies on the motivations of donors have found that there is an aspect of the donor's 'self' in the decision to engage in the philanthropic behavior (Aaker & Akutsu, 2009; Drezner, 2013a; Jackson, Bachmeier, Wood, & Craft, 1995; Martin, 1994; Oyserman & Destin, 2010; Schervish, 1993, 1995, 2003; Schervish & Havens, 1997). Schervish and Havens (1997) find that many donors see themselves in "the needs and aspirations of others" (p. 236). Jackson et al. (1995) find many voluntary gifts are made out of "the sense of being connected with another or categorizing another as a member of one's own group" (p. 74); they refer to this as "we-ness." In other words, when donors identify with a cause, this identification can trigger their motivation to give. This "we-ness" can take many forms, including kinship within groups of shared social identity (race, religion, gender, sexuality) or other shared identities. For example, within higher education, this shared identity can be in the form of former scholarship recipients. According to the **identification model**, an alumna who received a scholarship might decide to give a gift toward a scholarship to a student at her alma mater, while recognizing that she might not be as successful as she is, had not someone done the same for her (Monks, 2003). According to Martin (1994) there is mutual benefit to prosocial behavior, as "philanthropy unites individuals in caring relationships that enrich giver and receiver alike" (p. 1).

The identification model is based on Becker's (1974, 1976) **rational utilitarianism theory**. Becker's theory holds that pure altruism does not exist, arguing that while many who give of themselves have a desire to improve an aspect of society, donors are also motivated by forms of peer pressure, or extrinsic motivations "to avoid the scorn of others or to receive social acclaim" (1974, p. 1083). Schervish and Havens (1997) believe that Becker is pointing to a level of 'selfless' that is found within altruism. They note that this motivation is actually "grounded in a form of mutual self-interest" or, as Becker describes it, "multi-person altruism" (p. 237).

Schervish and Havens (1997) argue that the identification model encompasses five theoretical interrelated clusters:

(1) models and experiences;
(2) communities of participation;
(3) frameworks of consciousness;
(4) direct requests; and
(5) discretionary resources.

According to their model, a donor's experiences lead to a personal moral ideology. This moral ideology then affects the donor's participation in an organization based on his or her belief in the group's mission and the fact that the solicitation for support occurs within communities of participation. Finally, the amount that a donor gives is subjective and connected to disposable income.

Schervish and Havens (1997) used the 1992 National Survey of Giving and Volunteering (Gallup, 1992) through the lens of **identification theory**. Interestingly, they found that giving behaviors were more closely related to the donor's current communities of participation than his or her prior experiences. Yet, Jackson et al. (1995) found that religious participation increased philanthropic behaviors toward secular organizations. Jackson and colleagues' finding was more significant among those who defined themselves as actively involved in the church (p. 74). The influence of religion is not surprising, as charity and philanthropy are the cornerstones of all of the world's religions (Gasman, Drezner, Epstein, Freeman, & Avery, 2011).

Scholars have regularly found the concept of community to be an important motivation for giving. Martin (1994) defines community as "any group of people joined by shared caring, both reciprocal caring in which they care about the well-being of members of the group and of caring for the same activities, goals, or ideals" (p. 26). Within his definition of community is the idea of reciprocal caring relationships. Within a philanthropic context, this definition of community allows for a donor to have some reciprocal benefit, even when giving anonymously or when giving to someone the donor might not know.

Sugden (1984) refers to this as **reciprocity theory**. Within a higher education context, this concept of a reciprocal benefit is often espoused. One example is annual fund solicitations; often universities remind alumni, especially young alumni, that part of the *U.S. News & World Report* rankings is tied to alumni participation in giving. Therefore, development offices argue, by giving even small amounts or "participation gifts" to their alma mater, alumni might help increase the university's ranking and thereby the value of their degrees.

Many economists have considered the motivation for giving beyond the position of the public goods theorists who emphasize altruism. These economists argue that some donors give for private-good benefits (Andreoni, 1989, 1990, 1998; Cornes & Sandler, 1984; Palfrey & Prisbrey, 1996, 1997; Steinberg, 1987; Sugden, 1984). As mentioned earlier, Andreoni (1989) argues that philanthropic giving and volunteerism often provides the donor or volunteer with a "warm glow" (p. 1448). In economic terms, that **warm-effect theory** is an additional personal utility that a donor receives from engaging in prosocial behavior.

Andreoni (1988, 1989, 1990, 1998) refers to this as impure altruism. Andreoni's studies disagree with Roberts's (1984) and Warr's (1982) findings. He found that government's crowding-out effect is incomplete and that those who give to the public good do so for two reasons, one to increase the public good and the other to receive some aspect of private good from their gift (Andreoni, 1998).

Impact Philanthropy Model

Understanding both public- and private-good motivations for philanthropic behavior, Duncan (2004) suggested that some donors have an extreme desire to "make a difference" (p. 2159) with their philanthropy. Duncan refers to these donors as "impact philanthropists." Others have called this type of philanthropy "venture philanthropy" (Boverini, 2006). This recent philanthropic movement is associated with donors providing not only the means but also the expertise, typically in the area of organizational capacity building (Boverini, 2006). Similar to those who might give in order to create change, some donate to repair what they view as injustice (Drezner & Garvey, forthcoming).

SOCIAL PSYCHOLOGICAL PERSPECTIVES

Relationship Marketing

Relationships are the key to fundraising. Therefore, **relationship marketing** and s**ocial exchange theory** are often noted as conceptual foundations to understanding fundraising and philanthropic giving. The relationship fundraising model in development is derived from marketing theory (Burnett & International Fund Raising Group, 1992; Burnett, 2002; Kelly, 1998). Relationship marketing, defined as "establishing, developing, and maintaining successful relational exchanges," (Morgan & Hunt, 1994, p. 20) is one of the most prevalent models for engagement and fundraising. In other words, in the context of higher education, relationship marketing is the idea of establishing long-term relationships with alumni and friends in order to engage them and maintain their loyalty, involvement, and donations (Gamble, Stone, Woodcock, & Foss, 1999; Kotler, 1997; McKenna, 1991). Relationship marketing within the corporate world is predicated on the benefit of customer retention and a customer's lifetime value to a company (Buttle, 1996; Sargeant & McKenzie, 1998). The idea of customer retention—or within a non-profit context, retaining donors—is easily combined with the idea of **continuity theory**, borrowed originally from the medical world, which states that repeated actions are more likely to be continued and sustained (Atchley, 1989). Relationship marketing and continuity theory suggest, and have shown, that those who have established giving relationships are likely to give repeatedly (Lindahl & Winship, 1992; Okunade & Justice, 1991; Piliavin & Charng, 1990).

Relationship building between the institution and its current and prospective donors is one of the most important aspects of successful engagement and solicitation of the largest, or leadership, gifts. In the past, fundraising offices relied on transaction-based marketing rather than on sustained relationships. Transaction-based marketing within fundraising means a series of one-time transactions, or each year, donors were asked to give and then not engaged until the next 'ask.' Relationship marketing theory changes fundraising strategy from a series of one-time transactions to a focus on donor lifetime value and continued engagement (Sargeant & McKenzie, 1998).

Social Exchange Theory

Social exchange theory is another popular theory to explain philanthropic giving. Similar to the concept of mutual benefit, social exchange theory is based on the belief that "voluntary actions of individuals . . . are motivated by the returns they are expected to bring and typically do in fact bring from others," such as social recognition (Blau, 1992, p. 91). A number of scholars apply social exchange theory to philanthropic and volunteer motivations (Cook & Lasher, 1996; Gächter, Fehr, & Kment, 1996; Hollander, 1990; Kelly, 1991). Hollander (1990) and Gächter, Fehr, and Kment (1996) investigated the effects of social approval on voluntary actions. Gächter et al. (1996) used a controlled experiment and found that among strangers, social exchange theory is not effective in increasing voluntary cooperation. However, among groups of people that know each other, Gächter, Fehr, and Kment found an effect—increased participation and giving. They posit this was because of the influence of wanting acceptance and a level of social exchange with those they know.

The power within the relationships that are being built is important. Kelly (1991) states, "Fundraising predominantly involves a social exchange relationship between a charitable organization and a donor, in which the power of each relative to the other determines the outcome of the exchange" (p. 199). Within a higher education context, Cook and Lasher (1996) built upon Kelly (1991), and their study advances the idea of how different university players including presidents, trustees, volunteers, deans, and advancement professionals engage donors in different ways in order to connect the university and donors' needs. This idea of leadership within philanthropy and fundraising in higher education is further discussed in Chapter 5.

Cook and Lasher (1996) and Kelly (2002) use social exchange theory to explain the interdependent relationship that exists between an alumnus or alumna and the alma mater. Under Cook and Lasher (1996) and Kelly (2002) models, donors give when they realize that their interests align with the needs and interests of the institution. Kelly (2002) finds that, "based on social-exchange theory, the mixed motive model of giving describes two levels of donor motivation: (1) raising the amount of common good . . . and (2) receiving some private good in return" (p. 46). These mixed motives, evident in social exchange theory, align with the intrinsic (internally driven) and extrinsic (imposed from the outside) influences on prosocial behavior in Harbaugh's (1998) work.

Social Identity Theory and Organizational Identification

Organizational identification, a part of **social identity theory**, occurs when an individual defines him or herself by an organization. In the context of higher education, "I am a student at . . ." or "I am an alumna of . . ." are good examples of the embodiment of organizational identification (Ashforth & Mael, 1989; Mael & Ashforth, 1992). Mael and Ashforth (1992) suggest that college and university alumni conceptualize organizational identification perfectly because: (1) college can be considered a "holographic organization" (Albert & Whetten, 1985), that is, one where members share common organization-wide identity and are less likely to experience competing demands from, say, department-level or occupational identities, and (2) since alumni constitute a particularly critical source of support for colleges, alumni identification is likely to strongly affect the welfare of their respective alma maters. (p. 104)

Mael and Ashforth (1992) find aspects of both the institution and the individual that feed into a graduate's organizational identity. They propose that this identity then leads to a possible "organizational consequence" of the individual supporting his or her alma mater (Figure 1.1). Using social identity theory as a basis, Mael and Ashforth (1992) posit that alumni identification corresponds to philanthropic giving, participation in alumni reunions and events, and recruitment of others to attend the institution. Beyond different forms of alumni participation, Mael and Ashforth (1992) found that organizational characteristics including the perception of institutional distinctiveness and prestige have positive effects on organizational identity. Further, competition between institutions increases alumni identity. Similarly, institutional traditions influence alumni contributions (Leslie & Ramey, 1988). However, Mael and Ashforth also find that competition within an institution for alumni identity and participation has a negative effect. For example, if multiple departments or offices compete for alumni support without an organized full-institutional effort, alumni participation falls.

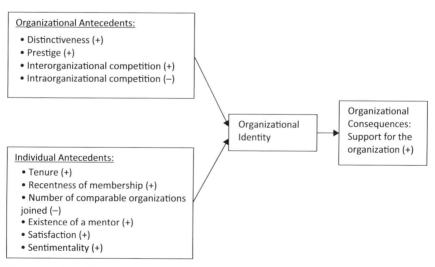

Figure 1.1 Proposed correlates of organizational identification

Additionally, beyond organizational characteristics, Mael and Ashforth (1992) identify individual characteristics that can affect a person's organizational identity. They find
that time spent at the institution, the existence of a mentor, overall satisfaction, and perception of one's own time at the college—sentimentality—all have positive effects. How
recently a graduate has had a positive experience with the alma mater also affects the person's organizational identity. However, those with more than one degree from multiple
institutions often have a weaker organizational identity with each institution than those
who attended only one university. This suggests that organizational identity has some
aspects of being a zero-sum game. Figure 1.1 pulls together Mael and Ashforth's (1992)
model. They conclude that having a positive institutional identification leads alumni to
donate to their alma mater.

The concept of organizational identity might change based on institutional type or
mission. For example, minority-serving institutions perhaps have a better opportunity
to create the personal and organizational identity that Mael and Ashforth (1992) suggest.
Gasman and Anderson-Thompkins (2003) find that:

> For many Black-college alumni, the bond to alma mater is formed long before they
> arrive on campus—especially in the case of legacies . . . The college is "alma mater"
> in the truest sense because it nurtured them much like a mother and gave them skills
> that they might not get elsewhere in a White-dominated society. If nurtured and
> re-kindled regularly, the surrogate parent image can be beneficial to institutional fund
> raising; if neglected, it can be devastating to alumni giving.

(pp. 37–38)

Drezner (2008, 2009, 2011, 2013a) finds that it is this "bond to alma mater" that develops
and enhances organizational identity through stimulating the interest of students while
they are enrolled at member institutions. There is a gap in the current literature in that
organizational identity within a philanthropic context has not been looked at beyond
historically Black colleges and universities (HBCUs) when it comes to institutional types.

Others expand Mael and Ashforth's findings to include student involvement. For
example, Miller and Casebeer (1990) find that the more a student is involved in college
activities, the larger positive effect there is on alumni giving. This was also supported by
Gaier (2005). He finds that "alumni who participated in at least one formal student activity during the undergraduate experience were 87 percent more likely to give" (p. 285)
than those who were not engaged as students. Others find that participating in alumni
activities can increase philanthropic giving (Bruggink & Siddiqui, 1995; Hunter, Jones, &
Boger, 1999; Mosser, 1993; Taylor & Martin, 1993; Young & Fischer, 1996). Moreover, Leslie and Ramey (1988) show that the economic success of alumni factors into two decisions
related to giving. Perhaps not surprising, financial success increases one's ability to give.
However, more interesting, Leslie and Ramey (1988) find that economic success increases
a person's interest in supporting his or her alma mater as well. Others find that emotional attachment between a graduate and his or her institution was a positive influence

on contributions (Brittingham & Pezzullo, 1989; Mosser, 1993; Spaeth & Greeley, 1970). Finally, alumni academic success and overall happiness with their student experience also increases the likelihood of alumni gifts (Gaier, 2005; Miller & Casebeer, 1990).

Model of Personal Donorship

Related to social exchange theory and organizational identity is Mount's (1996) **model of personal donorship**. Mount's theory posits that donors base how much they give on five criteria: (1) involvement in the organization; (2) the importance and alignment of the nonprofit's mission with respect to the donor's philanthropic interests; (3) self-interest; (4) the donor's disposable income; and (5) past giving behaviors. Additionally, Mount's research shows that tax incentives have only a nominal impact on whether and how much a person gives.

Aligned with Mount's model of personal donorship's criteria, involvement with the organization, the amount spent on a donor's involvement plays a role in engagement. William Harrison (1995), in his article entitled "College relations and fund-raising expenditures: Influencing the probability of alumni giving to higher education," predicted the probability of alumni giving based on the amount of money spent on fundraising and alumni relations. Using statistical modeling, Harrison showed that the old adage that "you have to spend money to make money" is true for alumni fundraising. He found that an increase in alumni relations spending of as little as $10 per current student could increase alumni participation from 25 percent to 26.4 percent, which could be a significant increase in dollars raised.

Justice Motivation Theory

Another theory to explain philanthropic giving is **justice motivation theory**. Justice motivation theory posits that the urge to fix an injustice motivates some people to engage in action (Lerner, 1975; Miller, 1977). Warren and Walker (1991) applied justice motivation theory to philanthropic giving in a study of mail solicitations in Australia and found that

> *if people witness undeserved suffering their "belief in a just world" is threatened; consequently they are motivated to restore their faith . . . this motivation may lead to helping behavior, but only if the person believes their actions will be of real and permanent help.*

(Warren & Walker, p. 328)

Warren and Walker's (1991) findings suggest that a solicitation within higher education needs to have a more complex case for support than just showing a need. For example, when considering a direct mail solicitation of a scholarship, according to their findings, the solicitation should not only build a case for support of the scholarship—the increasing need for the university to help with tuition costs—but also show how the gift will have a lasting impact on the students receiving the scholarship and on the institution.

Prosocial Behavior

Stemming from the discipline of psychology is another notable theory to explain philanthropic motivations, **prosocial behavior theory** (Clark, 1992; Dawes, Van de Kragt, & Orbell, 1990; Diamond & Kashyap, 1997; Hogg, 1987; Midlarsky, 1971; Piliavin, Dovidio, Gaertner & Clark, 1981; Schwartz & Ben David, 1976). Eisenberg and Mussen (1989) define prosocial behavior as "voluntary actions that are intended to help or benefit another individual or group of individuals" (p. 3). Unlike most of the other theories that we have examined in this chapter, prosocial behavior is examined from the vantage point of the recipient rather than from the donor's perspective. In other words, the consequence of the action—fixing an injustice, receiving a tax break, or feeling good, and so forth—is not necessarily the motivation for the donor to act. Prosocial behaviors are often defined very broadly. They can include volunteering, giving of money, comforting, rescuing, or helping others.

Prosocial behaviors should not be confused with the concept of altruism. Altruism, as discussed earlier, is a motivation to help others regardless of the benefits to the donor, while prosocial behavior is an action. Bentley and Nissan (1996) suggest that prosocial behavior explains the circumstances in which people act to help others and how the inclination to give of one's self exists.

The concept of prosocial behavior was first introduced by biologist Edward Wilson in 1975. He finds that there is evidence that humans and other animals help one another in different ways; this finding later led to the development of the field of sociobiology. Given that Wilson finds this helping nature in animals other than humans, developmental psychologists contend that prosocial behavior is a biological function rather than one that is solely nurtured or taught. In dialogue with the developmental psychologists, social psychologists show that prosocial behaviors, while a natural function, can also be taught, learned, and enhanced (Eisenberg, 1982; Rushton, 1982; Schroeder, Penner, Dovidio, & Piliavin, 1995). Therefore, the action of giving alumni donations to one's alma mater can be learned. Studies show that as a person ages, developmental and moral reasoning can evolve in terms of helping others.

Modeling Theories

There are a number of ways that prosocial behaviors can be taught; one is through modeling. There are different types of modeling within the emerging philanthropic studies literature. Philanthropic modeling, social justice modeling, and religious influences are three examples of this concept.

PHILANTHROPIC MODELING

Often, one generation transmits the concept, importance, and encouragement of philanthropic giving to another (Gasman et al., 2011). Bentley and Nissan (1996) found that elementary school students can learn philanthropic and altruistic behavior through witnessing an influential adult (e.g., parent or guardian, teacher, or a religious or youth organization leader) engage in acts of prosocial behavior. Bentley and Nissan (1996), along with Drezner (2005, 2008) and Gasman et al. (2011), noted that witnessing philanthropic actions is most effective in passing along the importance of helping others from one generation to the next, whether it be a parent or other influential adult. Further, using data from the 1992 Survey of Giving and Volunteering in the United States (Gallup, 1992), Schervish and Havens (1997) found that children's observation of volunteerism from at least one parent or guardian was associated with higher levels of giving as an adult. Hunt (1990) referred to this as **modeling theory**. Bar-Tal (1976) and Bentley and Nissan (1996) argued that philanthropic modeling was intensified when it was coupled with a discussion about the importance of such actions.

SOCIAL JUSTICE MODELING

Similar to philanthropic modeling, parents and other important individuals can model social justice beliefs and actions and pass along the importance of those beliefs and actions to others who observe them. For example, Rosenhan (1970) found that many people involved in the civil rights movement claimed that their sense of action and volunteerism had been born out of their home environment. Cascione (2003) found that the influence of family affects the motivations of major gift donors within higher education, noting that:

> *participation drew directly from their family backgrounds, [sic] and was assisted by the historical milieu in which they were living. Having individuals who are able to teach generosity through their actions and lifestyles plays a crucial role [in] carrying on a philanthropic tradition. Role modeling represents a form of teaching philanthropic values and individuals who represent such generosity encourage others by their actions. Extraordinary acts of generosity become ordinary events and since they are seen as ordinary events, the ability to replicate them would be a typical response in the course of an individual's life.*

(p. 69)

Gasman et al. (2011) observed that many of the foundation leaders in their study spoke of their religious experiences in the context of social justice and progressive rights movements, connecting their upbringing and their parent's involvement in the civil rights movement in the 1960s with their decision to pursue work focused on social justice and equality within the nonprofit sector.

MODELING THROUGH RELIGION

Philanthropic modeling also occurs within a religious context. Religion plays an important role in the philanthropic decisions of many Americans. Within a larger religious context, Hodgkinson and Weitzman (Gallup, 1996) determined that 73.6 percent of individuals who remembered observing a member of their family help another person also made philanthropic gifts. In contrast, among those who did not recall observing a helping action, the likelihood of giving declined to 50 percent. Other scholars have discussed adult influence in teaching prosocial values (Bremner, 1994; Grusec & Kuczynski, 1997; Steinberg & Wilhelm, 2003a, 2003b). Research by Wilhelm, Brown, Rooney, and Steinberg (2008) concluded that parents' giving to religion was strongly correlated to their children's giving to faith-based organizations. The same study determined that parents' philanthropic giving toward religion was "positively associated with children's secular giving, but in a more limited sense" than that of children's giving to religious organizations (p. 2146). In other words, children who know that their parents donate to religious organizations give more to secular nonprofits (about one-third more than those who only observe their parents' giving to nonreligious groups); however, the child's secular giving does not increase as the parents' religious giving increases. The influence of parental giving to religion has a significant effect on the philanthropic behaviors of their children. These findings are similar to those of a study by the Independent Sector (2002), a coalition of nonprofits, foundations, and corporate giving programs, regarding religious giving and volunteering for religious and secular nonprofit organizations.

African Americans have a particularly strong connection between the church and philanthropic giving outside of religion (Carson, 1987a, 1987b, 1987c, 1989a, 1989b, 1990a, 1990b, 2001, 2005; Drezner, 2013a; Ellison & Sherkat, 1995; Gasman et al., 2011). Ellison and Sherkat (1995) found that African Americans often look to the church for advocacy, guidance, and the promotion of social needs within the community—not only for religious uplift. Similarly, Trulear (2009) argued:

> *In many communities, the leadership of both the religious community and the local NAACP [National Association for the Advancement of Colored People] was one and the same, challenging the notion of a deradicalized Black church, and replacing it with the more nuanced view that churches often supplied the spiritual and moral vision for persons to exercise social advocacy work through secular organizations.*

(pp. 30–31)

Ellison and Sherkat's (1995) findings, as well as those of other scholars, indicate that African Americans are more closely affiliated with the church than other Americans (Glenn, 1964; Jacobson, Heaton, & Dennis, 1990; Roof & McKinney, 1987) and look to the church for advocacy, guidance, and the promotion of social needs within the community. African American communities are committed to financially support the church in order to gain the community support that they seek from the religious institution. Beyond the African American context, these concepts are true in many religious communities of color (Gasman & Bowman, 2013).

REINFORCING THE PHILANTHROPIC MODELING

As mentioned above, Bar-Tal (1976) and Bentley and Nissan (1996) find that philanthropic modeling is intensified when the observation is coupled with a discussion. Bentley and Nissan (1996) go further and find that participating in giving and volunteerism with a parent or guardian helps reinforce the positive feelings associated with helping others. Hodgkinson and Weitzman (Gallup, 1996) find that among those who observed a loved one help another person or family member, 73.6 percent are making charitable contributions. In contrast, of those who do not recall seeing a family member give, the probability of donating is only 50 percent. Parental actions also affect volunteering. Bekkers (2003) finds that an adult's volunteering correlates with recollections of his or her parents' volunteering. Additionally, scholars find that adults influence children through teaching values such as philanthropy (Bremner, 1994; Grusec & Kuczynski, 1997; Steinberg & Wilhelm, 2003a, 2003b).

Providing young adults with opportunities for community service allows them to experience the positive feelings associated with prosocial actions and gives them the ability to learn the importance of philanthropy (Daloz & Indiana University Center on Philanthropy, 1998; Schervish & Havens, 1997). Bjorhovde (2002a) concluded in her review of the literature that "the acquisition of the value of philanthropy and its resulting behaviors of giving and serving are the consequences of three primary types of learning: (1) modeling, which involves seeing and hearing, (2) cognitive learning, which combines thinking and discussing, and (3) experiential learning, which involves doing" (pp. 9–10). Having looked at many of the theoretical frameworks and theories that can guide one's research on philanthropic behavior, we now will look at some of the theoretical frameworks more specifically within a higher education context.

Applying the Theories to Higher Education Research

Fundraising professionals, whether working in higher education or in other nonprofits, often do not rely on theory to guide their practice. Most of the fundraising literature is written for practitioners by practitioners and consultants and offers "best" practices that are not grounded in theory but rather are based on case studies or the authors' successful experiences (Brittingham & Pezzullo, 1989; Carbone, 1986; Drezner, 2011; Kelly, 1991). While understanding what has worked for others and different methods of fundraising is important, further understanding of donor motivations and successful fundraising strategies from a theoretical standpoint will allow practitioners to enhance their advancement programs.

Donor motivation, the foundation of giving, includes the prior willingness to give and the factors that influence the action. Giving often occurs when a donor's motivation and the proper cultivation and solicitation by the institution align (Paton, 1986). Pezzullo and Brittingham (1993) find that there are a variety of donor motivations that can influence giving, including less altruistic motivations such as "the desire to buy acclaim and friendship, the need to assuage feelings of guilt, the wish to repay society for advantages received, egotism . . . investment in activities that have indirect utility to the donor . . . or tangible perquisites" (p. 31). Donor motivation also includes the belief in the organization's mission, a feeling of obligation, understanding community needs, ego positioning, self-interest, and self-actualization (Pickett, 1986).

Within the higher education context, Connolly and Blanchette (1986) suggest distance from graduation can affect donor motivation. They found that the desire to give declines steadily as alumni age, because they identify with their college or university less. Connolly and Blanchette's finding aligns with **organizational identity theory** (Mael & Ashforth, 1992). Understanding how a graduate's connection to his or her alma mater declines with time, it is very important to engage young alumni and students in order to encourage them to remain connected to their alma mater (Drezner, 2008, 2009, 2010; Nayman, Gianneschi, & Mandel, 1993; Van Nostrand, 1999). If they remain connected and engaged by their alma mater the desire to give does not necessarily decline, because they will still have a high organizational identity. Further, according to continuity theory (Atchley, 1989), once an alumnus or alumna makes a first gift, even as a student, the likelihood of future donations is enhanced.

Several studies show that having a satisfying educational experience positively impacts alumni giving (Gallo & Hubschman, 2003; Mael & Ashforth, 1992; Monks, 2003; Pearson, 1999; Sun, Hoffman & Grady, 2007). There are several specific educational experiences that, when a graduate was satisfied as a student, predict higher levels of giving. These include having a mentor and/or interactions with faculty outside of class (Cascione, 2003; Clotfelter, 2003; Monks, 2003), earning one or more degrees from an institution (Pezzullo & Brittingham, 1993), and receiving financial aid (as opposed to loans) (Monks, 2003; Pezzullo & Brittingham, 1993).

Having a high-quality relationship with a mentor while in college often motivates donors to give back to their alma mater (Cascione, 2003; Clotfelter, 2003; Monks, 2003). Most of the literature devoted to academic mentors is written about graduate students rather than undergraduates (Lovitts, 2001; Nettles & Millett, 2006). However, Cascione's (2003) study found that some donors gave to their undergraduate institutions in appreciation of a faculty mentor.

Researchers (Cascione, 2003; Monks, 2003; Pezzullo & Brittingham, 1993) and development professionals have long known that alumni who attend a university on scholarship are often motivated to return the generosity of a scholarship by contributing to—or creating—scholarships at their alma maters. Gregory Cascione (2003) found that major donors who themselves were on a grant as a student viewed their scholarship "as a form of institutional investment in individuals, and given that investment a form [sic] 'payback' was considered in order" (p. 99). Cascione's (2003) research participants discussed that receiving a scholarship was often the "first practical experience of the effects of . . . philanthropy" and that experience was a motivating factor for them to give when they felt that they had the disposable income to begin to give back to the institution (p. 99).

Satisfaction with educational experiences, cocurricular involvement, and alumni engagement leads to a form of kinship with one's alma mater. This kinship is often an important motivator for giving. Mael and Ashforth (1992) view this form of kinship as organizational identification, and their research shows that it correlates with alumni giving. Another way to view this connection between alumni and their alma mater is having 'school spirit.' Development officers often use a graduate's school spirit when soliciting donations, in impersonal annual fund solicitations or the very personal individual request for support.

Similarly, Diamond and Kashyap (1997) decided to look at how models of prosocial behavior explain alumni donations to universities. Using their own survey data merged with university contribution records from a randomly sampled set of alumni of a public university school of management who graduated between 1980 and 1988, they measured social psychological constructs from the literature on prosocial behavior. The determining factors that lead to a graduate feeling obligated to donate included perceived efficacy, perceived need, reciprocity, and individual attachment to the university (school spirit). Obligation and other constructs (intention to attend reunions and intention to contribute) explained the number of donations given over a six-year period. Their model also predicted intentions to support the university by working (and volunteering) for the alumni association or attending reunions. Diamond and Kashyap (1997) used their model to recommend how to design university fundraising communications.

The Use of Intrinsic and Extrinsic Motivations for Participation

Colleges and universities regularly solicit their alumni for donations, using intrinsic and extrinsic motivations. Extrinsic motivations include small gifts, invitations to campus or alumni activities, listing of names in annual reports, or membership in giving societies. Beyond physical acknowledgements of gifts, there are benefits of giving that are extrinsic, such as the belief that alumni participation and dollars raised can increase their alma mater's reputation, rankings, and/or the value of their own degrees. In contrast, intrinsic motivations for giving include the good feeling you feel by helping others—for example, giving to a scholarship to help others attend college (Harbaugh, 1998).

AVENUES FOR FUTURE RESEARCH

The theoretical frameworks that explain philanthropic motivations and guide the practice of fundraising come from multiple disciplines, including economics, psychology, and sociology. Each of the theories described in this chapter provides a possible conceptual home for the study of philanthropy and fundraising within higher education. Researchers have used these theories to understand motivations for giving, and practitioners can use them to create engagement strategies for their donors. On a cautionary note, many of these theories were developed using mostly a White wealthy male view of how philanthropy is defined. Therefore, the theories might not hold true in more diverse populations. Continued research is needed on how to expand and develop new theories on philanthropic motivations and behaviors that are more inclusive.

GEORGE EASTMAN CIRCLE AND
THE UNIVERSITY OF ROCHESTER
MULTIYEAR ANNUAL FUND

The University of Rochester, founded in 1850 in western New York, is a top-tier research university with more than 200 academic majors, over 2,000 faculty members, approximately 10,500 students, and more than 103,000 living alumni. The university is known for its small classes, with a low 10:1 student to teacher ratio, and increased interactions with faculty.

When Joel Seligman arrived at the University of Rochester as the tenth president in 2005, he brought with him, from Washington University in St. Louis, James Thompson as his new senior vice president for advancement. Prior to the arrivals of the administration, the advancement office lacked the financial resources and programmatic sophistication to launch a successful capital campaign. The university, and therefore the entire fundraising operation, was completely decentralized. The decentralized approach created an environment where immediate institutional needs drove fundraising priorities without regard for the donors' interests.

Advancement was generally seen as a tool to pay the bills or solve specific short-term problems and lacked an articulated purpose to inspire transformational contributions. At the time, the university was not pursuing long-term commitments and larger donations through the annual fund, and most of the larger gifts involved restricted funds, which offer less flexibility in spending. Fundraising and alumni, parent, and friend engagement at the University of Rochester required a major paradigm shift. The board of trustees hired Seligman "with the mandate to focus heavily on fundraising, to manage a comprehensive campaign, and to build a centralized advancement operation," said Jonathan Schwartz, senior associate vice president of advancement and director of university campaigns (Marts & Lundy, n.d.).

The new centralized Office of University Advancement adopted a donor-centric approach to its work. To develop the donor-centric philosophy, the new leadership employed a traditional three-part giving model. The first component of the model included listening to the donor prospects in order to become familiar with their philanthropic interests. When a better sense of the prospects' interest was understood, the university developed a donor strategy with an annual fund component followed by a major gift, and when appropriate, a conversation centered on an ultimate gift including a bequest. In order to be successful, the new administration believed that they needed this multiyear strategy built on a donor relationship strategy based on developing consistent and loyal leadership annual giving. To achieve this, a new annual fund program was developed, fostering a habit of giving over a minimum five-year period and embodying the philanthropic spirit of George Eastman.

George Eastman is considered to be Rochester's greatest benefactor. Eastman quietly donated tens of millions of dollars to higher education, including gifts to MIT, the Tuskegee Institute, and the University of Rochester. Within the first few decades of the 20th century, Eastman gave more than $50 million to Rochester. Eastman's legacy at the University of Rochester—including the Eastman School of Music, the Eastman Theatre, the River Campus, the Eastman Dental Center (now the Eastman Institute for Oral Health), and the School of Medicine and Dentistry—transformed the University of Rochester and its city.

PROGRAM OVERVIEW

The George Eastman Circle (GEC) is a university-wide leadership annual (unrestricted) giving society that recognizes aggregate giving of $1,500 to $50,000 per year for five consecutive years. Rochester established the GEC as the central portion of the university's Annual Fund Program, which has a $130 million goal within the larger $1.2 billion comprehensive campaign, *The Meliora Challenge*. This George Eastman Circle is the University of Rochester's first central platform to cultivate, engage, and steward alumni, friends, parents, grateful patients, faculty, and staff.

The University of Rochester established the George Eastman Circle to recognize alumni, parents, friends, grateful patients, community leaders, faculty, and staff who set an example of philanthropic leadership in the tradition of George Eastman. Donors are encouraged to designate their unrestricted gifts to over 200 schools and units funds throughout the university that align with their greatest interests. The stated mission of the program is to:

- *practice the donor-centric philosophy by listening to the donor's dreams and aspirations, thereby building a lifelong relationship;*
- *build a culture of leadership annual giving to the university, providing a highly flexible and reliable source of unrestricted operating funds;*
- *cultivate, steward, and delight donors, ultimately creating an expanded major gift prospect pool;*
- *elevate donor performance and identify prospects for major, leadership, and principal gifts;*
- *deploy a national, central sales force that will match the goals and aspirations of the donor and the institution.*

(Thompson, Katz, & Briechle, 2010, p. 276)

Originally established in March 2007, the university set the GEC a goal to successfully gain 250 members and $10 million in unrestricted commitments by the end of its Charter Phase on December 31, 2008, and to double the annual fund by the end of FY2012 (Thompson, Katz, & Briechle, 2010).

CHARTER PHASE

In order to engage the university's most committed donors and volunteers first, the George Eastman Circle was rolled out in several phases. "Staging the program in phases was a tactical decision to manage momentum and modulate expectations with operational readiness (i.e. to ensure adequate infrastructure is in place), as well as to enable the organization to engage its 'inner circle' of prospects prior to rolling the program out to a broad audience" (Thompson, Katz, & Briechle, 2010, pp. 276–277). The George Eastman Circle was unveiled before the public phase of the university's comprehensive campaign. However, the Advancement office unveiled the Circle similarly to a comprehensive campaign. The launch was modeled on the nucleus phase of a standard campaign, with the enlistment of key volunteers and stakeholders, a case statement and charter statement, and a defined period of time with special kickoff and closing events. The university chose to focus on those who had a high level of engagement with the institution, including the board of trustees, members of institutional advisory boards, and high-level administrators. Development officers made thousands of visits to cultivate and solicit the first GEC members.

THE USE OF VOLUNTEERS

In keeping with the donor-centric philosophy of engagement and involvement and modeling the George Eastman Circle after a campaign, the university built an extensive volunteer network. During the Charter Phase, a group of nine trustees served as an advisory committee to the program. The role of these volunteers was to assist in establishing the strategic direction of the George Eastman Circle, conduct peer-to-peer solicitations, and host cultivation and stewardship events. At the conclusion of the Charter Phase, the university created a number of regional leadership councils to engage others as volunteers.

BENEFITS FOR DONORS

The George Eastman Circle has a number of benefits, as forms of recognition and stewardship, for its members. Many of the recognition and stewardship protocols for members are designed to function more like those given to major gift donors than annual fund programs. There are five donor levels, each with their own benefits. Upon joining the GEC, new donors receive a welcome package with small tokens of appreciation and a welcome note from the national co-chairs. Additionally, donors are invited to high-end events featuring world-renowned speakers both in Rochester and New York City and are given access to a hospitality suite at events, VIP seating, special parking, and special receptions and photo opportunities with keynote speakers for top-level donors.

ENGAGING YOUNG ALUMNI

In the middle of Fiscal Year 2011, the university established a new young alumni giving level to the George Eastman Circle. The chairperson of the George Eastman Circle said that the university established the Associates Level "to engage our recent graduates and help them become leaders in the world, impacting their communities in every way, including philanthropically. . . . It gives them [recent graduates] a chance to join us at a more attainable level, getting them into the habit of giving back every year in support of the University" (University of Rochester, 2011). The Associates Level was open to any graduate from the prior 10 years. The Associates Level is a tiered, multiyear ask. Unlike the rest of GEC members who pledge to give at the same level ($1,500 or above for 5 years), recent graduates are invited to join the George Eastman Circle at a lower level and build up to their support over 5 years. In their fifth year their gift is $1,500, so that upon renewal, they are ready to renew at the "Member" level or greater, continuing the pledge at least $1,500 a year going forward.

RESULTS

The results of the George Eastman Circle are both tangible and intangible. In the first year of the program the board of trustees increased its annual fund contributions by over 300 percent. The initial goal of 250 charter members and $10 million raised was quickly surpassed as momentum increased. At the conclusion of the Charter Phase, 1,087 members joined, representing over $21.5 million in five-year commitments. One of the stated objectives of the program has been to drive the growth of the annual fund. In FY2009, when the national economy was in crisis mode, the annual fund was up over 12.3 percent, one of the stronger growth rates in the country. The loyal donor base has helped to mitigate the recent national decline in charitable giving. Approximately 33 percent of George Eastman Circle Charter Phase members joined between July 1, 2008, and December 31, 2008. The member growth rate from calendar year 2007 to 2008 was 280 percent. In 2010, as the economic crisis was still effecting philanthropic giving, the default rate on George Eastman Circle pledges was less than 5 percent.

According to the University of Rochester 2011–12 annual report, the Annual Fund (Figure 1.2) showed consistent strong growth, surpassing $12.3 million in cash received for FY2012. While this did not reach the original stated goal of doubling the FY2007 Annual Fund total ($7.6 million) by the end of FY2012, the performance marked the seventh consecutive year of growth and the fifth year of double-digit growth. The George Eastman Circle continued to be a significant driver of the growth, as was strong performance of the reunion giving program, which provided a surge of momentum to surpass the FY2012 projection of $11.8 million. The university claims that the Annual Fund is now on track to triple by FY2016 from its pre-campaign base FY2005.

By fall 2013, over 2,700 members have joined, having pledged and given over $43 million in unrestricted giving through the George Eastman Circle. Additionally, in the

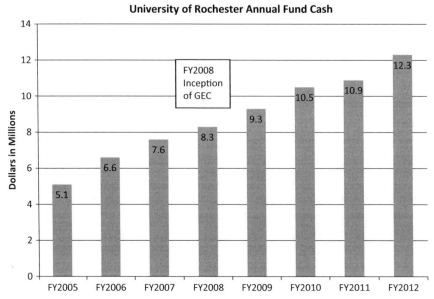

Figure 1.2 University of Rochester Annual Fund Cash

first 18 months after the introduction of the Associates Level for recent graduates, the GEC raised over $855,000 in new pledges from 165 young alumni, with an additional 30 young alumni joining at higher levels. Pledged unrestricted gifts through the George Eastman Circle totaled around $50 million since January 2007. George Eastman Circle members account for about 60 to 70 percent of the dollars raised for the Annual Fund. The university's board of trustees then approved a goal of securing 3,300 members by June 2016, when the comprehensive campaign is scheduled to conclude.

DISCUSSION QUESTIONS

1. What theories possibly explain the success of the George Eastman Circle at the University of Rochester?
2. Using the theories described in this chapter, how might you suggest improving the GEC?
3. As a researcher, how would you construct a research project to explore the GEC?

RESOURCES USED FOR THE CASE STUDY

Dougherty, N. (2012). New concept in giving fuels UR donor group. *Rochester Business Journal.* Retrieved from www.rbj.net/print_article.asp?aID=191226

Thompson, J. D., Katz, S., & Briechle, P. (2010). Notes from the field: A high level annual fund without the annual ask. *International Journal of Educational Advancement, 9*(4), 273–279.

Marts & Lundy (n.d.). Creating a new tradition of annual giving at University of Rochester: The George Eastman Circle. Retrieved from http://martsandlundy.com/reports-commentaries/client-stories/creating-a-new-tradition-of-annual-giving-at-university-of-roche

University of Rochester (2011). George Eastman Circle Newsletter. Retrieved from www.rochester.edu/giving/gec/newsletter/2011/i04/index.html

University of Rochester (n.d. a). Advancement. Retrieved from www.rochester.edu/advancement

University of Rochester (n.d. b). George Eastman Circle. Retrieved from www.rochester.edu/giving/gec/

University of Rochester (n.d. c). Meliora Challenge. Retrieved from http://campaign.rochester.edu/

University of Rochester (n.d. d). University of Rochester 2011–12 Annual Report. Retrieved from www.rochester.edu/aboutus/2011_2012/annual-report.pdf

2

GROUNDING INSTITUTIONAL MARKETING IN THEORY

Marketing takes place in two phases. The first is to match a general want with a specific service or product. The desire to go to college is a general desire for many women. The desire to go to Smith College because of its long history of tradition and excellence may in part be attributed to marketing. In the second phase of marketing, general wants are matched with specific products or services. Young women may have learned about Smith through guidance counselors, college recruiters, mail, social media, and contact with Smith alumnae (Truell, 2001).

Marketing is fundamentally rooted in the concept of and theories surrounding exchange. Exchange is a means of acquiring resources—goods or services—without having to produce them, steal them, obtain them through other forceful means, or by begging. In order to have an exchange, there must be two parties and each must have something that the other values. For organizations such as nonprofits—including universities and colleges—that deal primarily in providing services, there are two exchange paths. First, donors and other stakeholders exchange time and money with the organization and receive gratitude in return. Second, the organization provides services to clients/students in exchange for payment (Kotler, 1975).

Social exchange, which focuses on exchanges that are not purely economic in nature, has been the subject of discussion in the fields of both sociology and psychology and has been approached from a number of angles. It has been characterized as a process that is distinct from either giving or receiving and actually results when giving and receiving are simultaneously the cause and effect of each other (Simmel, 1908/1996). The roles of balanced exchanges within small groups (Homans, 1958), power (for example, Blau, 1964; Molm, 1997), and emotion (Lawler, 2001) have been part of the ongoing discussion of social exchange.

Reciprocity is a form of social exchange in general and specifically gift exchange. It is based in mutual obligation, with both parties having rights and duties in the exchange.

Transactions between parties not capable of reciprocation—such as children or the mentally incompetent—are, by definition, not exchanges. One party's act will, over time, result in the return of gifts and services of equivalent value (Gouldner, 1960; Levi-Strauss, 1957/1996; Malinowski, 1922/1996).

Relationship development and its application to gift exchanges are also germane to a discussion of marketing. Simmel (1908/1996) argued that relationships, once developed, tend to endure even after the initial forces and conditions that initiated the relationship are gone. He termed this 'faithfulness.' In reciprocal exchanges, he asserted that the gifts exchanged may not be exactly equal in value and are often not equal in kind. Gratitude is the motive for returning a gift even where there is no expectation or obligation to return it. Gratitude creates a relationship between parties that cannot be fully reciprocated.

Social exchange theory has been described in detail in the chapter on fundraising. Although fundraising and marketing share some common theoretical themes, the goals of marketing are broader. Marketing creates the relationship between an individual and an institution that should, if nurtured, result in mutual benefits including gift exchanges.

TRANSLATING MARKETING FOR THE NONPROFIT SECTOR AND HIGHER EDUCATION

In describing the role of marketing in higher education, Madden (2008) commented that "marketing research offers universities insights into the way students, alumni, and other prospective donors view the school. This enables the university decision-maker to raise the probabilities that students will choose to attend and donors may willingly give" (p. 286). In terms of 'exchange,' the focus of marketing shifts from transactions and relationships between individuals to transactions and relationships between individuals and institutions.

Academic researchers of marketing have been careful to distinguish marketing in nonprofit organizations, including higher education, from business. The theory of 'market failure' as an explanation for the existence of the nonprofit sector relies on the idea that the commercial market has failed to provide services or levels of services. In fact, the exchange of goods and services that is the goal of business marketing often does not occur in nonprofit organizations where the donors are not the beneficiaries of nonprofit services (Liao, 2008).

Scholars have adopted a social orientation construct for marketing in the nonprofit sector, including higher education, which distinguishes itself in terms of marketing focus, challenges, and stakeholders. The focus of marketing for nonprofit organizations is the provision of services as opposed to products (Kotler & Levy, 1969; Liao, Foreman, & Sargeant, 2001) and satisfaction of societal needs (Kotler & Fox, 1995; Kotler & Levy, 1969; Krachenberg, 1972; Liao et al., 2001). For higher education, marketing has been specifically defined as a long-term process (Kotler & Fox, 1995) with specific goals, including that of educating the whole person (Kotler & Levy, 1969).

This social orientation to marketing also invokes challenges. To begin with, benefits received by stakeholders are often intangible. Although quality standards are set by institutions, outcomes may not be subject to their control (Liao, 2008). These factors make it difficult to measure efficiency and effectiveness of services, key measures of marketing success (Liao et al., 2001). In addition, there is generally little direct competition between institutions. Competition comes more from the environment—the internal drive for excellence, the needs of the business community, and the needs and demands of students. Marketing is also tied to mission, and collaboration is often coupled with mission. Competitor institutions may collaborate to develop and share knowledge and to provide student services (Liao, 2008).

However, in a comparison of social orientation to traditional marketing, the variety of stakeholders may point to the largest difference. As has already been noted, stakeholders may not benefit directly from institutional services. In addition, the number of stakeholder groups is extensive. In higher education, they include students, parents, faculty, staff, accrediting bodies, trustees, businesses, competitor institutions, legislators, foundations, alumni, media, volunteers, and the general public (Kotler & Fox, 1995). **Stakeholder theory** suggests that in a complex environment, stakeholder groups may influence each other and the roles they play may change depending on the circumstances. Within higher education, there are internal stakeholders (students, faculty, and staff), external stakeholders (alumni, parents, donors, competitors, legislators, and the public), and interface stakeholders (trustees and administrators) who oversee internal operations while representing the institution to other stakeholder groups (Liao, 2008).

The focus of research in marketing has been the testing and refinement of **exchange theory**. Two areas of extensive development are relationship marketing and branding. Research in both of these areas will be reviewed.

RELATIONSHIP MARKETING

Relationship marketing represents a process of developing exchange relationships that will persist over time. These relationships may involve individuals beyond institutions and customers/clients, such as employees internal to the institution or indirect stakeholders. Research has focused heavily on defining and testing the antecedents to forming these lasting relationships. These studies operationalize what relational exchanges look like within real marketing operations.

Morgan and Hunt (1994) developed a theoretical model of relationship commitment and trust in relationship marketing and then tested it against data from the automotive tire industry. It is critical to review because nonprofit research has built on these findings. Their work was grounded in the idea that relationship marketing was based in a dynamic balance of competition versus cooperation in the market. The study found that relationship commitment and trust were key mediating factors in the development of long-term relationships. Relationship commitment exists where the relationship is perceived as so important that any amount of effort will be exerted to maintain it.

Five antecedents and five outcome factors gleaned from prior research on organizational behavior were tested and confirmed:

Antecedents of relationship commitment

- Relationship termination costs—When alternative partners appear to be in short supply, parties will tend to remain in a relationship;
- Relationship benefits—Parties will seek out partnerships where the potential benefits are perceived to be high (for example, profits and customer satisfaction);
- Shared values—Potential partners share common views and beliefs about factors such as goals and policies;
- Communication—Parties are willing to share information;
- Opportunistic behavior—Pursuit of self-interest by one party negatively influenced relationship commitment by killing trust.

Outcomes of relationship commitment

- Acquiescence—The likelihood that a partner will comply with what the other partner wants;
- Propensity to leave—The probability that a partner will end the relationship in the near future;
- Cooperation—Achievement of mutual goals by working together; develops from both relationship commitment and trust;
- Functional conflict—A direct result of trust; disputes are resolved in a productive way that builds the partnership;
- Decision-making uncertainty—Insufficient information exists to make decisions; outcomes of decisions and the degree of confidence in decisions cannot be predicted. Trust declines.

Morgan and Hunt (1994) concluded by saying:

We posit that relationship commitment and trust develop when firms attend to relationships by (1) providing resources, opportunities, and benefits that are superior to the offerings of alternative partners; (2) maintaining high standards of corporate values and allying oneself with exchange partners having similar values; (3) communicating valuable information, including expectations, market intelligence, and evaluations of the partner's performance; and (4) avoiding malevolently taking advantage of their exchange partners. Such actions will enable firms and their networks to enjoy sustainable competitive advantages over their rivals and their networks in the global marketplace.

(p. 34)

BUILDING AND TESTING RELATIONSHIP
MARKETING THEORY

A succession of six studies that built upon Morgan and Hunt's work demonstrate how their framework has been tested and refined for the nonprofit sector.

Garbarino and Johnson (1999) considered the level of commitment to a relationship exhibited by the customers of a repertory theater company. Transactional customers/relationships represented occasional ticket buyers. In contrast, relational customers/relationships represented those who consistently subscribed over a period of time. They demonstrated a higher stake in the organization than the transactional customers. Garbarino and Johnson were able to demonstrate that satisfaction, trust, and commitment were factors in the development of relational exchanges. In low relational exchanges, satisfaction guided future transactions, but for the high relational customers, future interaction was driven by the presence of trust and commitment.

In a series of studies, Sargeant and other researchers teased out the roles of trust and relationship commitment for donor relationships. Sargeant and Lee (2002) identified individual and contextual antecedents of trust development. Trust is distinguished from confidence in that confidence is based on being aware of alternatives. Trust is what maintains the relationship in the absence of information. Three contextual antecedents of trust development that they identified were role competence, the belief that the non-profit organization can actually accomplish what it claims; service quality, the provision of timely information to donors; and organizational judgment, the extent to which a donor believes that the organization will use gifts in line with organizational ethics. One individual antecedent was also identified—a predisposition toward philanthropy, altruism, and helping behaviors.

Sargeant and Lee (2004a, 2004b) operationalized 'trust' and asked if trust directly affected giving behavior or if it was mediated by commitment. Four measures of trust were found to contribute to relationship commitment:

- Relationship investment—Are donors willing to provide resources including money and time to develop the relationship with the nonprofit organization?
- Mutual influence—Does the donor feel that the nonprofit organization has influenced his or her thinking, and does the donor feel that he or she might have some influence on the goals and policies of the nonprofit?
- Communication acceptance—To what degree does the donor welcome and expect communication with the nonprofit?
- Forbearance from opportunism—Does the donor refrain from making donations to other organizations?

Increased relationship commitment also increased donation behavior. When relationship commitment was missing, trust had a minimal impact on giving behavior.

Sargeant and Woodliffe (2005) went beyond trust to look for other antecedents of relationship commitment. This study involved focus groups of long-term committed donors. Drivers of passive and active commitment were identified. Passive commitment was characterized as something that persisted unless one or more of the following factors became unacceptable:

- Risk—Fear that the beneficiary group will suffer if their support stops;
- Trust in the organization—Donor belief that the organization is doing what it claims to do;
- Organizational performance—Donors assume that an organization is performing well unless there is direct evidence to the contrary;
- Communication quality—The quality and content of messages sent is acceptable;
- Available alternatives—Many organizations represent the cause or need; the organization does not stand out as unique.

By contrast, active engagement had a cognitive component. Drivers included learning about the organization or cause; sharing beliefs with the organization; having a sense of control over communications with the organization; multiple levels of engagement; and a sense of connection with beneficiaries of the organization.

Sargeant, Ford, and West (2006) looked more specifically at the return that donors expect in their gift exchange. Social exchange theory predicts that potential donors will be influenced by the benefits that they expect to receive as a result of their gift. Trust in an organization is enhanced when the organization appears to be having a positive impact on its mission (positive impact on beneficiaries) and when it provides appropriate communications back to donors. Other returns that have a positive effect on the relationship are emotional benefits (enhanced self-esteem, recognition) and the perception that a family member will benefit from the relationship. When these two factors are present, commitment may develop even when trust is absent. Direct personal benefits to donors did not enhance either commitment or trust.

Money, Money, Downing, and Hillebrand (2008) utilized a case study to test the Morgan and Hunt model. The case organization was a crime-prevention nonprofit in South Africa with multiple funders. Focus groups and in-depth interviews were followed by a survey sent to funders to determine what drove funder trust and commitment for this organization.

The drivers of commitment they found were shared values, nonopportunistic behavior, communication, and benefits. Termination costs had no effect on funder commitment. Nonmaterial benefits were far more important to commitment than were material benefits. Communication was the most complex factor and the one that nonprofits could most effectively modify to encourage higher levels of trust.

This excellent body of research, which tells us a great deal about how relationships are formed between institutions and individuals, has yet to be tested in the context of higher education marketing. To the extent that enduring relationships or the lack of them impact so many areas of the academy, including student retention, alumni loyalty, public support, and donor development, researchers and practitioners alike would do well to study and test their implications.

BRANDING TO ENHANCE RELATIONSHIP FORMATION

A brand can be defined "as the totality of perceptions and experiences surrounding a product, a service, an organization or, indeed, a charity. Such perceptions and experiences may be grouped according to two dimensions: the functional, what the brand does; and the symbolic, what the brand represents" (Hankinson, 2001, p. 231). For a university, a brand represents the emotional reaction to the institution's name—who it represents, its physical presence, and the people associated with it (Bulotaite, 2003).

Brand orientation exists if an organization regards itself as a brand. It is reflected in what practices the organization uses to differentiate itself from others and to present itself to stakeholders. Brand-oriented organizations understand what values the brand represents, are able to communicate those values to internal and external stakeholders, and use the brand as a strategic resource to communicate mission, recruit employees, educate the public, and build trust. Managing the brand is an ongoing activity (Hankinson, 2001).

Development of a brand orientation requires the personal vision of individuals who will champion the cause, relevant education and training of marketing staff in brand management, a supportive organizational culture, and environmental factors that are conducive to brand development (e.g., donor demographics and changes in donor behaviors). Successful development of a brand orientation results in a strategic resource that can drive fulfillment of organizational objectives and enhance a cohesive internal organizational culture (Hankinson, 2001).

Brand personality has been defined as the essence of a brand (Hankinson, 2001) or the human attributes associated with it (Aaker, 1997). In order to apply social exchange theory—particularly **relationship development theory**—to interactions between institutions and individuals, the institutions need to take on human characteristics. Nonprofit sector research has tried to establish the existence of distinct personality attributes for nonprofit organizations as well as distinguish between causes and individual organizations.

Venable, Rose, Bush, and Gilbert (2005) argued that according to social exchange theory "nonprofit stakeholders perceive nonprofit organizations at an abstract level because of the organizations' intangibility and social ideals" (p. 295). They found four distinctly human attributes in nonprofits that they see as dimensions of brand personality—integrity, nurturance, sophistication, and ruggedness. These are described as:

- Integrity—Reputable, committed to the public good, purposeful, accessible, long term;
- Nurturance—Caring, empathy, love, compassion;
- Sophistication—Glamorous;
- Ruggedness—Strong, durable (Aaker, 1997).

Aaker (1997) noted that the qualities of sophistication and ruggedness are attributes that many people idealize but do not possess.

During the qualitative phase of their work, Venable et al. (2005) found clusters of characteristics that were particular to nonprofits:

- Thoughtfulness—Loving, compassionate, kind, helpful, caring;
- Integrity—Reputable, committed to the public good, purposeful, accessible, long term;
- Reliability—Cost-effective, financially sound.

Overall, their work confirmed that individuals do ascribe distinct human attributes to nonprofit organizations.

Building on Venable et al. (2005), Sargeant, Ford, and Hudson (2008) and Sargeant, Hudson, and West (2008) looked for characteristics that would help to differentiate specific nonprofit organizations. They wanted not only to be able to differentiate nonprofit organizations from other organizations in terms of brand personality characteristics but also to be able to distinguish what characteristics were common to all nonprofit organizations. Additionally, they wanted to be able to find relationships between brand personality characteristics and giving behavior.

From a marketing perspective, it does not make sense to focus on traits that are common across the sector. The common traits are not likely to encourage donations to a specific organization. These studies confirmed that there are many characteristics that nonprofit organizations as a whole have in common but also identified characteristics that could differentiate specific organizations. A successful brand distinguishes an organization from others, invokes emotional response from stakeholders, and communicates important messages about the institution. More than a logo, a brand carries an emotional dimension that stakeholders can identify with. Association with the brand becomes part of the stakeholder's identity and conveys information about the stakeholder to others.

McAlexander, Koenig, and Schouten (2006) took the brand/relationship concept one step further to develop a conceptual model of *brand community* within higher education. They utilized a definition for brand community developed for the commercial sector. Citing from their original source, the definition is:

> *A brand community is a specialized, non-geographically bound community, based on a structured set of social relationships among admirers of a brand. It is specialized because at its center is a branded good or service. Like other communities, it is marked by a shared consciousness, rituals and traditions, and a sense of moral responsibility.*

> (Muniz, Muniz, & O'Guinn, 2001, p. 412)

The model reflected four alumni relationships:

- Customer–product: Education becomes part of alumni identity. "The more centrally and positively a person's education figures in her identity, the more attached she is likely to be to the source of that education" (p. 109);

- Consumer–brand: Alumni take pride in association with the institution; the association helps convey information about the alumni to others;
- Customer–institution: Alumni develop interpersonal relationships with individuals within the institution; when that relationship is established, the reciprocity of gifts and goodwill is most likely to occur;
- Customer–customer: Alumni bond with other alumni; these affiliations form networks of relationships, further integrating the alumni into the institutional community.

Their work indicated that it is important to build multiple bridges between alumni and the institution. Developing these bridges during the student years is also critical to building enduring long-term relationships and loyalty to the institution.

AVENUES FOR FUTURE RESEARCH

Perhaps one of the starkest untouched areas of research is stakeholder studies. Kotler and Fox (1995) pointed to a wide base of stakeholders. In terms of both relationship formation and the effect of institutional branding, little work has been done to test how various stakeholders—other than alumni—respond to institutional marketing. We also do not know how diversity within populations of stakeholders affects marketing. In the studies cited here, we do not know the race, ethnicity, sexual orientation, gender identity, or religious orientation of the stakeholders involved. There are many opportunities for researchers to reproduce these methodologies with segment-identified stakeholder groups. Postmortem studies of branding initiatives would also add to our understanding of this theory. Although many good case examples of branding initiatives can be found in the literature, their long-term successes and failures are not assessed, either theoretically or practically.

=============================CASE STUDY=============================

A CASE OF FOUR BRANDS

A brand represents a set of functions and emotions that come to represent a college or university. Its goal is to distinguish one institution from another. A well-developed brand imparts human characteristics—a personality—to the institution that enhances relationship development with stakeholders. Four cases taken from the higher education literature are presented here, followed by a set of questions and exercises designed to help the reader understand the theoretical bases of branding.

The University of North Carolina at Chapel Hill (UNC-CH) has a long history of low tuition and affordability. It has consistently received a Kiplinger's Best Value Rating. In addition, UNC-CH was the first public university in the United States.

> *The Carolina Covenant—Carolina's Promise:*
> *Eligible low-income students who earn admission can have the opportunity to graduate debt-free. With grants, scholarships, and a work-study job, Carolina Covenant Scholars can earn a UNC degree without student loans. [carolinacovenant. unc.edu]*

In 2003, UNC-CH instituted a brand that represents the institutional commitment to maintaining economic access to higher education, even in times of continuously climbing tuition, and the stance that higher education is not reserved for the elite. The Covenant works like this:

Combining scholarships, grants, and work-study, UNC-Chapel Hill could guarantee the promise to admitted, full-time, low-income students to graduate with a bachelor's degree without accumulating loan debt. Nonresident students are also eligible for the Carolina Covenant program. No additional application is required beyond submission of the Free Application for Federal Student Aid (FAFSA) and the College Board's PROFILE application. Lastly, there is no limit to the number of Covenant Scholars awarded each year (Harris & Barnes, 2011, p. 37).

The message: If you meet the academic requirements for admission to UNC-Chapel Hill, finances will not bar you from attending:

The University of North Carolina at Chapel Hill's promise: Eligible low-income students who are admitted to Carolina can enroll without worrying about how they will pay for it. And, if they work 10–12 hours per week in a Federal Work-Study job, they can graduate debt-free. (http://carolinacovenant.unc.edu/)

The official Covenant website (https://carolinacovenant.unc.edu/) is linked to information for prospective students and includes an annual report of results, featuring Covenant scholars. The Covenant has also been featured in media coverage for football and basketball games.

 **The University of Ulster (Northern Ireland)** instituted branding in 2007 in response to austerity funding changes in the UK. Northern Ireland's largest university, Ulster operates four campuses for more than 24,000 students. Economic, social, and cultural engagement across Northern Ireland is a strong focus, as is providing access to higher education for students. Ulster is noted for excellence in teaching and research, which relates to the local economy.

Brand development was directed toward evoking an emotion-driven decision process in the students they were trying to recruit. Ulster wanted to be the institution of choice for sixth form students across Northern Ireland.

In response to the popularity and appeal of animation, a genderless animated character, Eddie, clad in Ulster colors, appeared in TV ads, on billboards, on bus shelters, in radio ads, and on the Ulster website. Eddie's image represented a contemporary and innovative means of engaging potential students. In one scenario, Eddie was shown dealing with confusing messages and decisions, finally choosing the route to Ulster. Postcampaign research showed that Eddie had a likeability rating of 69 percent.

www.missouristate.edu
In 2005, Southwest Missouri State University changed its name to **Missouri State University**. The new name more clearly reflected the scope of the institution than the regional designation implied. However, the marketing team did not want to brand as MSU, since so many other institutions could already claim that designation. Consequently, the official brand was "Missouri State University."

The change entailed a major communication outreach plan including phone messaging, on-hold phone messaging, publications, speeches, web pages, and email. The marketing team developed logos, stationery, and signage of all kinds and obtained a new Internet domain name. The name transition was coordinated with the institution's centennial celebration and was kicked off with a major event at midnight when the change became official.

To alleviate concerns with stakeholders, the public relations outreach included messaging that costs for the name change were not going to be paid from student fees or state appropriations. Alumni could also opt to receive a replacement diploma with the new name at a nominal cost. A historical exhibit covering all five name changes the institution has gone through is maintained on the website (www.missouristate.edu/about/history.htm). Original bronze seals on historical campus buildings have been left intact.

The **University of Kentucky** rolled out the Top 20 Business Plan at the end of 2005. The goal was to become a top-tier public research university by 2020. To do that would require more state appropriations for the university. To justify this commitment, the university adopted civic engagement as a brand—"UK: Catalyst for a New Commonwealth." The essence of the brand was accountability to the state of Kentucky. Through civic engagement, the university would strive to improve educational attainment, economic growth, and healthcare.

The mission of the Center for Community Outreach is to serve, connect, and unite the University of Kentucky with the surrounding community in collaborative efforts to promote life-long community service. [http://uky.volunteermatch.org/]

Dissemination of the plan involved multiple venues:

- Consistent news releases about the plan;
- Educational leaders toured the state, speaking to legislators, schoolchildren, alumni, and the media;
- Funded Commonwealth Collaboratives—Seed money for specific projects to address problems in Kentucky;
- Wide dissemination of the plan through media that emphasized university engagement in the state;
- Grassroots advocacy—Ongoing personal contact with legislators.

To guarantee the future of the brand, additional initiatives were planned. The university offices of external relations, government relations, and campus radio were consolidated to insure a consistent message. Offices of alumni relations and development were also combined. Plans were made to fund additional engagement collaboratives and to hold a statewide engagement conference. A 'Public Scholar' designation for faculty was proposed.

The university website front page features tabs for the three traditional areas of excellence—research, teaching, and service. The service message states:

"From training service dogs, to painting fences, to dancing all night, giving back to the community is a UK tradition that students, faculty and staff are passionate about" (www.uky.edu/).

The university's Center for Community Outreach currently oversees civic engagement activities including a volunteer sign-up site (http://uky.volunteermatch.org/).

DISCUSSION QUESTIONS

1. What exchange relationships were developed by each institution (internal and external)?
2. Who are the critical stakeholders in each case?
3. What human attributes can you link to each institution?
4. What means did the institutions use to help each institution take on these attributes?
5. Based on evidence you can find on each institution's website, does the brand still represent the institution's message? Is there evidence that the institution continues to maintain the brand?

RESOURCES USED FOR THE CASE STUDY

Blanton, J. (2007). Engagement as a brand position in the higher education marketplace. *International Journal of Educational Advancement, 7*(2), 143–154.

Durkin, M., McKenna, S., & Cummins, D. (2011). Emotional connections in higher education marketing. *International Journal of Educational Management, 26*(2), 153–161. Additional image of Eddie appears on page 157.

Harris, M. S., & Barnes, B. (2011). Branding access through the Carolina Covenant: Fostering institutional image and brand. *Journal of Student Financial Aid, 41*(2), 36–46.

Haytko, D. L., Burris, G., & Smith, S. M. (2008). Changing the name of a major university: A case study and how-to guide. *Journal of Marketing for Higher Education, 18*(2), 171–185.

Special thanks to the University of Ulster for permission to use the image of Eddie.

3

BOARDS OF TRUSTEES AND PHILANTHROPY

Boards of trustees are very important and potentially powerful organizations within the governance of higher education. They have the power to hire and fire the president, play a role in setting the vision and mission of the university, and have overall fiduciary responsibility for the institution. Under the scope of their fiduciary responsibility they not only have oversight over the university budget but also have a role in the fundraising for the university, often participating as major donors but also as those who evangelize the university's case for support and bring others on board as donors. While board governance is a critical aspect of American higher education, there is little literature that explores this work from a theoretical standpoint. This chapter will briefly recap the historical trajectory of board literature within higher education, enumerate theories used by nonprofit scholars to explain board behavior, and present a case study of a college board that will serve as a lens for deeper understanding of the theories presented.

THEORY IN THE STUDY OF HIGHER EDUCATION GOVERNANCE

Studies of board characteristics have dominated the literature. A few have touched on characteristics needed for effective philanthropy. For example, an early study concluded that private institution boards needed to be larger to accommodate fundraising (Ashbrook, 1932). Another examined the social qualities of trustees, citing social conscience, objectivity, and the ability to resist power players and pressure groups as key attributes (Chambers, 1938). A third looked at board roles, including understanding the role of philanthropy in sustaining the institution and keeping up with changes in fundraising processes and methods as important roles (Dana, 1947). These studies are significant for their timing as well as their findings, given that the early thirties was only the beginning of professionalized fundraising for American higher education. Harvard ushered in the first endowment campaign for private institutions in 1919. And it was not until after these studies that public institutions began a concerted and organized fundraising effort with the establishment of The Ohio State University Development Fund Association in 1940 (Cutlip, 1965; Drezner, 2011; Meuth, 1992).

In the second half of the 20th century, most of the literature was descriptive. However, in 1991, Chait, Holland, and Taylor set out to systematically study boards. Their first effort defined six aspects of trusteeship:

- Context: The trustee understands the culture and norms of the organization; responds to individual organization culture; uses mission and values as a guide, uses trusteeship to reinforce institutional values.
- Education: The institution actively insures that the trustees are prepared to do their job; creates opportunities for trustee education, self-evaluation, and self-reflection on performance.
- Interpersonal: Recognizes that the trustees are most effective when they are working as a group; actively work at being more cohesive; foster a sense of inclusion; have group goals; have leadership within the board.
- Analysis: Board understands that not all issues are clear cut and can live with some level of ambiguity; takes a broad institutional view; looks at all aspects of an issue; encourages difference of opinion.
- Politics: Board takes responsibility for working with multiple stakeholders; communicates regularly with stakeholders; works to minimize conflict.
- Strategy: Helps the institution shape its long-term goals and plans; focuses on processes that help formation of institutional goals; conducts board business within the priorities of the institution; acts to prevent situations from becoming crises; anticipates problems and acts to reduce potential consequences.

In their 1996 study, Chait, Holland, and Taylor further defined effective governance as "a collective effort, through smooth and suitable processes, to take actions that advance a shared purpose consistent with the institution's mission" (1996, p. 1). Four tensions that beset nonprofit boards were identified:

- Dispassionate analysts versus impassioned advocates: The need for objective decision making plays against the need for passionate advocacy for the organization; tension is also often seen in the relationship with the CEO; the board is an evaluator but also the biggest supporter.
- Part-time amateurs versus full-time professionals: Most trustees are amateurs with regard to the work of the organization and will tend to focus on their particular area of professional expertise rather than the primary mission of the organization; this sometimes leads to forcing a corporate model onto the nonprofit/academic environment.
- All-stars versus constellations: Trustees tend to be the stars and leaders of their own fields; they are rarely good at team approaches.
- Low stakes versus high rollers: There tends to be low individual accountability for board members.

These two studies are particularly important because they have both dominated the higher education literature and have also been utilized by nonprofit researchers to look more broadly at nonprofit boards. Minor (2008) evaluated the relationship between how public trustees are selected and the performance of public higher education institutions. He used seven criteria suggested by the work of Chait, Holland, and Taylor (1991)— "(a) a commitment to public education; (b) a record of public or community service; (c) knowledge of complex organizations and academic institutions; (d) demonstrated ability to lead collectively; (e) willingness and availability for constructive engagement; (f) a commitment to open-minded, nonpartisan decision making; and (g) a record of integrity and civic virtue" (p. 834)—to evaluate the selection criteria for trustees. These were correlated with institutional performance characteristics including access, completion rates, affordability, and economic benefits returned to the states. In the institutions he looked at, the high-performing institutions also had more stringent requirements for trustee selection. Unfortunately, these high-performing states are a minority of institutions. Rather than scrutinizing potential trustees for their qualifications, one-time orientations for new board members are the norm. Minor suggests that accountability to the public is compromised by inadequate and often politically motivated appointments that cannot be corrected by limited on-the-job training. Perhaps more important to our purposes, the work of Chait, Holland, Taylor, and Minor points to the value of systematic research and the development of theory for board behavior that can ultimately enhance the performance of institutions and accountability to the public.

For purposes of this discussion, 'philanthropy' includes board roles in fundraising, gift management, endowment management, and alignment of philanthropy with institutional mission. These activities have lurked in the literature but not been exploited as research topics. As Proper (2011) pointed out, most publication in this area is advisory and best practice rather than theoretical. Her 2011 comparative case study of independent college board involvement in fundraising is one of the few exceptions. Her review of literature is exceptionally thorough and comments directly on how little of this body of publication is meaningful to the serious researcher. Most is normative, descriptive, or prescriptive of what should be. Further, Caboni and Proper (2007) found that most fundraising research focuses on single institutions and donor versus non-donor scenarios and is largely unpublished as dissertations. Another factor confounding research is the lack of longitudinal data. What data can be found is aggregated in ways that make it difficult to use. There is little research that integrates theory.

Proper's (2011) exploratory case studies compared actual board members to what the literature says they should be like. Overall, the qualitative phase of the case studies concluded:

- Board roles did not include formulating policy or directing institutional vision;
- Fundraising was seen as an individual responsibility of the trustee and not as a collective responsibility of the board;
- Changes in board structure and responsibilities were initiated by the president;
- Board members did not describe their relationship to the president as a principal/agent scenario.

Nonprofit literature provides multiple theoretical lenses to understand and explain board behavior. Agency theory, the theoretical concept that Proper utilized in her study, is an excellent starting point.

AGENCY AND SUBSIDIARY THEORIES

Agency theory explains the dynamics of hierarchical relationships where there is interdependence of players. Agency is a concept that can be found in many fields, including law (for example, contact law and fiduciary relationships), business, and economics. This discussion is limited to the view from business and economics.

Typically, there is separation of ownership and control in organizations. Boards (principals) vest decision making and program implementation to administrators (agents). The administrators in turn deal with third parties (students, faculty, and clients, including parents and community partners). Administrators may have goals that do not agree in total with the goals of the board (goal incongruence). Boards may also have less information than administrators about the operations of the organization (information asymmetry). Principal/agent relationships are by definition deliberate and not accidental. Agents have a fiduciary relationship to the principal, owing them a duty of care in their actions on behalf of third parties. In other words, within a higher education context, trustees and administrators have a reciprocal relationship to care for their institution on behalf of faculty, students, alumni, and, in the case of public institutions, the citizens.

Steinberg (2010) provides a detailed explanation of the theory through the lens of economics. Although it would seem to be a given that nonprofits want to be accountable to stakeholders, the diversity of stakeholder groups can confound the best of intentions. Steinberg cites the case of the nonprofit university, which has stakeholders including students, faculty, staff, administrators, donors, alumni, and for-profit research partners. "Professors like to claim the primacy of academic freedom and the free dissemination of research results, but for-profit bio-technology partners see things differently. Unfortunately, accountability to one class of stakeholders can impair accountability to other classes" (p. 74).

Steinberg lists nine aspects of agency:

- Hidden action: where agents act without the principal's knowledge;
- Moral hazard: where the principal does not know if the agent is acting in the principal's best interests or if the agent is exerting optimum effort;
- Hidden information: where the agent has information that the principal needs. Adverse selection is a subset of this in which the principal cannot know all of the qualities of the agent before hiring him or her;
- Informed principal: where the principal has information that the agent needs;
- Lack of third-party verifiability: where the principal cannot easily verify that the agent has acted appropriately;

- Multitask agency: where more than one task is required and it is not possible to watch all tasks equally. If only observable tasks are rewarded, the agent will neglect the unobservable;
- Common agency: where many principals rely on one agent. If there is one common set of goals, principals may free ride;
- Common principal: where the net effect is teamwork. The focus is on collective outcomes;
- Chained agency: where there is one principal to one agent to subsequent agents.

Two subsidiary theories that try to create a better fit between agency theory and the non-profit sector are stakeholder theory and stewardship theory.

Stakeholder theory is sometimes discussed in terms of social networks or systems theory. The development of systems theory is attributed to the sociologist Talcott Parsons (1951). A stakeholder is someone who can make a claim on an organization's resources or services, whether they are internal or external to the organization. Stakeholder theory recognizes internal stakeholders (e.g., students, faculty, staff, and volunteers), external stakeholders (e.g., alumni, parents, donors, competitors, government, and citizens), and interface stakeholders (the board and administrators who represent the organization to the external stakeholders while overseeing internal operations). The board serves as an interface to various stakeholder groups and the organization itself. Agency theory is sometimes seen as a subset of stakeholder theory to the extent that who is identified as principal or agent may change depending on the stakeholder group being considered.

Stewardship theory originated in the fields of psychology and sociology. Traditional agency theory assumes that there will be conflict between principal and agent. However, in stewardship theory, agents may be motivated to act in the best interests of the principal and may accrue personal benefits from acting in the principal's best interests. On the other hand, the principal and agent may be in tune with each other and have common goals. The agent may identify with the organization's mission and find intrinsic motivation to act for the organization.

Stewardship theory has been discussed as a subset of agency theory (Caers et al., 2006). Principals of nonprofit organizations, or the trustees of a university, may be ineffective at controlling administrators. Combined with the difficulties in measuring nonprofit effectiveness, assessment of managerial performance or the creation of effective incentives for performance becomes problematic. On the other hand, nonprofit managers have been shown to act in the best interests of their clients rather than in their own interest. The nondistribution constraint deters managers from acting unethically toward clients. Individuals self-select into nonprofit work because the goals of nonprofits are closer to their personal goals. In this scenario, the lack of a strong board and evaluation measures loses its effect. Stewardship theory applies when a board elects weak controls because it believes that the manager's goals are in line with the mission. Agency theory prevails when the board cannot control because the manager exerts overruling influence.

Within higher education, stewardship theory can be observed in the fact that the typical trustees often have no experience in higher education beyond attending their alma mater and perhaps sending their children as students. Therefore, as lay leaders, their understanding of how to run the institution day to day is low. However, since presidents and other administrators ideally align with the mission of higher education and their institution more specifically, the lack of trustee understanding of the day-to-day work is mitigated.

RESOURCE MANAGEMENT THEORIES

Beyond agency theory and its subsidiaries are resource management theories—resource dependency theory, group decision/process theory, and social capital theory.

Resource dependency theory is based on the idea that institutional survival depends on being able to acquire needed resources—financial, human, and other intangibles. Organizations are interdependent and must interact with other parties (individuals, organizations, groups) in order to get resources. Because the relationships that develop between parties are often asymmetrical, institutions give up power in order to get resources while still attempting to maintain their autonomy. Institutions are effective if they can balance these competing dynamics. Board members bring valuable resources to an institution that enhance and strengthen institutional performance and provide networks to external resources. In addition to financial contributions, board members provide access to other donors, to legislators, and to community networks.

The works of organizational theorists Pfeffer (1972, 1973) and Pfeffer and Salancik (1978) are critically important reading. They predicted that in complex environments where there is dependence on outside resources, the board will be outwardly focused. Boards of institutions that are less dependent on outside resources will be more involved in administration. Other research, outside of higher education, has found that nonprofits with strategic boards had stronger financial performance and more often operated with a financial surplus. 'Strategic boards' refers specifically to the characteristic identified by Chait, Holland, and Taylor (1991). Strategic boards are instrumental in helping the institution shape its long-term goals and plans, focus on processes that help form institutional goals, conduct board business within the priorities of the institution, act to prevent situations from becoming crises, anticipate problems, and act to reduce potential consequences (Brown, 2005). Activity by boards will be influenced by the organization's dependence on external resources, the complexity of the organization, and its information needs (Harlan & Saidel, 1994). Building upon the idea that an organization depends on external resources, Melissa Middleton's chapter in the 1987 edition of *The Nonprofit Sector: A Research Handbook* presents an excellent discussion of how the nonprofit board is a border-spanning entity. Boards link the organization to the community, ensuring access to operating resources, recruiting board members, and building the organization's public image.

Beyond external resources, internal dynamics of boards are important in their functioning and, therefore, the organization's efficiency. **Group/decision process theory**, which finds its roots in the sociology of organizational effectiveness, posits that groups with effective decision-making processes foster a higher level of efficiency within the entire organization. Effective decision making may be grounded in the management of information or behavioral approaches, but the results are measurable against a standard and are future oriented (Seashore, 1983). In a board scenario, this means that if a board functions well as a group, the organization will also operate better. For example, there have been positive correlations found between analytical decision making by the board and stronger net revenue for the organization. Strong internal board collegiality and net financial surplus are also related (Brown, 2005).

Social capital theory, first conceptualized by sociologist James S. Coleman (1988), proposes that society is composed of individuals who, out of self-interest, use resources available to them to pursue their individual interests and goals. Relationships develop where people see benefit to themselves. However, some of the resources are inherently social things (collective things like trust, social norms, social networks) that are larger than the individual. Within social systems, these types of resources are 'social capital.'

Fredette and Bradshaw (2012) define social capital as "a resource embedded within a network of relationships that endows the capacity to mobilize both the network and the assets that may be accessed through the network" (p. 392). Social capital has been shown to impact organizational effectiveness. They found that greater sharing of information, a shared vision for the organization, and trust within the board enhanced board social capital. Enhanced board social capital leads to more effective governance.

INSTITUTIONAL THEORY

The third theoretical genre is institutional theory. In this context, the assumption is that the actions of those charged with institutional stewardship play an instrumental role in organizational growth and change.

Institutional theory, according to sociologists DiMaggio and Powell (1983), helps to explain why institutions—including colleges and universities—look and behave so much alike. The theory states that over time, organizations become more alike in response to environmental uncertainty. A field of organizations, such as higher education, once established, tends to become homogeneous over time.

Miller-Millesen (2003) helped to operationalize the theory to board practices in stating:

> Institutionalization occurs when boards enact similar behaviors (e.g. self-assessment practices), structure (e.g. advisory committees), and/or processes (e.g. Robert's Rules of Order) because these activities and courses of action have become the accepted way of doing things. The theory can be useful in understanding why many nonprofit boards of directors engage in similar activities, codify like practices, and develop

comparable structures. Institutional theory focuses analytical attention on the inter-
pretation of the norms, values, and beliefs that legitimate governance behaviors.

(pp. 522–523)

An organizational field is a group of entities that produce similar goods and services. In addition, they are connected through factors like professionalization that create associations and employee networks (e.g., American Association of University Professors [AAUP] or the Association of Governing Boards [AGB]) and 'structural equivalence'— within a network of organizations, institutions hold similar position and have similar ties to the organization (e.g., Division I within the National Collegiate Athletic Association [NCAA]). A field exists only to the extent that the organizations that compose it can be institutionally defined. Institutional definition or 'structuration' has four components:

- Increase in interaction among organizations in the field;
- Formation of formal coalitions;
- Increase in information load;
- Awareness for an organization that it is part of a group with common missions and goals.

Although organizations may institute new practices and new actors may enter the field, as time goes on the environment begins to produce constraints on change. At some point, attempts at change create reactions from the field that actually create more homogeneity.

Isomorphism is the term that captures homogeneity. When environmental conditions are the same, units in a population are forced to become more like each other. For organizations, the environment tends to select out the weak members, leaving the stronger more alike to survive. DiMaggio and Powell (1983) identify three mechanisms of organizational isomorphic change:

- Coercive isomorphism—responses to political influences and attaining legitimacy; pressures come from controlling organizations and the cultural expectations of society;
- Mimetic isomorphism—responses to uncertainty; organizations may model themselves after other organizations to reduce uncertainty;
- Normative isomorphism—related to professionalization; the need to be able to define and control the conditions and methods of work and establish legitimacy.

Two important sources of legitimacy are university-based training and educational programs and development of professional networks of organizations. When socialization of employees to the field occurs outside the workplace, it becomes an isomorphic factor.

DiMaggio and Powell predict isomorphic change at both the organizational and field levels. Dependence on another organization promotes isomorphism. If dependent for

resources, an organization will change to become more like the organization it is dependent on. Organizations will model after organizations they see as being successful, particularly when there is a lack of stability within the organization.

In organizations where there is goal ambiguity, the organization will tend to model
after organizations seen to be successful. Organizations that have set standards regarding
academic credentials for their managers and staff will become more like other organizations in the field than those that do not. Participation in trade and professional organizations promotes isomorphism.

Factors that encourage isomorphism within a field are dependency on a single type of
support and/or high levels of transactions with government agencies. Isomorphism will
be faster if there are relatively few organizational models in a field or if the goals or tech-
nologies of the field are ambiguous or uncertain. Professionalization and structuration
within a field also accelerate isomorphic change.

Stensaker and Norgård (2001) present a case study of organizational change at the
University of Tromsø (Norway) that illustrates how isomorphism can apply to higher
education. The case does not relate directly to board involvement in philanthropy but
does reflect the board role in strategic planning.

The University of Tromsø —part of the Norwegian national university—was established in the late 1960s. The three objectives that guided its early development were relevance for the region, establishing a democratic governance structure, and an emphasis
on innovative teaching and learning. The organizational changes over a 30-year period
for each objective illustrate an isomorphic shift toward a traditional university model.

- Relevance for the region: Tromsø's early curriculum emphasized programs that
  were both unique and relevant for northern Norway. These included fast-track
  medical training and programs on fisheries and ethnic languages. The strategy was
  effective for recruiting students, but demands for transferability of courses to other
  institutions resulted in a drift toward a more traditional curriculum. Although special programs are often seen to take funding that might have gone to traditional
  disciplines, schools with few unique programs do not attract as many students.
  Although Tromsø maintained its regional relevance, the curriculum needed to shift
  in a traditional direction to meet student needs.
- Democratic governance structure: Tromsø instituted a decentralized system that
  included student and staff representation but marginalized faculty influence. Large
  cross-disciplinary departments also tended to erode disciplinary strength within
  the faculty. The departments eventually developed a de facto faculty governance
  structure and the faculty moved back toward a disciplinary orientation as the need
  for recognition and discipline-based research cooperation increased. Over time,
  the governance structure has become more traditional.
- Innovative teaching and learning: Tromsø focused at its inception on interdisciplinary programs and instituted innovations such as abolishing grades and a shift
  to a problem-based learning curriculum. As the student body has increased and

students have demanded the ability to transfer coursework to other institutions in the university system, grading has become standardized. The medical program has been able to maintain its unique stature within the university system. Problem-based learning has also maintained a certain status as the ideal model for teaching and learning.

The institution was challenged by the need to be innovative and unique while also meeting the standards of a national system of higher education that dictated standardization and compatibility. A statement from the institution's strategic plan suggests that the isomorphic shifts Tromsø experienced were not reactive:

> *It is important to remember the old when one changes to something new. Evolution is better than revolution in this respect. Many changes in processes have failed due to beliefs in radical change, where old structures are taken away without having new structures to replace them. The old must be administered at the same time as new things evolve.*

> (Stensaker and Norgård, 2001, p. 490)

Although institutional adjustments—whether isomorphic or innovative—were made for economic reasons, they were made to achieve compatibility and not strictly for economic opportunity. The process of change was strategic and long term.

Institutional isomorphism within the context of board development and fundraising in higher education takes on many roles (DiMaggio & Powell, 1983; Milem, Berger, & Dey, 2000; Morphew, 2002; Riesman, 1956). One aspect of considerable research is institutional isomorphism in the form of striving. O'Meara (2007) defines striving "as the pursuit of prestige within the academic hierarchy" (p. 122). Institutional decision making, policies, and behaviors within the contexts of admissions process, reward structures, resource allocation decisions, donor engagement, and fundraising can all be affected by the interest of an institution to morph into the likes of an aspirational peer (Aldersley, 1995; Dichev, 2001; Ehrenberg, 2003; Meredith, 2004; Morphew, 2002; Winston, 2000). David Riesman (1956) was one of the first to consider institutional isomorphism within American higher education. Riesman (1956) noted, "there is no doubt that colleges and universities in this country model themselves upon each other . . . All one has to do is read catalogues to realize the extent of this isomorphism" (p. 25).

Boards of trustees are often part of the decision making that leads to isomorphism on campus. Often the decision to strive and pursue prestige leads to boards deciding to borrow fundraising programs from other institutions. Perhaps the most recognizable, in terms of fundraising, is the growth and standardization of capital and comprehensive campaigns, as well as the evolution and professionalization of in-house advancement offices at colleges and universities.

The first comprehensive campaign was at Harvard. Throughout the 20th century, campaigns spread throughout American higher education, first through private institutions and then to public higher education. At first, institutions hired professional fundraising firms to manage their campaigns and even make the solicitations. Harvard hired John Price Jones in 1919 to administer their first full-fledged organized campaign that asked "regular" alumni for their support (Cutlip, 1965). This extended to historically Black colleges and universities, who used fundraising firms through the 1970s (Gasman & Drezner, 2008, 2009, 2010). In the latter half of the 20th century, fundraising moved to within the university's own staff.

The size and reach of comprehensive campaigns have also grown in the last few decades, with top universities often competing within their peer group for the largest campaign goal and dollars raised—akin to an arms race—but certainly can be viewed in terms of the theoretical lens of isomorphism. As of May 2013, there were 109 campaigns (up from 75 in 2010—a sign of additional confidence after the 2008 great recession), either announced or completed, with goals over $1 billion at institutions in the United States. Of those 109 campaigns, 71 campaigns were successfully completed and in fact exceeded their original goals (goals totaled $107.29 billion, yet $125.75 billion was raised). The amount raised is higher than the stated goals because all of the campaigns that were active during the late 1990s and early 2000s closed significantly above their original goals. The remaining 39 are currently in the public phase of their campaign. Further, of the 109 campaigns, 19 of them are at institutions that are currently in or have completed a second billion-dollar-plus campaign, and 2 (Johns Hopkins and Stanford Universities) are in their third billion-dollar-plus campaign (Grezenbach, Glier, & Associates, 2013). The University of Southern California is currently in the largest campaign ever announced—it is seeking to raise $6 billion by the end of 2018—and the University of Virginia is the largest campaign for a public institution; it is looking to raise $3 billion by the end of 2013 and is nearly there.

THE NO SINGLE THEORY SCHOOL OF THOUGHT

Nonprofit researchers generally agree that there is no single theory that explains board behavior. The trend has been to look at combinations of theory. There is no consensus on a combination, but the following studies illustrate this approach. Not all of the studies discussed involved an experimental design. They are useful here to illustrate the value of a combined theory approach. This research also reflects work done in non-higher education contexts.

Miller-Millesen (2003) developed a model that integrated agency, resource dependency, and institutional theories. She argued that board behavior is sensitive to two environmental factors—the resource environment and the regulatory environment. Many board behaviors can be interpreted through agency, resource dependency, and institutional theory. For example, boards may become involved in strategic planning to set policy, obtain resources, or because it is required by a funder. However, none of the theories applied individually may explain board dynamics. Miller-Millesen advocates a multi-theoretical analysis based on actual board behavior. When applied to board performance evaluation, assuming the criteria for the wrong theory may result in flawed analysis. As she explained:

> For example, if board members were recruited to legitimize the organization, it would be unacceptable to assess board performance by measuring its contribution to the oversight function. Similarly, if the board engages in self-assessment activities in order to position itself for a capital campaign, it would be inappropriate to evaluate the effectiveness of the self-assessment from an agency theory perspective. The problem is that, as this article has demonstrated, the assumptions of the three different theoretical perspectives underlie the best practice literature.

> (p. 543)

More research on actual board behavior will yield better studies linking board behavior to organizational performance.

Brown (2005) applied agency theory, resource dependency theory, and group/decision process theory to the six dimensions of effective boards suggested by Chait, Holland, and Taylor (1991) in order to simultaneously look at board and organizational performance. All three theoretical constructs were supported with strategic contributions of the board most strongly associated with organizational performance. In support of agency theory, Brown (2005) found that boards of nonprofit organizations not only monitor ethical and financial behavior but also adherence to mission and charitable purpose. Resource dependency was supported by a correlation between stronger financial performance and strategic contributions by the board. Also supporting the theory was a positive relationship between a board that fosters external relationships and net financial surplus. Educational, analytical, and interpersonal factors were related to decision/group process theory. In particular, the analytical aspect of debating important issues correlated positively with net revenue and perceived organizational effectiveness. Reflecting the interpersonal factor, the board's ability to work together effectively and form interpersonal relationships correlated positively with net financial surplus and perceived organizational performance. Overall, time developing a cohesive board is good for organizational performance.

In a subsequent study, Brown and Guo (2010) looked at executive perceptions of the board's role and how board roles are contingent on organizational and environmental factors. They found that organizational factors like environmental uncertainty and organizational complexity have an effect on board roles. For example, where resources are constrained, board participation is considered critical. Board involvement in strategy formation was more important in complex organizations, while board oversight was more critical for larger, more diverse organizations. Agency theory and resource dependency informed some key roles like strategy formation but did not explain all of the roles of nonprofit boards or even role prevalence. Looking at board behavior as group or interpersonal process captured a more holistic view of board activity encompassing both control and resource activities. Brown and Guo also noted that work needs to be done on how board engagement is fostered.

Guo (2007) focused on the effect of government funding on board roles, using a combination of resource dependency and institutional theory. He found that more government funding led to boards that had both weaker community ties and a weaker relationship to the executive director. Increased dependency on government funding led to boards that had connections to funding agencies and/or had expertise in grant writing. Due to the limited number of board seats, the government insiders crowded out the community representation on the board, reflecting resource dependency. Because of funding dependency, organizations were more likely to be compliant with government expectations. The professionalization needed to comply with funding requirements also reduced the number of volunteers, creating distance between the organization and the community, as well as vesting power in the executive director, reflecting institutional theory.

Although this work has not yet been applied to higher education, it is possible to see its value to the expansion of our understanding of the role of government on public institutions of higher education. The political nature of these trustee appointments has been pointed out (Minor, 2008; Taylor & Machado, 2008), but the effects have not been explored. Weakened board connections to community and executive leaders could result in a loss of donor networks, reducing the potential for philanthropic gifts.

A fourth theoretical combination considered governance through the lenses of agency theory, stewardship theory, and stakeholder theory (Van Puyvelde, Caers, Du Bois, & Jegers, 2011). In nonprofit situations, principals and agents may not be clearly defined. Although there are no shareholders, there are many stakeholders both internal and external to the organization. Incorporating stakeholder and stewardship theory provides a broader perspective on the principal/agent dynamic. Stakeholder theory allows for the consideration of both inside and outside stakeholder groups as principals and agents. Multiple principal/agent relationships can be found that involve stakeholder groups where there is a contractual relationship between the parties and some transfer of decision-making authority occurs. These may include board members, managers, employees, volunteers, funders, or members. The use of stewardship theory also allows for additional perspectives. For example, a donor may be a principal that delegates the decision of how to spend the gift to the organization (agent). Stewardship theory assumes that the nonprofit wants to act in the best interests of the donor about how the gift is used. When board members are donors, the relationship becomes more complicated. The board member is an interface stakeholder and a principal in setting organizational strategy, and a steward of organizational resources.

Although the research in this area is steadily evolving, one constant is the connection of board behavior and effectiveness to organizational effectiveness. The nonprofit research does not generally attempt to look at boards separated from that context. It also bears repeating that much of the nonprofit literature at this point suggests hypotheses but is not densely experimental.

AVENUES FOR FUTURE RESEARCH

The nonprofit theories discussed in this chapter have rarely been explored within the context of American higher education, thereby leaving the directions for future research wide open. There are a number of ways that higher education scholars, practitioners, and students can use these theories to guide their work. For example, looking at institutional theory and the concept of isomorphism, future research can look at campaigns, their cases for support, marketing materials, and fundraising strategies. This research can be guided by the work of Hartley and Morphew (2008), whose study looked at admissions view books throughout American higher education and found few essential differences. When looking at fundraising campaigns in this manner, it is imperative that institutions critically analyze whether the isomorphism and benchmarking being done is best for the institution or if successful work at other institutions is being replicated without critical thought as to the individual campus context.

Further, building off of Proper's (2011) finding that higher education trustees view fundraising as an individual responsibility rather than a collective one of the board, research exploring trustee involvement in the conceptualization and implementation of campaigns is warranted. This work could use a number of theories discussed in this chapter as a starting point. For example, agency theory could be used to explore how administrators and trustees interact, stakeholder theory could explain the lack of involvement of trustees in the process beyond approval of ideas presented by administrators, and resource dependency theory could be used to show that trustees should be more involved in the fundraising enterprise of the university.

The role of isomorphism has yet to be explored in many areas, including how the composition of boards changes in response to levels of government funding and public policy and how both of these factors influence donor networks. Researchers in higher education would do well to take the lead of nonprofit scholars and consider a multiple theory perspective in their work. As complex institutions, the principals, agents, stakeholders, and stewards may reverse roles as the need to gather and sustain resources changes and as the field of institutions changes on a grander scale. Governance of higher education deserves to be studied and analyzed in all of its dimensions. The thoughtful consideration of theory can accomplish that goal.

Just as theories provide lenses for understanding board behavior, case studies are lenses that help us develop a deeper understanding of those theories. The case study that is presented here incorporates all board roles related to philanthropy—fundraising, gift management, endowment management, and alignment of philanthropy with institutional mission. Important contexts to consider are donor intent and the effect of time on the relationship of institutions and donors, the stakeholder populations of both Earlham College and Conner Prairie, and the missions of the two organizations.

================================== **CASE STUDY** ==================================

EARLHAM COLLEGE AND CONNER PRAIRIE

Earlham College is located in Richmond, Indiana, and enrolls around 1,200 undergraduate students. The institution's strong Quaker roots reach back to the early 19th century. Reflecting this heritage, the Earlham board makes all decisions by consensus. The board is composed of members from the Indiana Yearly Meeting of Friends, the Western Yearly Meeting of Friends, alumni, at-large members elected by the Friends and alumni, and the college president (ex officio).

The Conner Prairie Interactive History Park is located in Fishers, Indiana, some 75 miles from Earlham College. Its mission is "to inspire curiosity and foster learning about Indiana's past by providing engaging, individualized, and unique experiences." (Conner Prairie Museum, 2013)

From 1964 until 2005, these two entities shared a history rooted in a philanthropic gift. The long history of this gift provides a unique lens for examining board theory within the context of philanthropy.

Eli Lilly acquired the Conner Prairie property in 1934. He continued to acquire land, expanding his holdings to more than 1,400 acres. Lilly was keenly interested in historic preservation and had visited Williamsburg and other living museums. The site, which included an experimental farm, offered educational programs as early as 1935. From the beginning, it was obvious that Lilly wanted to develop something of long-term significance for Indiana.

Lilly transferred Conner Prairie to Earlham College in 1964. He had approached both Purdue University and the Indiana Historical Society, but they were not interested. The manager of the Conner Prairie experimental farm at that time was a Quaker, Tillman Bubeznar, who knew Thomas Jones, an Earlham trustee. Through Jones, a conversation started between Lilly and Landrum Bolling, president of Earlham.

Fifty-eight acres, including the original Conner House and several outbuildings brought in by Lilly, were transferred to be held in perpetuity by Earlham as trustee. The property was to be maintained and access provided to the public. An additional 1,371 acres were transferred without restrictions. Lilly's expectation was that if land was sold, the proceeds would go to an endowment to maintain the public facilities. Earlham's board accepted the terms, understanding that the public charitable trust that had been created obligated the Earlham board to the public at large. When a public charitable trust is created, the "trustee becomes legally bound by fiduciary duties of loyalty and care in its administration of the trust, and it assumes the obligation to act in the best interests of the public as the beneficiary of the trust." (Duck, 2011, p. 8)

During 1964 and 1965, the Earlham trustees continued the educational programs at Conner Prairie but began to look at ways to develop it as well, including a master plan.

Between 1965 and 1968, the farm operations received the most attention, but museum attendance grew from 28 visitors in 1964 to 26,000 in 1968.

In 1968, the business officer for Earlham reported that the museum was operating at a loss. An endowment of half a million dollars was needed to sustain operations. Earlham preferred not to sell off acreage to fund an endowment. The sentiment was that the museum either needed to be developed to the fullest to make it profitable or potentially closed down. Closing down the museum would have violated the deed of trust, since it stipulated that the museum must remain open to the public. Lilly liked the idea of expanding the museum to help it become self-sustaining rather than selling off land to fund an endowment. Earlham appointed an advisory council of Indianapolis residents to guide a master plan for Conner Prairie.

Lilly's intent as a donor was also apparent in subsequent gifts. When President Bolling visited Lilly in 1968 and asked for a gift for the Earlham endowment, he came away with $50,000 for Conner Prairie but nothing for the college. Lilly followed this up with a gift of $3 million in Lilly stock in 1969. According to the gift agreement, funds were to be kept separate from the Earlham general endowment. Income from the fund as well as principal was to be used for development and operation of Conner Prairie. Earlham was permitted to use income but no principal after all of Conner Prairie's needs had been met. All funds donated principally for the benefit of Conner Prairie eventually came to be known as the Eli Lilly Endowment Fund. Lilly also did not favor restrictions on Conner Prairie expenditures. At one point, President Bolling attempted to get Lilly to formally agree to a cap on capital expenditures for Conner Prairie as well as a limit of $60,000 for annual income for operations, including an allocation for college overhead. Lilly specifically rejected this proposal.

In 1969, the Conner Prairie advisory board solicited proposals for the preparation of a comprehensive feasibility study to expand the scope of the museum. The proposed expansion for Prairietown—a re-creation of an 1836 Indiana community—came in with a budget of $1,725,000. Potential separation of the museum from the college appears to have come up for the first time in 1970, just as the expansion was getting underway. Edward Wilson, chair of the Earlham board, rejected a proposal from a member of the Conner Prairie advisory council to create a separate foundation to manage the finances for Conner Prairie. Wilson communicated to the Earlham board the need to keep their priorities straight. Earlham's obligations to undergraduate students came first. Conner Prairie was an asset of the college to be used to further their first priority. He acknowledged that Earlham had an obligation to Conner Prairie based on accepting the gift of stock. To fulfill their obligation under the gift, they should be prepared to spend $600,000 for capital improvements and some portion of the income. The sum of $50,000 income per year was suggested as an appropriate amount. The available income would have been around $190,000, far in excess of what Wilson was suggesting was appropriate. Lilly, unaware of the trustees' decision and very excited about the expansion plan for the museum, sent an additional $100,000 for the fund.

In 1972, the executive committee approved the expenditure of $600,000 for the construction of Prairietown but also approved a 50/50 split of the income from the 1969

Lilly gift between the college and Conner Prairie. This division became the operating principle for allocation of income from the Lilly endowed funds. There is no indication that Lilly was informed of the allocation decision. That year, he made an additional gift of $1.4 million in Lilly stock for Conner Prairie.

Lilly's third and largest gift of $16 million in shares of Lilly stock came in 1973. Principal could be used for the construction of Prairietown and income used to sustain its operations. Funds were to be separate from other Earlham endowments in the Eli Lilly Endowment Fund. As with prior gifts, Conner Prairie had first use of all income until all of its needs were met. Income not needed by the museum could be used by the college. Earlham was specifically barred from using the principal for its own purposes.

Although Lilly had not been formally notified of board action that changed the division of income, he apparently was aware that Conner Prairie was not receiving all of the income it was entitled to under the gift agreements. In 1974, Lilly asked President Bolling for an accounting of endowment income and what had been used for Conner Prairie development and operations. He expressed concern that the Earlham trustees were withholding funds that the museum needed. Landrum Bolling had moved on to the presidency of the Lilly Endowment, and Earlham had a new president—Franklin Wallin. Wilson, the Earlham board chair, wrote to Lilly that they had plans to proceed with the museum development and that the plan was that the income from the 1973 gift would be divided between Conner Prairie and Earlham on a 50/50 basis. Lilly's response indicated a strong preference to revert to the original agreement that all principal was for Conner Prairie and income was only available to Earlham if it was not needed by the museum. Despite this, Earlham continued to restrict what was available to Conner Prairie. A report to the advisory council in 1975 stated that further expansion of the museum would be limited to $1.2 million. Although the museum advisory council requested clarification on how the 1969 gift was being used, President Wallin did not provide it.

Eli Lilly died in 1977. His will, signed in 1973, provided for a gift to Earlham of 10 percent of the value of his residuary estate, which was to be used for Conner Prairie under the conditions specified in the prior gifts. The value was $10 million in stock.

Earlham put an endowment policy in place the year after Lilly's death, which was applied to the 1969 and 1973 gifts and the bequest. It reintroduced the idea that Lilly's intent was to provide a portion for the college and referred to the 1974 50/50 split as the basis for managing the endowment, even though these terms were not supported by Lilly's will. The 50 percent share of Conner Prairie's income that was not needed for current operations was allocated to the college, not reinvested for museum expansion. The board also stated the intent to control costs at the museum so that it would not need more than its 'share' of income. Members of the Conner Prairie advisory council saw that this arrangement was in opposition to Lilly's will, which was the controlling document for the bequest. The allocation of income favored the college, and the museum advisory council resented it. Because the capital expenditures to expand Conner Prairie were charged against their 50 percent instead of against the entire principal, eventually the college began to receive more income from the endowment than did the museum.

A capital campaign was mounted in the 1980s to finance the construction of the Conner Prairie Museum Center—a facility to house administrative offices, collections, meeting rooms, and food service. By the end of 1986, $7 million out of the $8.6 million needed had been raised. The Earlham trustees voted to go ahead with the project. When completed, the asset was placed on the books of the college, a further indication that the college did not see Conner Prairie as a public trust.

After construction of the Museum Center, Earlham approved a new management structure for the museum and formed Conner Prairie, Inc., an Earlham Museum. The board of directors was appointed by the college and was made up of former members of the advisory group, four Earlham appointees, and the executive director of the museum. The operation became a subsidiary of the college. The advisory board was allowed to manage operations with oversight from the college but had no fiscal control. The hope was that with this modified structure, Conner Prairie would be able to garner more philanthropic support.

The next major expansion to revitalize Conner Prairie began in 1997. By 2001, they would add the Lenape Indian camp, Liberty Corner (a re-creation of an 1886 town), hands-on workshops, and summer camp programs. By this time, Conner Prairie was deeply embedded in the culture of Central Indiana due to years of fourth grade field trips. The expansion was part of a five-year strategic plan developed under the direction of Conner Prairie CEO Marsha Semmel.

In 1997 and 1998 there were again changes in leadership. Douglas Bennett replaced Richard Wood as president of Earlham, and John Herbst became CEO of Conner Prairie. During his presidency of Earlham, Wood had issued regular reports about the endowment that took on the aura of institutional memory. In 1997, the museum board passed a resolution asking Earlham for a 1 percent increase in endowment spending (up to 5 percent) and $2.5 million from the endowment for the first phase of the strategic plan. It was also at this time that Berkley Duck, a member of the Conner Prairie board, began to look into the legal issues surrounding Earlham's endowment management policies. Although the issues surrounding the endowment were brought to President Bennett's attention by the chair of the museum board, no action was taken by either Bennett or the Earlham board. In 1998, the college adopted a repositioning plan to try to get both the college and the museum on more solid footing. It approved an additional 1 percent and a $3.7 million draw on the endowment for capital improvements that would be repaid through fundraising. Costs proved to be higher than projected, causing the college board to demand management controls that would prevent future cost overruns. Although the museum board complied, the question of why Conner Prairie could not use endowment principal without promising to repay it began to come up regularly.

From 2000 on, there were conversations among the Conner Prairie board chairs, past and present, that reached Earlham about not only management of the endowment but also about the possibility of separating the museum from the college. That year, the Earlham board would not approve an additional $1 million draw from the endowment. President Bennett advised Herbst to find the money in his operating budget. There was no progress in the discussion regarding separation. Despite the disparity in mission of the college and the museum, Earlham refused to consider any fundamental change in the arrangements. The museum board was urged to raise money for its endowment. The Earlham board failed to realize that it was impossible for the museum to garner that level of philanthropic support while it was under Earlham's budgetary control.

In 2001 the museum executive committee requested a special distribution of $974,000, referring formally to the Lilly gift agreements. The request never made it to the full Earlham board. Herbst requested again in March and was turned down. Earlham offered a loan against the endowment, which would be repaid by Conner Prairie with interest. The current fundraising effort had stalled, and it was apparent that support would not be forthcoming while Earlham listed Conner Prairie as one of its financial assets. Conner Prairie also wanted relief from the administrative fees that Earlham was charging against the museum—for payroll, health insurance, and rent for land that Earlham had not paid for. Earlham responded by proposing creation of a firewall to protect the college's share of endowment principal. Some adjustments were made in the administrative fees, and the museum was allowed to manage its health insurance plan. Conner Prairie agreed to take the endowment funds as a loan, hoping for resolution of the separation issue. In November, Earlham advised the museum board that the two organizations could not be separated under the conditions of the Lilly gifts.

In January of 2002, the museum governance committee wrote a position paper that argued for separation on the basis that the administration of the Lilly gifts conflicted with the terms of the Eli Lilly will and other bequests. When the museum board met that month, two of the Earlham representatives vetoed the proposed budget. A third Earlham representative abstained and then resigned from the board. Because of the impasse, museum board members considered meeting with Steve Carter, the attorney general. Under Indiana law, only the attorney general was empowered to act on the behalf of the public when there had been a breach by a trustee of the terms of a public charitable trust. The museum board suggested to Earlham that this meeting should take place, but Earlham did not consent. The museum board decided not to pursue an independent meeting at that time.

By May of 2002, Conner Prairie was ready to pursue formal mediation. The board felt that the museum was at the point of no return. If it could not separate from Earlham, it would stagnate. The September board meeting of the college provided no solutions. The Earlham board would not agree to any changes in endowment management. The museum board representatives saw the proposed firewall as a direct violation of the gift agreements. A mediation agreement drafted by Earlham would have given the museum additional operational independence, some control over endowment spending, and cessation of administrative fees. It did not give Conner Prairie any voice in endowment management, which the board considered crucial. The museum board returned a revised draft that the Earlham board did not act on.

Earlham was having serious financial problems. The college was suffering chronic deficits as well as serious recruitment and retention issues. All areas of operation were in trouble—enrollment, financial aid, faculty salaries, physical management, and technology. The revised agreement presented by Earlham prior to the February 2003 board meeting showed the need to gain a stronger measure of control over the endowment. Under the revision, the museum would have to agree to an endowment firewall and a mandatory depreciation allowance and would be barred from suing Earlham for past acts. The museum board feared that if the attorney general approved this agreement that he might be barred in future from filing suit against Earlham. The Conner Prairie board informed Earlham's attorney that it could not accept the agreement. If Earlham would not resolve the endowment issue, the museum would put the matter before the attorney general. Neither Conner Prairie nor Earlham could change the terms of the Lilly gifts, and only the court could decide the issue of the endowment.

The Earlham trustees rejected the next Conner Prairie revised agreement and terminated mediation. Their next proposal clearly partitioned Earlham's portion of the endowment, separating it completely from the Lilly gifts. In subsequent revisions in the document, Earlham remained firm in its partitioning of the gift and the firewall. The museum board went so far as to devise a plan to divide the remaining endowment based on the original agreements and the present value of the funds. They notified Earlham's lawyer that they could not accept the latest proposal because they would violate their fiduciary duties to the museum and to the Lilly gifts. The museum board made a final counterproposal based on its division plan. Earlham suspended negotiations.

On June 11, 2003, the Earlham and museum governance committees met at Conner Prairie. Earlham rejected the most recent museum board proposal and reinstated their March 31 offer. The museum governance committee declined to take the offer to their full board. Bennett then fired the non-Earlham members of the museum board and Conner Prairie CEO John Herbst. Press releases issued minutes later by Earlham cited the budget deficits and poor financial management of the museum as the reasons for terminating the board. The terminated board members regrouped to form a new nonprofit, Save the Prairie, Inc., to represent the museum's interests to the public and to work with the Indiana attorney general to investigate Earlham's management of Conner Prairie. On June 23, Attorney General Carter agreed to conduct a formal review.

A major issue that needed to be resolved was the relationship of the museum and the college. Was Conner Prairie a part of or separate from the mission of Earlham? Earlham claimed that they were one entity and that the gifts that created the endowment were not part of the public charitable trust. Myron Vourax, CEO of Conner Prairie from 1971–1976, had met regularly with Lilly during the construction of Prairietown. He did not believe that Earlham saw the museum as part of its overall mission but saw it as a way to get money from Lilly.

On January 17, 2004, Carter filed a lawsuit seeking a formal accounting for Earlham's management of the Lilly gifts. He called for the appointment of a new trustee for Conner Prairie as the best way to resolve the financial conflicts of interest that existed between Earlham and the museum. Carter's strategy was to focus on the future of Conner Prairie while allowing Earlham to save face. His position was that for a college to be both trustee and beneficiary of a trust created a conflict of interest that was not good public policy.

On July 5, 2005, Attorney General Carter's negotiated agreement was signed by both parties. Under the new structure, a foundation was created to manage the Eli Lilly Endowment Fund. A separate operating company would run the museum and raise funds. Earlham would have representation on both boards but not control of either. The Conner Prairie Foundation, Inc., would serve as trustee of the public charitable trust. Without going into the particulars, the Conner Prairie side of the equation received 48.25 percent of the value of the Eli Lilly Endowment Fund (not less than $85 million), a promise from Earlham to repay an additional $6.5 million within five years, and a majority of the land. The agreement also required Earlham to forgive $5.8 million in loans to the Conner Prairie Museum. Earlham retained some land and the remainder of the endowment—around $80 million.

EXERCISES AND DISCUSSION QUESTIONS

1. As a small group exercise, analyze and evaluate individual theories for 'best fit' as it applies to the case study.
2. Using the results of the group exercise, develop a theory concept map to do a macro analysis of the case.
3. In terms of agency and its subsidiary theories, what are the relationships between the Earlham board and other stakeholders—Eli Lilly, the Conner Prairie board and staff, Earlham students, and the public?
4. Resource theories go beyond the need to attract financial resources for an institution. Did Earlham fail to garner other types of resources such as social capital and other broader community supports?
5. Institutional theory makes a case for institutions sharing common characteristics and behaviors. In its actions regarding the Lilly gifts and bequests, did Earlham's board behave in the way that would be expected of college trustees?
6. Reflect on how an understanding of board dynamics could have changed the outcome from the vantage point of the various stakeholders.

RESOURCES USED FOR THE CASE STUDY

Conner Prairie Museum (2013). *Mission statement*. Guidestar. Retrieved from www2.guidestar.org/Home.aspx

Duck, B. W. (2011). *Twilight at Conner Prairie: The creation, betrayal, and rescue of a museum*. Lanham, MD: AltaMira.

Bingmann, M., Lewis, R., Rosenthal, E., Simic, C. R., & Yerkovich, S. (2012). What happened at Conner Prairie? An IMH Roundtable. *Indiana Magazine of History, 108*(1), 35–52.

Myers, M. B., Bennett, D. C., & Young, J. G. (2004). *A report on Earlham's stewardship of Conner Prairie, an Eli Lilly legacy*. Richmond, IN: Earlham College.

4

LEADERSHIP FOR PHILANTHROPY

Fund-raising in an institution is often led by a champion. The champion should be either the president or someone at the senior management level working closely with the president. The champion should be totally convinced about the importance of institutional advancement, taking that as a mission. Given the essential nature of fund-raising, institutional advancement should occupy a major position in the institution's policy agenda.

(Cheng, 2011, p. 171)

Leadership intersects philanthropy in building relationships with donors, engaging alumni and alumnae, and monitoring endowment performance. The role of the president—with boards, development staff, and other stakeholders—is of particular interest. The vast majority of advertised positions for higher education leadership include fundraising as part of the position description (Hunt, 2012). In an era when the major campaigns end only to begin anew and presidents and other top leadership transition between institutions with unnerving regularity, coordinating leadership changes within campaign strategy is a necessity (Nehls, 2008).

Although there is nothing close to the last word on how best to conceptualize leadership for either higher education or the third sector, five theoretical frameworks dominate the literature. They will be discussed in turn, including applications in both higher education and the nonprofit sector more broadly. The first three focus on individuals as leaders.

LEADERSHIP AS AN INDIVIDUAL ENTERPRISE

Transactional and Transformational Leaders

The development of **transactional** versus **transformational leadership theory** is attributed to historian and political scientist James McGregor Burns (1978). The prevailing view of leadership at that time was that leaders were born and not made. Burns's work marked a transition to a focus on how leaders could be developed and understanding how leadership style affects organizational growth and change. Transactional leaders focus on balancing the organization's mission against the motives and interests of employees. Leaders achieve compliance through providing resources needed by employees to achieve organizational goals as well as the use of rewards such as pay increases and praise or through disciplinary action (Burns, 1978; Nicholson, 2007; Ronquillo, 2011). However, the key characteristic of transactional-style leadership is that the organization's culture is maintained in a steady state. The transactional leader's goal for the organization is to maintain the status quo (Ronquillo, 2011).

In contrast, transformational leaders are characterized as charismatic and inspiring role models. They motivate employees to achieve organizational goals and to put aside self-interest for the good of the organization. They encourage their followers to envision a better future. By promoting creative thinking and focusing on coaching rather than using criticism as a motivating force, the organizational status quo is replaced by positive organizational change. Transformational leadership elevates leaders and followers to a higher level of both motivation and morality (Nicholson, 2007; Riggio, Bass, & Orr, 2004; Ronquillo, 2011).

Bass (1998) described four aspects of transformational leaders:

- Idealized influence—The leader is a charismatic role model who builds commitment to the organizational cause. The leader embodies the mission of the organization.
- Inspirational motivation—The leader infuses enthusiasm and team spirit.
- Intellectual stimulation—The leader encourages innovation and creativity.
- Individualized consideration—The leader is able to focus on the individual needs of followers.

Some weaknesses of the theory have been noted. The process of how transformational leadership affects emotion and commitment is ambiguous. Also, the theory does not take into account that the effects of leadership may be indirect and affect group processes rather than individuals. It can also be difficult to distinguish between transactional and transformational situations. How rewards are classified may be ambiguous. Contingent rewards may be financial or something transformational like praise or recognition. Behavioral descriptions of transformational leaders are not consistent. Finally, transformational leadership is never criticized but is always viewed as a positive characteristic of a single leader. The situation in which leadership takes place may warrant a different, non-transformational style. Invariably, the leader will always receive credit when things are going well, a scenario that does not take into account possibilities like shared leadership (Yukl, 1999).

Two papers illustrate use of transformational leadership theory in higher education research. Both focus on the role of leadership in fundraising. Success of a college president in fundraising depends on the ability to develop an effective leadership style for that task. Nicholson (2007) looked at characteristics of top fundraising presidents and specifically at their transactional and transformational leadership traits. He observed that presidents use both transactional and transformational approaches in their fundraising role. The choice of approach is contextual. A transactional approach is used to build trust and relationship with donors. A transformational approach in the ongoing relationship then increases motivation and donation behavior. Of particular importance to success are inspirational motivation (vision) and individualized consideration (individual needs of the donors).

Curry, Rodin, and Carlson (2012) utilized a survey to look at fundraising best practices for a range of Christian educational institutions, including higher education. The purpose was to determine the effect of a poor economic climate on donations. They found a transformational leadership style that focused on communicating mission to be far more important to success than regional economic conditions, development staff size, or fundraising budget size. This trend was pronounced for all institution types other than higher education. The authors attributed the result to the particular challenges faced by Christian higher education, such as declining enrollments that require stronger leadership, a clear message, more highly developed information systems, and stewardship of resources.

Nonprofit research on transformational leadership has focused more on tying leadership to organizational effectiveness and change. The importance of inspirational motivation and individualized consideration have been cited as being critical to working with volunteers and staff in nonprofit organizations where financial rewards may not be comparable with the business world (Riggio, Bass, & Orr, 2004; Anheier, 2005). The link between transformational leadership and organizational innovation is not conclusive. Jaskyte (2012) found a negative relationship. In her analysis, a strong consensus in values among employees when coupled with a transformational leader actually mediated against organizational change.

Two studies from the nonprofit literature further illustrate efforts to define the effects of transformational leadership on organizational behavior. Both are in the context of religious/church-based nonprofit organizations. McMurray, Pirola-Merlo, Sarros, and Islam (2010) looked at the "effects of leadership on organizational climate, employee psychological capital, commitment, and wellbeing" (p. 436). Psychological capital is defined as resilience, optimism, self-efficacy, and hope. They found that employees who rated their supervisors higher in transformational leadership skills also rated organizational climate higher and experienced higher levels of well-being, organizational commitment, and psychological capital. Their analysis also showed higher levels of psychological capital among older employees but higher levels of leadership among those in mid-life. The highest levels of transformational leadership were seen in the most highly educated employees.

In a second study—again with a religious/church-based nonprofit organization—the researchers looked for connections between leadership, work group climate, and performance (McMurray, Islam, Sarros, & Pirola-Merlo, 2012). Organizational culture appears to be a mediating factor. In a volunteer-driven organization, transactional leadership style influenced work group climate, perhaps due to the level of direction required.

Transformational leadership style and workgroup climate both influenced workgroup performance. Intragroup influences appeared to prevent either transactional or transformational leadership style from influencing performance through workgroup climate. In this religious environment, intellectual stimulation was not a motivator. It was perhaps viewed as being competitive and, therefore, not charitable.

Leaders as Servants

Robert Greenleaf's (1991) classic definition of **servant leadership** states that servant leaders are servants first and then make a conscious decision to become leaders. A retired business executive, Greenleaf drew inspiration from Herman Hesse's *Journey to the East* in developing his ideas. Servant leadership evokes the leadership styles of great religious figures of all faiths, whether it describes behavior or an ideal inner life. Three central characteristics are virtue, leadership behavior, and motivation to lead. Virtue refers to integrity in action. A leader's character is defined by integrity rather than reputation. A servant leader enacts the core values of an organization in order to build community within that organization.

Servant leaders speak through their behavior. They use their power to achieve the goals of the group rather than for personal ends. Their motivation to lead is driven by the desire to serve. Servant leadership does not ignore traditional leadership theory but directs it toward allowing and encouraging followers to achieve both individual and collective goals.

Spears (2010) identified ten characteristics of servant leaders:

- Deep listening;
- Empathy;
- Ability to facilitate emotional healing in followers;
- Self-awareness;
- Use of persuasion rather than issuing orders;
- Ability to conceptualize;
- Ability to learn from the past;
- Stewardship;
- Belief in the inherent value of individuals;
- Commitment to building community.

Ebener and O'Connell (2010) tried to operationalize servant leadership through a study of three high-performing Catholic parishes and demonstrated that servant leader behaviors encourage the development of organizational citizenship. The goal was to identify the patterns of behavior that explain the mechanisms of servant leadership or how it initiates the citizenship behaviors that were identified. The research shows a relationship between servant leadership, organizational citizenship, and high performance.

Case study organizations were chosen from the results of a self-study of churches in the Catholic Diocese of Davenport, Iowa. Eighty-four parishes completed a 43-question instrument that included both operational measures such as attendance and behavioral measures designed to detect both servant leadership behaviors and organizational citizenship behaviors. Diocesan leaders were asked to score the parishes. After ranking, the highest-scoring small, medium, and large parishes were chosen for the case studies. The focus at the parish level was on identifying and describing servant leadership and organizational citizenship behaviors. Data gathering included observation, focus groups, interviews, and examination of archival records.

The initial case sites looked at three specific servant leadership behaviors:

- Recognizing—Calling on the skills and talents of followers;
- Serving—Placing the needs of followers ahead of personal needs;
- Empowering—Providing opportunity and license for followers to act on behalf of the organization and themselves.

Four specific follower behaviors were also examined. The inquiry assumed that if leaders were exhibiting servant leadership behaviors, the followers would respond with organizational citizenship behaviors.

- Helping—Refers to informal outreach that is driven by altruism; this behavior has been linked to organizational effectiveness;
- Initiating—Followers voluntarily initiate projects, make suggestions, and generate ideas on behalf of the organization;
- Participating—Followers are actively involved in the formal activities of the organization; this behavior has been directly linked to organizational effectiveness;
- Self-developing—Followers take responsibility for their ongoing education and growth as a person and a member of the organization.

In the second stage of the research, an inductive grounded theory approach was used to discover patterns of behavior that would explain the mechanism of servant leadership in relation to citizenship behaviors. Through iterative listening to recordings and transcript readings, the transcripts were coded to find servant leadership and citizenship behaviors in close proximity to each other. Five themes emerged—three interpersonal links and two organizational—that led to development of a model linking servant leadership behaviors to organizational citizenship behaviors.

The interpersonal links were:

- Invitation—A servant leader invites a follower to participate, which encourages the four citizenship behaviors;
- Inspiration—Followers are motivated to participate through inspiration, example, and leader involvement; participation is chosen, not coerced;

- Affection—The leader expresses concern and compassion, often by listening and then taking care of follower needs. This behavior inspires followers to want to help, as well as establishing trust and commitment.

The two organizational links transformed both individuals and the organization:

- Culture of service—"Through a network of help and support, service became a norm in the parish" (p. 327);
- Structures of service—Committee or other small group structure permitted and encouraged citizenship behaviors. This created opportunities for volunteers to take initiative and lead, as well as for shared decision making.

Two additional leadership mechanisms noted by the authors were strategic influence and the role of religion in this setting. Although transformational leaders can help create a sense of shared vision in an organization (strategic influence), this theme did not stand out in the analysis as a factor that influenced citizenship behaviors. The five links, unique to servant leadership, were what encouraged these behaviors. The authors also note that the results may have been at least in part due to the emphasis the church places on parish life. Although hierarchies in organizations may pose challenges to servant leadership, these can be overcome. Organizational change occurs when a leader adopts the philosophy of servant leadership and actively integrates servant behaviors into the organization.

Irving (2005) found a statistically significant relationship between servant leadership and team effectiveness. Using a combination of assessment tools, he looked at servant leadership at the organizational level and at the level of the individual leader. The instruments used were the Organizational Leadership Assessment, the Servant Leadership Assessment Instrument, and the Team Effectiveness Questionnaire. The participants included over seven hundred employees of the U.S. division of an international nonprofit organization. Irving acknowledged that the relationship he found was mediated by job satisfaction. Despite this limitation, he called for formal efforts to develop servant leaders at both the organizational and individual level.

Authentic Leaders

A third concept that focuses on the individual as leader is **authentic leadership**. The notion of authenticity was popularized by Bill George (2003) as a response to corporate misconduct. It is based on the idea that it is not possible to legislate qualities of leadership such as integrity and stewardship. These qualities must flow from the authentic self— one that reflects a leadership style that is in harmony with the leader's personality and character and is grounded in a genuine desire to serve others through leadership. Most leadership training focuses on developing a persona of leadership rather than developing the unique individual. George outlines five dimensions to authentic leadership:

- Purpose—Passion for the cause or organizational goals;
- Values—Behavior that adheres to a personal code of ethics;

- Heart—Compassion for people;
- Relationships—Connections to other stakeholders;
- Self-discipline—Consistency in leadership behavior.

In addition, George felt it was important for leaders to remember that leadership is only one aspect of life. The most successful leaders work at having a balanced and well-rounded life.

The academic version of authentic leadership was developed within the field of business management by Luthans and Avolio (2003). Their goal was to develop a theory of genuine leadership development based in positive psychology. They wanted to define what actually was effective in developing leaders rather than looking at leadership as a remedial process of fixing deficiencies so that one could lead. Central to their conception is the idea that leadership has to consider followers and organizational context. Leadership does not exist in a psychological vacuum. They defined authentic leadership as "a process that draws from both positive psychological capacities and a highly developed organizational context, which results in both greater self-awareness and self-regulated positive behaviors on the part of leaders and associates, fostering positive self-development" (p. 243). It is characterized by four components:

- Balanced processing—Objective analysis of relevant data before making decisions;
- Internalized moral perspective—Internal moral standards guide and regulate behavior;
- Relational transparency—Open sharing of information and feelings in an appropriate manner;
- Self-awareness—An "understanding of one's strengths, weaknesses, and the way one makes sense of the world" (Avolio, Walumbwa, & Weber, 2009, p. 424).

Siddiq, Meyer, and Ashleigh (2013) have proposed a nonprofit research agenda to test the relationship between authentic leadership and leader accountability. Their definition of authentic leadership stated that the "leaders' actions, decisions, responsibilities and behaviours are accountable to themselves and others" (p. 396) and reflect the qualities of "openness, responsibility, and answerability" (p. 398). They propose to test the four components of authentic leadership defined by Luthans and Avolio (2003).

LEADERSHIP AS A COLLECTIVE ENTERPRISE

Shared Leadership

The final two theories, shared leadership and leader-member exchange theory, also have roots in business theory. They take into account the dynamic relationship between leaders and followers. **Shared leadership**—also referred to as distributed or collective leadership—describes a nonhierarchical or team-based style of leadership. Authority is shared across a group rather than being vested in a single individual. Three features of organizational climate that influence the diffusion of shared leadership are:

- Shared purpose—A common understanding and sharing of goals;
- Social support—Team members provide emotional and psychological support to each other;
- Voice—Members of the group have input into decision making.

The interaction of these three factors produces a dynamic and self-reinforcing system of group shared leadership (Avolio et al. 2009).

Shared leadership has not been ignored in the literature of higher education. In the early 1990s, Bensimon and Neumann (1993) conceptualized leadership in terms of team building. However, their executive leadership teams did not embrace the conception of shared leadership that is in the current literature. They described the ideal leader as "someone who knows how to find and bring together diverse minds—minds that reflect variety in their points of view, in their thinking processes, and in their question-asking and problem-solving strategies; minds that differ in their unique capacities as well as in their unique limitations" (p. 1). This leader was somewhat the antithesis of the superhero, great man ideal of a leader that had dominated conceptions of leadership, but their leader remained embodied in a single individual who was clearly in charge. Shared leadership has also made an appearance in research about student outcomes in higher education and in leadership at the elementary and secondary levels.

However, shared leadership has only been lightly touched on in relation to philanthropy in higher education. Sturgis (2006) examined the team relationship of presidents and vice presidents for institutional advancement at a sample of private baccalaureate colleges and universities. She found that these two levels of leaders did not share common perspectives about presidential leadership in the development arena. Vice presidents felt that the presidents overrated their ability to lead and to create an effective team environment.

Research in the arenas of nonprofit and philanthropy have also not exploited shared leadership theory to any extent. Crutchfield and Grant (2008) incorporated the concept into their description of high-impact nonprofit organizations. A scenario of shared power was characterized by:

- Distributed leadership, including a highly engaged board; power is shared;
- Collaborative initiatives, which are more effective in the nonprofit world, where leaders operate through influence instead of authority;
- Sublimation of personal interest to the interests of the organization;
- Belief that leadership does not translate to a particular personality type; both introverts and extroverts can fit the model;
- Presence of a strong second-in-command;
- Executive longevity, where work is viewed as a calling;

- Avoidance of founder's syndrome;
- Succession planning.

One compelling area of potential for application in both higher education and in non-profit organizations is the effect of leadership style on the board involvement in fundraising. Does executive leadership style have an impact on board willingness to participate in solicitation and other development activities? The intersection of executive and advancement leadership is also a ripe area for exploration of shared leadership theory.

Leader-Member Exchange

Leader-member exchange theory (LMX) stresses the relationship between leaders and followers. The quality of that relationship affects workplace outcomes. This work originated in psychology and is attributed to Graen and Uhl-Bien (1995). Effective leadership is predicated upon developing "high quality social exchange relationships between dyadic partners (leaders and followers, leaders and board members, team members and teammates, etc.), which bring all parties numerous benefits" (Jaskyte, 2012, p. 447). High-quality relationships result in benefits for all parties—greater access to resources, stronger influence over each other, and stronger support from each other. These relationships are characterized by trust, respect, and commitment to common goals (Avolio et al., 2009; Jaskyte, 2012). Parallels can be drawn between transformational leadership and high-level LMX relationships that encompass psychological factors including trust and support. Lower-level LMX relationships are more like transactional leadership, where compensation for doing the job is sufficient. LMX has been criticized for not taking into account the network of relationships within which leader/follower relationships exist.

In discussing this theory from the nonprofit perspective, Jaskyte (2012) suggested that it is not appropriate to see the board chair/executive director relationship as being strictly superior/subordinate since they essentially share the leadership role. She suggested that because this theory captures the relationship between the board chair and the executive director, it may prove to be useful in making connections between these relationships and organizational innovation.

ROLE OF INSTITUTIONAL LEADERSHIP IN FUNDRAISING

The role of institutional leaders in fundraising has increased substantially in the past four decades. Fundraising is a shared responsibility of many institutional leaders, with notable responsibility resting with presidents and deans (Glier, 2004; Miller, 1991). There is a lack of rigorous academic work that looks at the role of institutional leaders in fundraising; this void has been filled by atheoretical literature by practitioners, consultants, and journalists. Few published empirical studies look at the role of academic leaders within fundraising (e.g., Cook, 1997; Cook & Lasher, 1996; Nicholson, 2007). Additionally, there are a few unpublished dissertations looking at aspects of the topic (e.g., Rodriguez, 1991; Satterwhite, 2004; Slinker, 1988; Winfree, 1989).

Presidents and deans have key roles in creating, sustaining, and executing a successful culture of philanthropy at their institutions (Slinker, 1988). Kaufman (2004) noted, "Fundraising is one of the most visible and demanding roles expected from campus leaders today" (p. 50). Cook (1997), in his qualitative study on fundraising and the university presidency, found that presidents at that time were estimating spending between 50 percent and 80 percent of their time engaging in different aspects of fundraising for their institutions. While institutional leaders are not responsible for cultivating and soliciting the majority of gifts, presidents create the vision (Fisher, 1985; Nicholson, 2007), establish priorities (Essex & Ansbach, 1993; Willmer, 1993), articulate the case for support (Weidner, 2008), and inspire donor confidence (Satterwhite, 2004), which are the most important elements of successful fundraising (Boardman, 1993; Bornstein, 1989; Brown, 1988; Cowley, 1980; Dowden, 1990; Drucker, 1990; Fisher, 1985; 1989; Flawn, 1990; Foote, 1986; Francis, 1975; Hardin, 1984; Hesburgh, 1988; Howe, 1991; Kohr, 1977; McGoldrick, 1989; Rodriguez, 1991; Skelly, 1991; Slinker, 1988; Smith, 1986; West, 1983).

In many ways presidents and deans, as fundraisers, are required to be transformational leaders. **Transformational leadership theory** suggests that leaders convert followers into agents of the organization, with the express purpose to advance the mission of the institution (Bass, 1990, 1997; Burns, 1978). Within a philanthropic context, academic leaders must convince both internal (professional fundraisers, faculty, staff, and students) and external (alumni and other donors) stakeholders of their long-term vision of the institution. Fundraising success is only achieved if all of these constituents partner in the efforts.

University fundraising has become more sophisticated in last few decades, with an increasing number of private and public institutions engaged in multibillion-dollar campaigns. As such, presidents are still intimately involved in the success or failure of fundraising efforts (Altizer, 1992; Cook & Lasher, 1996; Panas, 1984; Winfree, 1989; Winship, 1984). The ability to fundraise and having a proven track record of success is nearly a requirement for all incoming presidents (Cook, 1997). According to Cook (1997) "fundraising considerations permeate all aspects of the presidential selection process" (p. 68). Cook mentioned that alumni and other donors' reactions to a president's identity and appearance are considered in the selection of an academic leader.

AVENUES FOR FUTURE RESEARCH

Progress in understanding leadership for philanthropy will depend on studying both individuals and processes. Questions remain about whether leaders can be developed and how that would actually take place. Can we really distinguish transactional, transformational, and authentic leaders based on psychological characteristics? If we can, is it meaningful outside the context of a specific institution or situation? Qualitative studies, including in-depth interviews and oral histories with all members of development teams, would provide more of the inside story on leadership and followership. Presidents can provide us with one view of their leadership, but an accompanying view from their development teams and other 'followers'—alumni, major donors, and board members—would be illuminating. Researchers undertaking inquiries from the follower side would do well to study the emerging literature on followership.

On the process side, the research methodology of McMurray et al. (2010) and McMurray et al. (2012) in their studies of religious nonprofit organizations would translate to higher education. It would enable scholars to look at the outcomes of leadership on organizational climate and well-being within development departments and with governing boards.

As noted, shared leadership is also an area that is ripe for exploration. Sturgis's (2006) unexpected finding that presidents and vice presidents do not share common views about presidential leadership deserves further exploration. In addition to replicating her methodology with additional institutions, in-depth interviews with members of development teams would provide valuable insight into the working of these teams. Nehls's (2008) research on presidential transitions during capital campaigns provides additional incentive to pursue this vein of inquiry. She noted that campaigns have increased in duration while presidential tenures have become shorter. Campaign stability during these transitions would seem to necessitate a shared approach or at least well-developed team processes.

======= CASE STUDY =======

PRESIDENTIAL LEADERSHIP AT THE UNIVERSITY OF OREGON

This case study on leadership uses the retrospective view of oral history. In 2007, Miles Brand recorded two oral history interviews as part of an initiative sponsored by the Randall L. Tobias Center for Leadership Excellence at Indiana University-Purdue University Indianapolis. The interviews were conducted by historian Philip V. Scarpino. As an analytical tool, narrative analysis can be used to extract the essence of lived experience.

Miles Brand was a philosopher by training, receiving his BS in philosophy from Rensselaer Polytechnic Institute in 1964 and his Ph.D. from the University of Rochester in 1967. In 1986, he was appointed provost and vice president for Academic Affairs at The Ohio State University. This was followed in 1989 by a call to the presidency of the University of Oregon, where he served until 1994, when he became Indiana University's sixteenth president. He retired from university life in 2002 to become the president of the National Collegiate Athletic Association.

In this case study, Brand's own words will be used to present and describe his personal vision of leadership and his immersion in the world of philanthropy during his tenure as president of the University of Oregon. The transcripts are presented as three themes:

- Brand's views on leadership
- Brand's views on his own leadership style
- Brand's leadership at the University of Oregon during a financial crisis

VIEWS ON LEADERSHIP

SCARPINO: Who, in your opinion, do you think are important leaders?

BRAND: I think some of our scientists are important leaders. I think some of our political leaders are very important. They help shape our lives. I think those who have direct influence on people—mentors, if you like—faculty members, teachers, elementary school teachers are important. I think parents are important. Anyone who affects the lives, particularly in the developmental phase of people, young people, are important leaders.

SCARPINO: Do you think the ability to ask hard questions is the mark of a leader?

BRAND: Oh, yes. Oh, yes. I think that's a critical part of being a leader. To get to the strategic core of what the issue is. To break away from the distractions and the provocative marginal issues but figure out what's really going on here. What's the core. And to draw that out of people. For example, I've been engaged in the university administration many times in creating plans of action for people and what I learned was that you don't impose a plan of action, a strategic plan on anyone. You draw it out of them and sometimes they don't even know that they have it. So asking those hard questions and pressing them, and engaging in that dialogue, always seemed to me to be a critical part of leadership.

SCARPINO: Do you think that part of the exercise of intelligence as a leader is the ability to identify intelligence in other people and surround yourself with people who may even be smarter than you are?

BRAND: Absolutely. I couldn't agree with that more. I mean I, I think someone if they find themselves in a leadership position, has to get the very best people they can find and if they're smarter and know more than you, what a great advantage that is. But then you have to be able to depend upon them and trust them. I mean the last thing you should do is tell them what you think the answer is or try to micromanage them. If you're going to bring in smart, productive, insightful people, turn them loose and get out of the way.

SCARPINO: What do you think are the qualities that distinguish effective leadership?

BRAND: That's an important and difficult question. I think a deep sense of honesty is critical, certainly with yourself, but about the issues too—truthfulness and honesty. I think an unbridled respect for other people—their opinions and their well-being. I think a willingness to examine in depth, the issues, and that's both time consuming and could be intellectually draining. And I do have a bias. I mean, I think to be a good leader one has to be smart. To be a demagogue you don't have to be smart, but to be a leader you do. I think that is an essential ingredient and how you use that ability to understand the issues, to create the background and context you need to understand it and then apply it in a socially conscious way is important.

SCARPINO: Do you think that the exercise of power or authority are qualities that a leader should possess? The ability to exercise power and authority?

BRAND: If that's the goal, the likelihood is you're going to be a bad leader. I mean, power and authority comes with leadership positions. I think they have to be used very carefully and understand that more often than not that's a deficit and a problem you have to overcome in order to provide the kind of leadership that is productive.

SCARPINO: As you look at other leaders, what criteria do you use to define successful leadership?

BRAND: I believe in getting things done, so there's feel-good politics, so to speak, where it makes you feel good if you're pursuing a certain goal and it seems to be the socially responsible goal, but nothing's going to happen. I think that's a waste of time, but I think practical politics—you have to pick out the right goals and have to know why you're pursuing them. But how you get there and what it takes to get there is part of being a good leader. You have to accomplish your goals. It isn't just having good goals.

SCARPINO: How did you go about picking your goals?

BRAND: Well, my personal goals were more opportunistic. But in terms of goals, for example, whenever I was in an administrative position, whether it was chairman of the philosophy department at Circle or president of the university, I always identified myself with the institution. So I saw myself as the philosophy department. I saw myself as the university. And so my success as a university president was tied exactly to whether the university succeeded. If the university succeeded, I succeeded. If not, I don't care what I did, I wasn't a success. So tying myself to the group that I represented was critically important.

PERSONAL STYLE OF LEADERSHIP

SCARPINO: How would you describe your leadership style?

BRAND: I started off, as you heard earlier, very consultative, consensus-building. I think over the years I have found that sometimes you have to be a bit more directive and I think it has something to do with where you are in the organization. So when you're a department head or even a dean you could be much more consensus-building. When you start to be a leader of the entire organization and their vested interests, you try and build consensus, but if you just build consensus I don't think you get too much done. So I suspect most people would characterize me as highly directive. And I am more directive now than I was in the past. I still try and build consensus and work hard at that. So I think it's awfully dependent upon where you fit in. These absolute rules you should do this rather than that doesn't work. It's dependent upon the organization, the circumstances, and where you are in that institution. I think a leader also has to be hard-working. You know, I think a university presidency is 26 hours a day, seven days a week, 365 days a year. I mean you've just got to continually do it, and that goes for the NCAA too. So you can't be a leader if you don't roll up your sleeves and work hard at it and get it done, and depending upon what the situation is and where you are in the organization, being more or less directive is a matter—it's impossible from the president's office to create total consensus in a university. But you can sitting and having pizzas with your colleagues around the philosophy table. It's just not the same.

SCARPINO: Do you see a distinction between leadership and management?

BRAND: Oh, sure. In university presidencies I think, you know, that's the area I know best, but you know, there are operational, transactional presidents as they call them, people who are really good managers and keep them going and keep the roof on and keep the fires down. And then there are transformational leaders who want to create change and those are the leaders as opposed to managers. And I always saw myself as a transformational leader and I'm a change agent. I think that's why IU hired me from Oregon. They saw me as a change agent. There are some costs to being a change agent as we talked about before. Not everyone particularly in universities likes to see change. So there's some personal risk involved in doing that, but I think those are—transactional leaders aren't doing the university any good. I mean, I think they're people who just want to get comfortable in their positions rather than actually forward the well-being of the institution.

UNIVERSITY OF OREGON

Miles Brand was named president of the University of Oregon in 1989. His first goal was to develop a strategic plan to start moving the university forward. As the plan was being completed in 1990, Oregon passed Measure 5. The ballot initiative eliminated property taxes, having the end effect of slashing funding for higher education. With a 75 percent reduction in state funding over three years, the cost of tuition tripled. Brand was forced to eliminate over 1,000 positions. The College of Human Development and Performance was closed along with many programs in the College of Education. Tenured professors were moved to other schools and departments, but pre-tenure faculty contracts were not renewed and administrative positions were cut. In the following narrative, Brand describes the process of rebuilding the university:

SCARPINO: What did you do to bring the budget, to put it in better shape if you lost all that state funding?

BRAND: I spent a lot of time thinking about that and essentially what we did is we made the university semi-private. We looked for other revenue sources. For example, we had about eight or ten percent out of state students, many of them from Asia when I started there. Out of state students pay much higher tuition and so we went from about eight or ten percent to forty percent out of state students and we got to keep all that additional revenue.

SCARPINO: How did you persuade the out of state students to come to Oregon?

BRAND: It was—that was easy. We had students wearing T-shirts that said University of California, Eugene, Oregon. I would be on TV saying it's clean, green, and you could take a twenty minute shower. There was a drought in southern California at the time.

SCARPINO: I remember that. (laughter)

BRAND: And so we worked very hard at it. We changed our whole approach to recruiting. We opened up an office in L.A. and an office in San Francisco. I actually went down to speak to the chancellor there in the University of California system and said could we become a campus of the University of

California? I was serious about it because, and the state at the same time was happy to do it. Some states say, well we don't want all these out of state students. The state of Oregon said go to it. Do whatever you want. I totally reshaped the fundraising efforts. They were very poor there. We started the first major campaign and raised a lot of private money.

SCARPINO: So you got involved in philanthropy.

BRAND: Oh, yes. Big time.

SCARPINO: And how did you organize the campaign?

BRAND: Well, what I did was I went to the board. I remember we had a Come to Jesus meeting in Bend, Oregon and I said. . .

SCARPINO: This is with the board of?

BRAND: Foundation Board. Give, get, or get off. And we lost about a third of the board which was fine, invited new people on and got everyone very excited and set up a—hired new development offices, new vice president for development and spent a lot of time doing it myself. Very successful campaign.

SCARPINO: So this would have been the first time where you were combining your activities in higher education administration with philanthropy.

BRAND: Yes.

SCARPINO: And you did it out of necessity, I assume.

BRAND: Well, I had been doing it before—university presidents have to do it but, when that Measure 5 hit we turned to that big time and the alumni, friends of the university, really came through. Big time. And we sought out research grants. I mean we just, it's a system and so I didn't have my own board. I had a state system and constant fighting with the central offices of the university to keep all the revenue we were raising because we had cut back and solved our problem, as painful as it was, and then we were moving forward and so we developed new revenue streams. Meanwhile, our sister institutions, particularly Oregon State, had put off the cutbacks, had cut across the board and they were receiving some great pain. So there was a constant movement by those in the systems office to see if they could take some of the resources we were generating and give it to other campuses.

SCARPINO: So part of your role as a leader was to raise money and part of it was to hang onto it.

BRAND: And hanging onto it was, after we, you know, were getting going and the engine was working. It was very frustrating that the system was making it more difficult for us even though the times were very hard. And we were doing it ourselves, autonomously, self-starting, and the state legislators and the public were happy with us, but from the—that office of the board, they were trying to move money around and I wasn't real happy about that.

SCARPINO: Were you able to solve that problem?

BRAND: Mostly. Not a hundred percent. That was one of the reasons why I began to look after—I didn't want to leave the University of Oregon until they were on very strong footing. I mean I felt, now I identified with the university and I felt really responsible for them. So I wanted to make sure they were successful before I'd even think of moving and these plans that were put in action, some of which I'm talking about now, were successful. So after about four or five years the university was starting to go great guns and the momentum was building, I said I don't need to fight with that central office anymore. I want to go to a place, a fine public university that has its own board that I can work with so I don't have to continue to see money come in one door and go out the others. That was very frustrating to me.

SCARPINO: How would you assess the strength of the University of Oregon today? Have you kept up with what they're doing?

BRAND: I have and I still have very good friends there and in fact, the president there, Dave Frohnmayer, was someone who was a state's attorney general and ran for governor and lost, so I hired him as dean of the law school and before I left worked with him to become president and he's still president there. So I certainly keep up with them and they're doing very well. They're in another major campaign. The out of state approach has worked. They managed after a lot of political pressure to finally stop the leakage out the back or mostly at least and I think they're doing very well—much, much better. They're far more engaged in athletics than when I was there, but that's not so bad.

SCARPINO: Did you learn anything about how a leader has to function in times of adversity?

BRAND: Yeah, I did. I think that was trial under fire and there was no one there to teach me. It was just learning how to do it. I think I saw the direction we wanted to go overall and I think my willingness to stand up and take the heat and responsibility was important. It wouldn't have happened—no one else was going to take the responsibility. I thought the way Oregon State did it was dead wrong, cutting across the board. So you really had to target it and of course that made some people unhappy and those who weren't cut, in empathy for those who were, didn't exactly come to my rescue or say anything. So, survivor's guilt. They just kind of hunkered down. But the university started to do well and I think it's been on a, with bumps and starts, on a reasonable course since. Not a wealthy university now but I think they're in good shape.

SCARPINO: Do you think the way in which a leader deals with adversity is a measure, in the end, of that leader's success?

BRAND: Oh, of course. It's easy when everything's working well. The real challenge is when things go to hell in a handbag and when you've got to figure out what to do and stand up and take the responsibility. I spent a lot of sleepless nights thinking about where we want to go, where are our opportunities and that's when I hit upon the out of state approach.

SCARPINO: Some of the literature on leadership argues that leadership style, leadership success, is often forged in a crisis. Was there an event or a crisis that helped forge your own view of leadership?

BRAND: Well, I think that Measure 5 was that one incident I was talking about but it was actually a three- or four-year period and certainly I learned a lot about leadership, learned a lot about myself, learned where my backbone was and what I thought was important. And that was forged in crisis, yes.

SCARPINO: What do you think you learned about yourself in that crisis?

BRAND: I was stronger than I thought. You know, I'm sure I thought through it the best I possibly could. I thought I knew the right direction and what we had to do. I did not take the path of least resistance. I took the path that would be best for the university. Frankly, the path that was most difficult for me, personally. And I stood up and was counted and I found that I could do this.

DISCUSSION QUESTIONS

1. What does narrative analysis of Brand's transcript reveal about his approach to leadership?
2. Brand saw himself as a transformational leader. Do you agree with his assessment?
3. In view of the crisis at Oregon, how would a different type of leader have affected the outcome?

RESOURCES USED FOR THE CASE STUDY

Brand, M. (2007). *Oral history*. Indianapolis, IN: Randall L. Tobias Center for Leadership Excellence at Indiana University-Purdue University Indianapolis.

Kerlin, S. P., & Dunlap, D. M. (1993). For richer, for poorer: Faculty morale in periods of austerity and retrenchment. *Journal of Higher Education, 64*(3), 348–377.

Indiana University. (2013). *Remembering Miles Brand, 1942–2009*. Retrieved from www.iu.edu/brand/

5

YOUTH AND STUDENT VOLUNTEERISM
AND PHILANTHROPY

The basic assumption within theory and most people's experience is that parents have a strong influence on their children's lives and decision making. Parents decide what religion, if any, to expose their children to, what schools and activities their children participate in, and how their children are exposed to culture. As a partial function of these exposures that our parents give us, we are more likely to vote like our parents (Achen, 2002), follow their religion (Flor & Knapp, 2001), and participate in similar cultural activities (De Graaf, De Graaf, & Kraaykamp, 2000; Grolnick & Slowiaczek, 1994). Prosocial behaviors, such as philanthropy and volunteerism, are no different. Parents' giving of time and treasure influences their children's giving as well.

An Independent Sector report (2000) found that people who volunteer are more likely to recall their parents' volunteerism and other acts of philanthropy than are people who do not volunteer. Bekkers (2005) points out this finding does not prove that children volunteer because their parents volunteer or give charity. He notes that there could be other reasons why children who remember seeing their parents volunteer are more likely to volunteer themselves. Bekkers (2004a, 2004b), Janoski and Wilson (1995), and Smith and Baldwin (1974) have found that the transmission of certain characteristics from parent to child increases the prospect of volunteering. For example, parents who volunteer are more likely to have a higher level of education and participate in religious activities, and since their children are also more likely to be college educated and be more religious, their children are more likely to volunteer than children whose parents are less educated and less religious.

Research in the 1990s (Segal, 1993; Wuthnow, 1995) found a gender difference in the transmission of volunteer habits from parent to child. Segal and Wuthnow both found that a mother's volunteerism is more influential than a father's. They argue this is because of how a mother might be more likely to include her children in her volunteer activities and that she is more likely to volunteer for child-related activities, such as school or cocurricular activities. It is important to note that this research was done in the early 1990s and this gender difference might have changed as gender roles have changed in the past two to two and a half decades. For example, the number of stay-at-home moms has decreased (and stay-at-home dads has increased) and household responsibilities have changed. So, although the generational transmission of behaviors may seem obvious, theory and supporting research suggest more complexity.

RESOURCE THEORY, SELECTIVE MOBILIZATION THEORY, AND STATUS TRANSMISSION THEORY

There are three theories that argue that a person's social status influences prosocial behaviors. The first, **resource theory** (Wilson & Musick, 1997), assumes that a person's social status is linked to the amount of disposable human, social, and financial capital they have. Therefore, as one's social status increases and disposable capital increases, the cost for one to participate in volunteerism or philanthropic giving decreases (Figure 5.1).

The second theory, **selective mobilization theory** (Brady, Schlozman & Verba, 1999), assumes that nonprofit organizations understand resource theory and direct their solicitation programs to engage donors and volunteers with more resources. In other words, as disposable resources increase within a family, the interest and engagement in nonprofit engagement increases (Figure 5.2). Kraaykamp (1996), Bekkers and De Graaf (2002), and Bekkers (2004a, 2004b) found that within the context of the Netherlands, voluntary participation in organizations is stratified by education. Others have found that income level in the United States and other countries has a statistically significant effect on volunteerism and giving (Musick & Wilson, 2008).

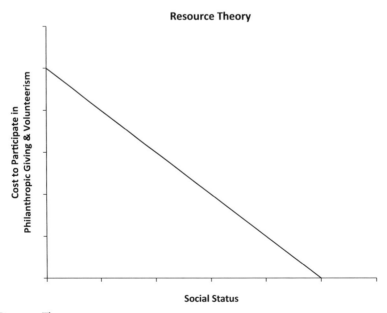

Figure 5.1 Resource Theory

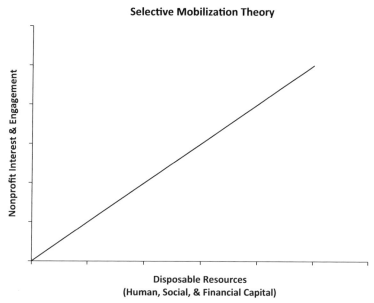

Figure 5.2 Selective Mobilization Theory

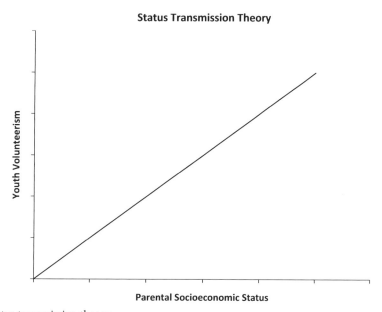

Figure 5.3 Status transmission theory

Status transmission theory (Figure 5.3) argues that parents' socioeconomic status (SES) influences a child's volunteerism; as family SES increases, youth participation in volunteerism increases as well (Brown, 1999; Child Trend Databank, 2003; Hart, Atkins, & Ford, 1998; Sundeen & Raskoff, 1994; Yates & Youniss, 1999). Some postulate that socioeconomic status has a positive effect on volunteering since higher socioeconomic families are more likely to be two-parent homes and there is a level of stability in these families that allows the parents to volunteer more themselves. However, this hypothesis has yet to be tested.

SOCIAL INTEGRATION THEORY AND SOCIALIZATION THEORY

Beyond social status, researchers have found participation in voluntary associations differs among belonging to more or less cohesive social groups. For example, those that are members of a religious community and who attend more frequently are more likely to volunteer (Bekkers, 2003; Dekker & De Hart, 2002; Musick & Wilson, 2008). **Social integration theory** is espoused to explain the influence of social cohesion on participation in voluntary associations. Social integration theory (Figure 5.4), which builds off of Durkheim's (1897/1930) theory on suicide, assumes that (1) those in groups with a higher level of cohesion are more likely to conform to social norms of desirable behavior and (2) participation in voluntary associations is understood as socially desirable behavior (Wilson & Musick, 1998). Lin (2001) combined social integration theory with resource theory, explaining that a higher level of cohesion increases the availability of resources of others; therefore, Lin equates 'cohesion' in integration theory with 'social capital' in resource theory.

However, **socialization theory** (Grusec & Hastings, 2007, 2008; Musick & Wilson, 2008) assumes that there are different levels of importance given to prosocial behaviors within groups. Socialization theory is therefore potentially in conflict with the second assumption of social integration theory, in that there is no assumption that voluntary association is considered socially desirable in all groups. According to socialization theory, groups that have attributed a higher level of importance and value to volunteering and giving will encourage their members to participate in prosocial behaviors. Socialization theory has also been used to understand parental influence on children's volunteerism (Keeter & Center for Information and Research in Civic Learning & Engagement, 2002; Lake Snell Perry and Associates & The Tarrance Group, 2002; Musick & Wilson, 2008). Within higher education, researchers should consider using social integration theory

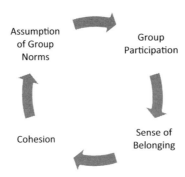

Figure 5.4 Social integration theory

and socialization theory to understand volunteer and giving behaviors of alumni from institutions that have high levels of community service, service learning, and philanthropic activity among students.

While this would be an interesting line of inquiry, Bekkers (2005) points out that the four theories (resource, selective mobilization, social integration, and socialization) *are not meant to* explain how youth participation in giving and volunteering affect prosocial behaviors in adulthood. In other words, while these theories explain the causes of youth participation, they are not meant to explain how an adult's volunteerism and giving are affected by participation as a child or young adult. Durkheim (1897/1930), in laying the foundation of these theories, argued that participation in a group results in group cohesion and a strengthened sense of belonging. This loop (Figure 5.4) is evident in volunteering. As people volunteer for an organization they develop friendships with the people they meet while volunteering. The development of these social relations is one of the intended outcomes of volunteering. In fact, Clary et al. (1998) found that volunteers often mention the contacts they make through volunteering as not only a benefit of participation but as a motivation to do so.

De Tocqueville (1835) argued that involvement in community life is a factor in the development of democratic values. Over 150 years later, Putnam (2000) built on de Tocqueville in his now-famous *Bowling Alone* and argued that participation in voluntary associations increases a person's trust. In the years after Putnam published his work, many scholars explored the socialization effects of participation in voluntary associations in adulthood (Bekkers, 2005; Uslaner, 2002; Wollebaek & Selle, 2002). They found that, as Bekkers (2005) puts it, "social values are rather stable in adulthood." Youth participation in prosocial behaviors, however, is at a stage of life when social values can still be influenced. Beutel and Johnson (2004) and Grimm, Dietz, Spring, and Foster-Bey (2005) found that children observing current parental volunteering promotes prosocial values in the children. However, observation of prosocial behaviors is not the only way that volunteerism is transmitted intergenerationally.

PARENTAL STYLE THEORY

Others have researched parental styles with regard to volunteering (Clary & Miller, 1986; Pancer & Pratt, 1999). The educational practices and family experiences of youth volunteers often contribute to the development of or inhibit individual prosocial behavior (Eisenberg & Fabes, 1998; Fletcher, Elder, Glen, & Mekos, 2000). The quality of family relationships and support structures are important factors in predicting participation in volunteerism and sustained service (Clary & Miller, 1986; Hart & Fegley, 1995; Rosenhan, 1973). Fletcher, Elder, and Mekos (2000), through their longitudinal study, found a complex relationship between educational styles, parenting (support and warmth), and educational practices (parental reinforcement and modeling) in predicting young adult participation as a volunteer. Their research highlights that support-oriented parental styles are perhaps more important at predicting youth volunteerism over the parents' own social commitment. While there has been some encouraging research on this topic, Musick and Wilson (2008) point out in their extensive review of the volunteerism scholarship that longitudinal data sets to test the theory that parental style influences future volunteering are scarce.

ROLE MODELING THEORY

Like with philanthropic role modeling (discussed in Chapter 1), volunteering is influenced by role modeling as well. In a 2005 survey of American teenagers, Grimm, Jr., et al. (2005) found that 78 percent of adolescents whose parents volunteered were volunteers, while only 48 percent of teenagers volunteered when their parents were not volunteers themselves. The number of role models was important as well. For example, when both parents and siblings volunteered, 86 percent of respondents were volunteers themselves, compared to 38 percent when no one in the family volunteered. Additionally, this study found that the regularity of observed volunteering had an influence. Those who observed regular volunteering (at least 12 weeks a year) were more greatly influenced then those who observed more episodic volunteering.

Bekkers (2005) builds on many of these theories and prior findings in order to study his four pathways of influence on youth participation in volunteerism and philanthropic giving. His first pathway is through the socialization of prosocial values. The second pathway is the development of social capital. Bekkers's third pathway is through the learning of skills, and his fourth pathway is caused by reducing the social distance between the young adult and other nonprofit organizations looking to recruit volunteers and solicit donations.

Using the Giving in the Netherlands Panel Survey, Bekkers (2005) found that:

(1) parents who volunteer and it is observed by their children promote giving and volunteering among their children when they become adults;

(2) the intensity with which a child participates in nonprofit organizations as a volunteer has a positive relationship with giving and volunteering of that same person as an adult;

(3) both observing parents volunteering and children volunteering themselves promote later adult volunteering because it is seen as enhancing human and social capital; and finally

(4) that parental volunteering and youth participation promote philanthropic giving, as at the young age these observations and actions teach and promote prosocial values while building social capital.

Bekkers's findings align well with the literature on prosocial behavior in sociology and social psychology. Studies show that as a person ages, developmental and moral reasoning can evolve in terms of helping others (Drezner, 2010). Social psychologists have observed that evolution; for example, young children offer help as a result of extrinsic motivation: being told to help, wishing to avoid punishment, or being promised a gift or prize. However, as a child grows older, less tangible benefits, such as peer approval, become a motivation for the adolescent to help others. The evolution continues in adulthood, in which intrinsic feelings motivate prosocial behavior (Bar-Tal, 1982; Cialdini & Kenrick, 1976; Eisenberg, 1982; Kohlberg, 1984; Schroeder et al. 1995). Researchers have also found that reinforcing the importance of prosocial behaviors to children is important. For example, when children perform prosocial acts and receive positive feedback, they internalize the praise and think of themselves as "good" (Miley, 1980; Rosenhan, 1978). As youth repeat these actions and grow older, they experience increased levels of moral obligation and their need for external motivations is reduced (Piliavin & Charng, 1990). This follows the later developed socialization theory (Grusec & Hastings, 2007, 2008). Schroeder et al. (1995), reviewing other research, suggested that prosocial behavior can be taught and learned. Many believe that direct reinforcement, as well as observing and discussing altruism, influences prosocial behavior (Ahammer & Murray, 1979; Grusec, 1982, 1991; Israel, 1978; Moore & Eisenberg, 1984; Rushton, 1975, 1982; Smith, Gelfand, Hartmann, & Partlow, 1979).

YOUNG ADULT VOLUNTEERISM

Young adult volunteerism has increased over the past few decades. Some of this has been attributed to the increase in high school community service requirements (Oates, 2005). Like philanthropic giving, volunteerism as a young adult has been found to affect future giving of time. However, Johnson, Beebe, Mortimer, and Snyder (1998) found that research on adult volunteerism could not be generalized to the young adult population. Adolescence is a key period for personal and social identity development (Alwin, Cohen, & Newcomb, 1991; Mortimer, Finch, & Kumka, 1982; Scabini & Rossi, 1997). Similarly, young adulthood is an important time period for prosocial behavior development, especially within a volunteer context (Erikson, 1963). This development occurs as young adults have more complex interpersonal relationships and experience cognitive and emotive development and changes in their social context (Carlo, Eisenberg, & Knight, 1992; Carlo, Fabes, Laible, & Kupanoff, 1999; Marta & Scabini, 2003). As adolescence transitions into adulthood, many psychological dimensions, including prosocial behaviors, crystallize and become more stable (Alwin et al., 1991; Fischer & Schaffer, 1993; Hanks & Eckland, 1978; Johnson et al., 1998; Mortimer et al., 1982; Mortimer, Pimentel, Ryu, Nash, & Lee, 1996).

Volunteerism supports and empowers identity construction (Erikson, 1963; Logan, 1985). Additionally, identity is a factor in the intention to volunteer (Youniss & Yates, 1997). For example, those who indicate that they have a commitment to prosocial role identity development are more likely to participate in more prosocial activities (Piliavin, Grube, & Callero, 2002). While exploring college freshman, Lee (1997) found that a student's volunteer role identity was related to his or her parents' volunteering, the perceived expectations to volunteer by peers, and the student's intention to volunteer during college.

While there are only a limited number of studies that have focused on philanthropic prosocial behavior development among young adults, including college students, very few focus on volunteerism in this age group (Carlo & Randall 2001, 2002; Drezner, 2010; Eisenberg & Fabes, 1998; Johnson et al., 1998; Yates & Youniss, 1996a). The youth volunteerism literature generally focuses on volunteer characteristics and the effects of giving of time.

Young adult volunteers:

- Are more extroverted,
- Are less autonomous,
- Have stronger egos (Smith & Nelson, 1975),
- Have higher internalized moral standards (Allen & Rushton, 1983),
- Have a more positive attitude toward self and others (Hart & Fegley, 1995),
- Have a greater degree of self-efficacy and optimism (Pancer & Pratt, 1999),
- Have more emotional stability, and
- Have greater empathy (Yates & Youniss, 1996a).

Beyond the characteristics of a volunteer, scholars have looked at the motivations of those who give their time. Chacon and Vecina (2000) found that motivations differ between long- and short-term volunteers. Others have looked at the difference between the motivations to volunteer and those that influence volunteer retention (Gidron, 1985; Oda, 1991; Winniford, Stanley, & Grider, 1995). Capanna, Steca, and Imbimbo (2002) found that those who saw the volunteer opportunity as a venue to learn capacities and competencies useful to themselves were often short-term volunteers, while those who were volunteering for other reasons, often out of community concerns, often remained in their volunteer capacities for a longer period of time (Capanna et al., 2002; Omoto & Snyder, 2000; Sundeen & Raskoff, 1994; Wuthnow, 1995).

The effects of volunteerism in young adults are great in many different aspects of socialization:

- Increasing social context of belonging (Sundeen & Raskoff, 1994);
- Increasing political participation (Flanagan, Bowes, Jonsson, Csapo, & Sheblanova, 1998; Hanks, 1981);
- Promoting civic engagement and prosocial behavioral norms (Youniss & Yates, 1997);
- Increasing self-esteem, self-acceptance, and self-efficacy (Conrad & Hedin, 1982; Hart & Fegley, 1995; King, Walder, & Pavey, 1970; Omoto & Snyder, 1990; Pancer, Pratt, & Hunsberger, 1998; Primavera, 1999; Tierney & Branch, 1992; Yates & Youniss, 1999);
- Sustaining cognitive and moral development (Yates & Youniss, 1996b).

Larson (1994) found that the effects of volunteerism were different than those that were received from family or at school. Understanding youth volunteerism sets the stage nicely to look at service while in college.

VOLUNTEERING IN COLLEGE OR UNIVERSITY

Musick and Wilson (2008) note that the transition from adolescence to adulthood occurs at the same time that traditionally aged students attend college. Additionally, they note that colleges and universities typically have environments that are conducive and supportive of volunteerism. Boraas (2003) found that the volunteer rate of college students, aged 16–24, was double the rate of those the same age but not enrolled in school or college. Institutional type plays a role in the amount of volunteering a student performs. Interestingly, Horn and Berktold (1998) and Horn, Peter, and Rooney (2002) found that the gap between those not attending college and those who attend private colleges or universities is greater than the gap between non-college goers and public university students.

Astin, Gardner, and Sax (1998), using a longitudinal study of college freshman collected in 1985, 1989, and then again in 1994–95, found that there is a strong effect of volunteering during high school on volunteering as an adult, regardless of the person volunteering in college. However, the effect was even stronger if they volunteered in college as well. Astin et al. report that of those who did not volunteer in high school or college, only 13 percent reported volunteering at least one hour per week nine years after graduation. However, nearly 50 percent of those who volunteered in high school and college gave of their time nine years later. Therefore, the continued participation in volunteer activities from high school through college appears to be important.

ENGAGING YOUTH IN PHILANTHROPY

Youth engagement in philanthropy is the focus of many nonprofit organizations and foundations. Between 1988 and 2003, the W. K. Kellogg Foundation gave over $100 million in grants "to help fund the promotion and development of youth engagement in social, civic, and community building" through volunteerism, service, and philanthropy (Ho, 2003, p. 2). Since then the challenge grants that the W. K. Kellogg Foundation has given have resulted in 1,500 young people serving on 86 grant-making committees, $62 million in endowment funds, and $1.5 million of yearly grants given by young adults (Council of Michigan Foundations, 2014).

Teaching Philanthropy

Bjorhovde (2002a, 2002b) identified four concepts that she believes should be part of any formal or informal philanthropy curriculum: (1) factual, (2) motivational, (3) procedural, and (4) personal development concepts. The factual concept introduces the learner to giving as the "critical societal force" within American culture through teaching about philanthropy's history, relationship with government, and role in the community (Bjorhovde, 2002b, p. 13). The reasons why people are philanthropic and the idea that anyone, regardless of personal wealth, can be a philanthropist through in-kind gifts of time and service are part of Bjorhovde's motivational concept. Finally, the procedural and personal development concepts include teaching ways for students to get involved and how their actions help others (Bjorhovde, 2002a, 2002b).

Combining Bjorhovde's types of philanthropic learning and curricular concepts provides an interesting model to use within the ivory tower. Drezner (2008, 2009, 2010) found that by engaging college students with opportunities to learn about and participate in community service, civic engagement, service learning projects, and student alumni associations such as the National Pre-Alumni Council (NPAC) at private historically Black colleges and universities, the institution cultivates a generation of engaged alumni dedicated to future service to the university. Astin and Sax (1998) and Avalos, Sax, and Astin (1999) also discuss how participation in service during college impacts students' philanthropic behavior.

NPAC, according to Drezner (2008, 2009, 2010), socializes and cultivates new groups of donors from the millennial generation by motivating students with gifts and opportunities that are appropriate for the developmental stage of college students. NPAC's education of students on the importance of giving and needs of the institutions was vital in students' decisions to be involved as donors and fundraisers.

Undergraduate student involvement in alumni and fundraising activities at institutions is a community of participation that creates a strong foundation for active alumni support after graduation. In a 1981 interview about his involvement in the founding of the United Negro College Fund in 1944, James P. Brawley, then president of historically Black, Clark College (now Clark-Atlanta University), understood the importance of instilling a culture of giving in undergraduates so that they are more likely to donate as alumni. Brawley believed:

> If you are going to develop responsive alumni you don't do it by talking to them when they are in their caps and gowns ready to go, and then expect them to respond by giving handsome gifts to the college . . . the need is to develop a systematic plan for the alumni to contribute and stimulate their interest through what is done while they are at the college for four years, and if you don't get a good response out of them during those four years, the chances are 99 [percent] that you won't get much of a response after they have gone.

> (Brawley, 1981, n.p.)

There is substantial literature that agrees with Brawley's principle and discusses the importance of engaging students in fundraising programming (for example, as solicitation callers) and even as donors early in their careers at both two- and four-year institutions (Chewning, 1993; Kerns, 1986; Nakada, 1993; Nayman, Gianneschi, & Mandel, 1993; Purpura, 1980; Shanley, 1985; van Nostrand, 1999).

Robbie Nayman et al. (1993) suggest that "turning students into donors is a socialization process that involves orienting students to the notion of voluntary giving, actively engaging them in varied institutional advancement activities, and strategically timing program initiatives" (p. 90). By socializing the students in this way, Nayman et al. (1993) found that students are more likely to participate in future fundraising campaigns. According to Atchley's (1989) continuity theory, established patterns are likely to be followed in the future. Further research shows that giving from young alumni, even in small amounts, has potentially large effects on lifetime donating (Lindahl & Winship, 1992; Monks, 2003; Nayman et al., 1993; Okunade & Justice, 1991; Piliavin & Charng, 1990). The impact of engaging young alumni in giving to their alma mater can be significant. In fact, some research from other private research universities shows that the vast majority of $1 million-plus donors begin to give in their first ten years out of school (Monks, 2003). Jonathan Meer (2008) finds that alumni who gave to their alma mater on an annual basis in the five years after graduation gave, on average, eight times more to their institution by their twentieth reunion than even those alumni who donated the same amount in the first few years but did not develop a steady habit. The gifts that Monks (2003) and Meer (2008) looked at were given by alumni long after their graduation.

AVENUES FOR FUTURE RESEARCH

While there are many theoretical frameworks to understand youth volunteerism and philanthropic giving, few scholars have looked at college students or young alumni through these frames. Given the complexity and developmental stage of traditional college students and some of the caveats that Bekkers (2005) and others have placed on the applicability of these theories to adult participants, future researchers should consider exploring these frameworks alongside the substantial literature on student development theory.

========================= CASE STUDY =========================

STUDENT FUNDRAISING AT PRAIRIE VIEW A&M UNIVERSITY: TEACHING PHILANTHROPY THROUGH INNOVATIVE GIVING

The information for this case study comes from popular press articles and the institutional website.

Understanding that when students are exposed to the importance of philanthropic giving while still in college, they are more likely to give as alumni, some colleges and universities have decided to create student giving programs. While some majority institutions are developing these programs, few historically Black colleges and universities are focusing on future alumni. About 5 percent of the alumni of public, historically Black schools give to their institutions, while about 10 percent of private Black institutions' alumni donate. With the exception of the United Negro College Fund's National Pre-Alumni Councils, talking to students about philanthropy has not been the norm at most HBCUs. However, this situation is changing.

Development officers at Prairie View A&M University, a public, historically Black university outside of Houston, Texas, with approximately 8,400 students, have created a new student philanthropy program that is based on the concept of "philanthropy by the students, for the students." Beginning in academic year 2012–13 students made their first contributions, creating an endowment that will provide scholarships to their fellow students.

The initiative, known as the Student Development Initiative (SDI), has several components that engage students in giving and decision making around philanthropy while they are still students. In 2012, the university administration approached the student leadership with the idea of creating a student-funded endowment. The student body responded by overwhelmingly passing a referendum to increase their fees by $10 per semester. This additional fee is optional. Beyond creating the easy way to give, the Student Government Association leaders set a participation goal of 15 percent of the university's 8,400 students.

Students have adopted this program, as the creation of an endowment is "for students, by students." While students can opt out of the additional fee, the majority of students are giving to the endowment. As a show of support, Prairie View is making a one-to-one match to all of the students' contributions. In order to build the principal of the endowment to a significant level, the first five years of interest will be reinvested. Beginning in 2018, or the sixth year, PVAMU will begin to award scholarships.

Students and administrators developed scholarship eligibility requirements that both encourage giving and thank student donors at the same time. Only students that contribute to the fund are eligible to receive scholarships. In reviewing the Student Development Initiative, Marybeth Gasman provided the potential results of the program (Table 5.1).

Table 5.1 Potential Results for PVA&M Student Development Initiative

Year	Student Pop.	Student Giving over 4 Years	Total Student Giving	University Match (1:1)	Annual Endowment Total	Annual Interest Earned (4%)	Endowment Total with Interest (Years 15)	Endowment Total without Interest (Year 6 and Beyond)	Available to Award Annually (Beginning in Year 6)
2013	8,400	$80	$168,000	$168,000	$336,000	$13,440	$349,440		
2014	8,400	$80	$168,000	$168,000	$685,440	$27,418	$712,858		
2015	8,400	$80	$168,000	$168,000	$1,048,858	$41,954	$1,090,812		
2016	8,400	$80	$168,000	$168,000	$1,426,812	$57,072	$1,483,884		
2017	8,400	$80	$168,000	$168,000	$1,819,884	$72,795	$1,892,680		
2018	8,400	$80	$168,000	$168,000	$2,228,680	$89,147		$2,228,680	**$89,147**
2019	8,400	$80	$168,000	$168,000	$2,564,680	$102,587		$2,564,680	**$102,587**
2020	8,400	$80	$168,000	$168,000	$2,900,680	$116,027		$2,900,680	**$116,027**
2021	8,400	$80	$168,000	$168,000	$3,236,680	$129,467		$3,236,680	**$129,467**
2022	8,400	$80	$168,000	$168,000	$3,572,680	$142,907		$3,572,680	**$142,907**

Gasman (2013, n.p.) notes that "Not only does this program aid current students, it also teaches them how to give and about the power of philanthropy."

An additional portion of the Student Development Initiative at PVAMU is the student-driven fundraising campaign. In order to drum up enthusiasm, student leaders are encouraging healthy competition in their fundraising, having residence halls and student organizations compete against each other to raise the most money for Prairie View. Additionally, as an incentive for students to give, they get to decide on the designation of the funds (e.g., book funds, scholarships, class projects). By giving the student donors a part in the decision-making process they hope to give students a sense of ownership in their philanthropic giving.

Priscilla Barbour, the then-chief of staff of the Student Government Association, said she was excited about the endowment campaign because it was new—never been done at the campus. "I'm all about philanthropy," said Barbour, a junior. "Ten dollars is less than what we pay for a parking decal. It's not a massive amount of money, but $10 per student adds up."

Biology major Edna Idan, who was co-chair of the student campaign, said she wanted to give back because she was on a scholarship and she felt an obligation to give back to the university. Her goal was that her classmates understood that the university depends on more than just their tuition to provide an education. "When we teach and educate students about the importance of giving, they will give and we will start a tradition of giving."

DISCUSSION QUESTIONS

1. What theoretical frames might explain the student participation in this campaign?
2. How should Prairie View A&M University consider extending this campaign to young alumni as they graduate? Base your answer in theory.
3. What are the potential concerns about the $10 optional fee as a form of philanthropy? How might those concerns be mitigated?

6

SOCIAL IDENTITY AND PHILANTHROPY

A person's social identity is a portion of their own self-concept that is derived from a perceived membership in a relevant social group. In other words, social identity is a person's sense of who he or she is based on a group with whom the person is associated (Turner & Oakes, 1986). The social groups often associated with social identity and a person's self-concept are social class, academic performance (Bong & Clark, 1999; Byrne, 1984; Byrne & Gavin, 1996; Shavelson & Bolus, 1982; Shavelson, Hubner, & Stanton, 1976), gender and gender roles, sexuality (Hoffman, 2004; Hoffman, Hattie, & Borders, 2005; Wade, 1998), religion, ability, and racial identity (Aries et al., 1998). People can be members of multiple social groups. These groups give us a sense of social identity or a sense of belonging to the social world.

Social identity theory was originally theorized by Henri Tajfel and John Turner in the 1970s and the 1980s (Turner & Reynolds, 2010) as a way to explain intergroup behavior (Tajfel, 1978; Tajfel & Turner, 1979, 1986; Turner, 1999). Tajfel and Turner (1979) find that the groups (e.g., social class, family, race, alma mater, etc.) that people belong to are important sources of pride and self-esteem. As a result, we break ourselves into "them" and "us" through a process of social categorization (i.e., we put ourselves and others into social groups). This is known as in-group (us) and out-group (them).

Tajfel and Turner (1979) propose that the in-groups and out-groups are created through a three-step process of social categorization, identification, and comparison. In the **categorization stage** we place people, including ourselves, in groups in order to understand and identify them and the social environment. In the **social identification stage**, we begin to adopt the identity of the group we have categorized ourselves as belonging in and conform to the perceived norms of the group. At this point, a person's self-esteem is usually bound up, to some extent, with the group membership, based on the saliency of the identity. In the third and final stage, **social comparison**, we begin to compare our group with other groups.

Social identity theory has been used and confused in different academic literatures. Social identity theory predicts intergroup behaviors that are based on perceived status differences of groups and the potential ability for a person to affect status change (Tajfel & Turner, 1979; Turner, 1999). Social identity theory is not meant to be used as a general theory of social categorization (Turner & Reynolds, 2010). Building on social identity theory and its limitations, John Turner and his colleagues (Turner & Oakes, 1986; Turner, 1999; Haslam, 2001) developed the related **self-categorization theory**, which speaks more generally to the self and group processes (Turner & Reynolds, 2010). There are a number of different aspects to social identity theory.

THE INTERPERSONAL–INTERGROUP CONTINUUM

Social identity theory postulates that social behavior varies along a continuum between interpersonal and intergroup behaviors. This continuum ranges from completely interpersonal, or solely individual characteristics, through interpersonal relationships where the relationship between two or more people help determine someone's behavior, and completely intergroup behavior where actions are determined solely by social category memberships that are shared or not shared by those involved (Tajfel & Turner, 1979). Like with other continuums, it is not likely that there are purely interpersonal or purely intergroup behaviors. Rather, behaviors fall between the two extremes of the continuum (Tajfel & Turner, 1979; Tajfel, 1970). Social identity theory focuses on the aspects of social structure that predict what aspect of the interpersonal–intergroup continuum most influences individual behavior and how those actions might look and in what forms the behavior may take (Haslam, 2001; Turner, 1999; Turner & Reynolds, 2010).

POSITIVE DISTINCTIVENESS

When Tajfel and Turner (1979) theorized on social identity, they made the assumption that individuals have an intrinsic motivation to be distinct and strive for a positive self-concept. According to social identity theory, individuals, to varying degrees, may define themselves or be informed by their own social identities. The interpersonal–intergroup continuum and assumption of positive distinctiveness motivation were tested in a number of studies that used the minimal group paradigm as their methodology (Turner & Reynolds, 2010). The **minimal group paradigm** is a methodology employed in social psychology that looks at the minimal conditions required for discrimination to occur between groups. Arbitrary social categorizations resulted in discrimination between groups (Tajfel, 1970). One study, Turner (1978), asked students to choose groups to donate to—either in-group, out-group, or intergroup. Self-interest was not an issue because the participants were anonymous to each other. Those who opted for an intergroup donation tended to slightly favor donations to their own group even when there was an option to get slightly more absolute donations for their group had they chosen to give to differently and help other groups. This option was not taken because the other group would have received even more than the participant's group. In other words, Turner (1978) found that students would endorse resource distributions that would maximize the positive distinctiveness of their ingroup, in contrast to an other's outgroup, even at the expense of personal self-interest. In these cases, greater positive distinctiveness, or greater distance between in-group and out-group, was more important than absolute dollars received. When a participant chose either an in-group or out-group donation, distributions tended toward 'fairness.'

There are a number of positive distinctiveness strategies that are associated with social identity theory, including, but not limited to, individual mobility and in-group favoritism. Social identity theory posits that an individual's behavior is influenced by the perceived intergroup relationship and the belief in the permeability of group boundaries and intergroup status hierarchy (Tajfel & Turner, 1979; Haslam, 2001). While many of the strategies are from the perspective of those in the less privileged status group, comparable behaviors may also be adopted by those in privileged groups (Haslam, 2001).

Individual Mobility. Haslam (2001) found that when group boundaries are considered permeable, individuals are more likely to disassociate from their group in order to find personal positive distinctiveness.

In-Group Favoritism. In-group favoritism, or sometimes referred to as in-group bias, is when individuals give preferential treatment to others that are perceived to be in the same group (Tajfel & Turner, 1979; Ellemers & Barreto, 2001). Social identity theory explains this form of favoritism or bias as the psychological need for positive distinctiveness. Researchers have observed in-group favoritism in both arbitrary in-groups and nonarbitrary in-groups (e.g., groups based on religion, race, culture, gender, sexual orientation, and first language) (Ahmed, 2007; Brewer, 1979; Giannakakis & Fritsche, 2011; Hogg & Turner, 1987; Krumm & Corning, 2008).

SELF-CATEGORIZATION THEORY

Self-categorization theory is a social psychological theory that was developed to explain the underpinnings of social identification that social identity theory did not originally address (Haslam, 2001; Haslam, Oakes, Turner, & McGarty, 1996; Turner, 1999; Turner & Oakes, 1986). The theory describes how a person perceives groups of people (including one's self) and the consequences of perceiving these groups (Haslam, 1997). Self-categorization theory originally was used to explain group formation. However, the theory also looks at the social perceptions and the interactions of both individuals and groups (Oakes, Haslam, & Turner, 1994). For example, self-categorization theory asks: Why do people place themselves within one group over another? Figure 6.1 explains the difference between self-categorization theory and social identity theory.

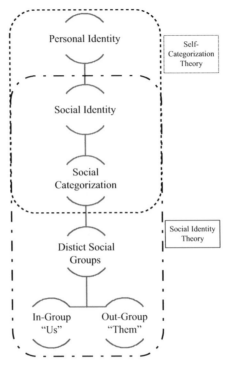

Figure 6.1 The distinction and overlap between social identity and self-categorization theories

THE IDENTITY-BASED MOTIVATION MODEL

Daphna Oyserman, through a series of single-author and coauthored articles, has developed and furthered the **identity-based motivation (IBM) model** (Oyserman, 2008, 2009a, 2009b; Oyserman & Destin, 2010). Within the IBM there is an assumption that identities matter as they allow for meaning making and are the basis for a person's actions (Oyserman & Markus, 1998). Oyserman (2007) found that people are motivated to act in identity-congruent ways, and when they feel that actions are aligned with their identity and within context, those actions feel natural. Further, Oyserman implies that the reverse is true; behaviors that do not feel identity congruent within a context, do not feel natural.

According to the IBM model, both personal and social identities evoke identity-congruent behaviors and cognitive processes. Further, the IBM model builds on other theories, such as social identity (Tajfel & Turner, 1986), self-categorization (Turner, 1987), and **symbolic self-completion** (Wicklund & Gollwitzer, 1981), in that people decide to act in a way that aligns with salient social identities, especially when that identity might feel threatened. Oyserman and Destin (2010) point out that the IBM model draws on cultural psychology (Triandis, 1989, 1995) in that when people express their identity different ways, they should be understood as differences in the relative salience of individual and collective identities, not that the individuals do not possess those identities.

The IBM model moves beyond these prior models in a number of ways. What advances the IBM model beyond the other theories that it is built on is that it assumes that what identity means and, therefore, what is identity congruent is dynamically constructed at the time of a person's actions. In other words, identity saliency and situational context are taken into account when explaining a person's actions. These actions can be either positive or even self-destructive behaviors.

Further, Oyserman and Destin (2010) contend that the IBM model links to many of the modern motivation theories with a situated social cognition perspective (Schwarz, 2007, 2010; Smith & Semin, 2004, 2007) that proposes that perception and action are not separate from situated contexts but are dynamically shaped by those contexts. The integration of this united framework allows us to understand the social and cultural nature of identity, identity-based processes, and outcomes (Oyserman, 2007, 2009a, 2009b). For example, the IBM model predicts that a salient identity can trigger a mental process that will guide subsequent perceptions and actions. Therefore, the IBM model is a potential theoretical framework to explore philanthropic actions. For example, the IBM model might be able to explain why a specific solicitation of an alumna might be more successful than another engagement strategy of the same alumna at a different time.

Aaker and Akutsu (2009) used the IBM model to develop a tripartite framework to understand the role of identity in philanthropic giving. Although the work of Aaker and Akutsu and colleagues is outside of the higher education context, it is helpful in thinking about future higher education research. Understanding that Oyserman (2009a, 2009b) argues that IBM assumes identity-congruent action and cognitive procedures, Aaker and Akutsu's framework is based on three concepts:

(1) Identities are highly malleable and context sensitive (identity saliency)
(2) Identity influences people's actions (action-readiness)
(3) Identity has a role in how a person makes sense of the world (procedural-readiness)

Identity Saliency

Aaker, Akutsu, and Liu (2009) found that there were three different identities that people most frequently claimed when asked why they give:

(1) Familial identity (e.g., "I am a first-generation college student.")
(2) Community or social identity (e.g., "I am a gay man.")
(3) Personal identity ("I am a scholarship recipient.")

Using the IBM model, Aaker and Akutsu (2009) claim whether a person gives and how much the person gives can, therefore, be activated by the context in which a person is solicited. For example, if a solicitation for a gift or volunteer opportunity surrounded the support of first-generation college students, the chance of the alumnus giving or volunteering should increase significantly when his family identity is salient.

Aaker and Akutsu (2009) point out that there is no research that examines the bidirectional relationship between giving and identity. For example, when does giving to an institution have a subsequent impact on one's identity? In other words, how does a person's giving (or not giving) to an alma mater affect the person's identity as an alumnus or alumna of their alma mater? This could be a very interesting way to look at giving toward higher education. Given that there is ample evidence that those who are already donors to their alma mater are more likely to give than those who have yet to give, understanding how philanthropic giving increases one's organizational identity can better explain the consistent giving (Drezner, 2010; Meer, 2008). There is also a need for research on how identity shifts over the life span. For example, how does one's identity with one's alma mater change as one moves further away from graduation? How do identity shifts manifest in giving to one's alma mater?

Identity and Action-Readiness

It is clear that a person's identity can influence his or her actions and the ease in which the person acts (Oyserman & Destin, 2010). Within the context of giving and volunteering, while a cued identity might stimulate action-readiness (i.e., whether to give), Aaker and Akutsu (2009) point out that it is unclear how much identity saliency causes a person to give. Shang, Reed, and Croson (2008) found that donors give more to their local public radio campaign if they are told by the caller that the prior donor shared their social identity (e.g., gender). Within higher education, because an alumna identifies as a scholarship recipient, her identity as having been helped by prior alumni giving might cue her to give to a scholarship fund when asked, especially if she is told other scholarship recipients have given, but it is unclear how much she will give based on her identity.

Identity and Procedural-Readiness

As noted, identity helps people make sense of their world (procedural-readiness). However, how that sense is understood depends on what identity is evoked. Within the context of higher education, the current literature has not explored how institutions best evoke identities in their solicitations. For example, what is the best way to evoke an alumna's different identities that might be salient and relevant to her experience with her alma mater?

MULTIPLE AND INTERSECTING IDENTITIES

Given that a person's sense of self is understood in relation to others and is "continuously emergent, re-formed, and redirected as one moves through the sea of ever-changing relationships" (Gergen, 1991, p. 139) and, in different situations and environments, "different senses of self and identity" emerge (Alvesson, 1994, p. 552), much of our identity is context dependent (Godley, 2003). In other words, a person has multiple identities that are dynamic and contextually situated, and one might draw on a different identity in different contexts (Gergen, 1991).

Some researchers have referred to the multiple identities (Gergen, 1991) as subidentities (Hall, 1986), or co-identities (Hecht, Jackson, & Ribeau, 2003). Deaux and Martin (2003) found that most people describe themselves as a collection of identities. While people are a collection of multiple, intersecting identities, the degree of salience, or importance of each identity, differs by individual and often by specific context (Hogg, Terry, & White, 1995). As research on how different social identities affect a person's philanthropic behaviors begins to emerge on a larger scale, researchers have yet to explore how intersecting identities and identity salience might affect prosocial behaviors.

THE USE OF SOCIAL IDENTITY, SELF-CATEGORIZATION, AND IDENTITY-BASED MOTIVATION THEORIES

Within the discipline of economics, social identity concepts, including both social identity and self-categorization theories, have been applied, resulting in the emerging field of identity economics (Akerlof & Kranton, 2010). Nobel laureate George Akerlof and Rachel Kranton (2000, 2005, 2010) incorporate social identity as a factor in the principal–agent model. The **principal–agent model** describes the difficulty to motivate an individual (the "agent") to act in the best interests of another person (the "principal") over his or her own interests. In essence, the concept of identity economics shows that people make economic decisions both on monetary incentives and their identity. This is important when thinking about how identity might effect a person's philanthropic decisions.

Identity-Based Philanthropy. An emerging area of study, both within the more general philanthropic studies literature and within the subfield exploring giving toward higher education, is identity-based fundraising. The authors of a 2012 *Cultures of Giving* report by the W. K. Kellogg Foundation and funded by the Rockefeller Philanthropy Advisors found that:

> . . . *identity-based philanthropy is a growing movement to democratize philanthropy from the grassroots up by activating and organizing its practice in marginalized communities, particularly communities of color. Simply described, it is the practice of raising and leveraging resources by and from a community on its own behalf, where "community" is defined not by geography but by race, ethnicity, gender, or sexual orientation.*

(p. 2)

Scholars who have explored the importance of identity within philanthropy toward higher education (Drezner, 2013b) have engaged their research along the lines of race and ethnicity (e.g., Cabrales, 2013; Drezner, 2008, 2009, 2010, 2013a, 2013b; Gasman & Anderson-Thompkins, 2003; Gasman & Bowman, 2013; Smith, Shue, Vest, & Villarreal, 1999; Tsunoda, 2011, 2013), gender (Gasman, Drezner, Epstein, Freeman, & Avery,

2011; Ginsberg & Gasman, 2007; Walton, 2005), ability (e.g., Drezner, 2005), religion (e.g., Gasman et al., 2011), and sexuality (e.g., Drezner & Garvey, forthcoming; Garvey & Drezner, 2013a, 2013b).

Ability. Drezner (2005, 2008) explored alumni participation at Gallaudet University, using a combination of historical and qualitative analysis coupled with descriptive statistics from institutional data and the Voluntary Support of Education Survey. Drezner found that within the deaf culture there was a nontraditional view of philanthropy, specifically toward Gallaudet, where alumni saw themselves as recipients rather than having an obligation to give back.

Race. The study of race and ethnicity is by far the most studied identity within philanthropy. Numerous scholars have shown that motivations for and ways of philanthropic giving in communities of color differ from the White majority (Berry & Chao, 2001; Cabrales, 2011, 2013; Campoamor, Diaz, & Ramos, 1999; Chao, 1999, 2001, 2002/2008; Cortés, 1999; Drezner, 2008, 2009, 2011; Gasman & Anderson-Thompkins, 2003; Gasman & Bowman, 2013; Gasman et al., 2011; Kasper, Ramos, & Walker, 1999; Ramos, 1999; Ramos & Kasper, 2000; Rivas-Vásquez, 1999; Tsunoda, 2010, 2011). Studies about racially and ethnically diverse community giving demonstrate unique cultural meanings of philanthropy in relation to families, communities, and religion. These cultural understandings of philanthropy often manifest as forms of obligation, social and racial uplift (Gasman, 2002; Gasman & Anderson-Thompkins, 2003; Gasman et al., 2011; Smith et al., 1999).

Racial Uplift. Racial uplift is the use of both individual and collective agency within a minority community to help advance the race within the larger majority society. The first research on racial uplift surrounded the African American communities. However, these concepts cut across minority races.

The ways in which racial uplift has manifested within African American communities has changed throughout history. During the 18th and 19th centuries, racial uplift was viewed as "organized social activities consciously designed to raise the status of the group as a whole" (Drake & Cayton, 1945/1993, p. 716). During slavery, these racial uplift efforts included the creation and support of mutual aid and benevolent societies—forms of early African American philanthropy—that helped Blacks support themselves in times of economic crisis (Perkins, 1981a, 1981b). The minutes of the 1879 National Negro Conference at Nashville, Tennessee, describe this need of the newly freed slaves to help themselves: "We are to an extent the architects of our own fortune, and must rely mainly upon our own exertions for success" (Meier, 1963, p. 44). After emancipation, racial uplift efforts included the struggle to educate the newly freed slaves for active citizenship (Anderson, 1988).

Black elites viewed racial uplift differently in the late 19th and early 20th centuries. No longer was racial uplift the collective struggle for equal citizenship rights, but it became an individual effort to continue to enhance Black Americans' status within American society (Gaines, 1996). Racial uplift still exists within the African American communities as well as the Latino, Asian, and Native American communities. Today racial uplift is predicated on how individual members of the community can help one another through their own success and actions. In other words, modern racial uplift emphasizes the upper and middle classes' responsibility to use their resources to advance the larger racial minority communities (Drake & Cayton, 1945/1993). Often this manifests in philanthropic giving (money and time). The concept of racial uplift fits well within the positive distinctiveness section of social identity theory and the action-readiness and procedural-readiness aspects of the identity-based motivation model discussed earlier in this chapter.

Role of Wealth. When considering race and philanthropy, Dalton Conley (2000) cautions researchers to consider net worth in addition to income in their work. Conley argues that "it is in the area of wealth that the greatest degree of racial inequality exists, with Black families owning about one eighth the assets of White families" (p. 530). One result of this wealth gap is the difference in intergenerational wealth transfer, or inheritance. Inheritance is important with regard to philanthropic giving, as it is a time where significant sums of money are given to nonprofits through bequests from those who pass away or those who are receiving the inheritance.

Gender. Gender has been considered in four genres of research. In the first three, sex (male/female) is invariably used as a proxy for gender. The presumption is that gender is a fixed, biologically determined characteristic.

First, the empathy/altruism literature reflects a lack of evidence and consensus on gender differences. Hoffman (1977) found differences between males and females in empathy responses but only in females when guilt was injected as a mediating factor. Socialization to gender roles was cited as the primary reason for differences in prosocial behavior. Subsequent studies attributed apparent differences in gender response to research methodology (Eisenberg & Lennon, 1983) and social stereotyping (Eisenberg & Lennon, 1983; Erdle, Sansom, Cole, & Heapy, 1992; Piliavin & Charng, 1990). Overall, gender does not appear to define or determine expression of empathy/altruism or the development of prosocial behavior.

The second genre, dictator studies (e.g., Andreoni & Vesterlund, 2001; Ben-Ner, Kong, & Putterman, 2004; Dufwenberg & Muren, 2006; Eckel & Grossman, 2001), has attempted to look at generosity and gender. What these studies have primarily shown is that giving is highly contextual. Changing the rules of the game (e.g., anonymity, partnering pairs, the cost of giving) affects the outcome. Dictator studies have provided little clarity with regard to the relationship of gender and giving.

The third genre, donor behavior studies look at how people respond in giving situations. For example, Kottasz (2004) analyzed the giving habits of wealthy young men and women. Differences were found primarily in preferences for where gifts are directed and how important various types of rewards (premiums and/or recognition) are for donors. A series of studies on the role of social information in donor behavior also attempted to shed light on the relationship of gender and giving behavior. As mentioned before, Shang, Reed, and Croson (2008) tested the idea that a person is more likely to make a donation if he or she shares a mutual identity with another donor. In this case, the 'identity' was gender. During a telethon fundraising call-in, prospective donors were typed for gender by the sound of their voice and were then told that another individual of their presumed gender had made a donation in a certain amount. The results indicated a positive effect on donation if the caller identified with another individual of the same gender. In a follow-up study by Croson, Handy and Shang (2009), participants identified themselves as male or female. Although they did not find that motivations and sensitivity to social information were mutually exclusive by gender, the results suggested that men were more likely to be influenced by social information than were women.

Within the higher education literature, donor studies most frequently examine alumni giving. Longitudinal studies of alumni giving have shown no significant overall differences in giving between males and females (Okunade, Wunnava, & Walsh, 1994; Wunnava & Lauze, 2001), although size of gift and frequency of gifts varies by gender (Dvorak & Toubman, 2013). Data on male/female giving to college athletics is contradictory (Shapiro & Ridinger, 2011; Tsiotsou, 2006). When the data set is more particular, a few effects of gender are seen:

- Within graduate student populations, men appear to give more (Okunade, 1996);
- Among occasional donors, men are more likely to give (Wunnava & Lauze, 2001);
- Within a household, women make the decision about giving to education (Rooney, Brown, & Mesch, 2007).

A fourth genre—gender identity studies—has tried to differentiate gender identity from biological sex. Winterich, Mittal, and Ross (2009) studied the effects of gender and moral identity on donations to in-groups and out-groups, as well as the mediating effect of how much a person identifies and feels connected to others. The Bem Sex Role Inventory (Bem, 1974) gender identity scale was used to indicate gender rather than the typical male/female identifiers. They found that strong moral identity and feminine gender identity was related to donations to out-groups. Strong moral identity and masculine identity was related to in-group donations. Overall, those with feminine gender identity donated more than those with male gender identity. The authors were careful to define gender by embedded characteristics rather than sex characteristics, recognizing that those who do not clearly identify as masculine or feminine were likely to experience identity conflicts. In their study population, those subjects that were androgynous or undifferentiated showed donation patterns that were not consistent with the feminine- and masculine-identified subjects.

Kemp, Kennett-Hensel, and Kees (2013) used the short form Bem Sex Role Inventory to differentiate gender in their study of gender, emotional response to fundraising, and the exhibition of prosocial behavior. Subjects who scored high on both masculinity and femininity (androgyny) were excluded from the study. Their data indicated at least some correlation between specific emotions and gender identity. When their study was repeated using male/female sex indicators instead of gender identity, the results were the same. Their study subjects were nonstudent adults, as opposed to Winterich et al. (2009), who worked with traditional-age college students.

Sexual Orientation and Gender Identity. There is very little research examining how sexual orientation and gender identities affect a person's philanthropic behavior. In fact, at this point there is only one empirical study (Drezner & Garvey, forthcoming; Garvey & Drezner, 2013a, 2013b) that exists on the lesbian, gay, bisexual, transgender, and queer (LGBTQ) communities' involvement in philanthropy and motivation to be philanthropic, let alone be philanthropic toward higher education.

Identity-based philanthropy scholars have found that marginalized communities approach and participate in philanthropy in different ways than the majority community. Therefore, it makes sense that giving in the LGBTQ communities might manifest itself differently than in the straight community. Because there is little research on philanthropy in the LGBTQ communities, Drezner and Garvey chose a constructivist paradigm for their research. The constructivist paradigm treats participants in this study as agents rather than objects of research and, therefore, relied on participants' perspectives within bounded systems, understanding the context and experiences of both the institutions and individuals involved. Drezner and Garvey's multi-institutional case study consisted of eight institutions of diverse types and over 135 participants.

Garvey and Drezner (2013a, 2013b) found the importance of advancement staff and alumni in promoting LGBTQ alumni philanthropy. Specifically, participants discussed LGBTQ advancement staff, accounts of microaggressions and overt discrimination, and taking a leadership role in promoting culturally sensitive practices. Both advancement staff and alumni spoke of how alumni volunteering can lead to deeper engagement and of the difficulty of recruiting and retaining volunteer leaders within the LGBTQ communities.

In a second study, Drezner and Garvey (forthcoming) examined how a person's LGBTQ identity and experiences (un)consciously affects his, her, or hir[1] decision to give philanthropically. Their findings revealed that there were often unconscious influences of LGBTQ identities on giving.

Most of their participants, when directly asked if their sexual identity affected their philanthropic giving toward their alma mater or nonprofits more generally, simply said "no." However, when delving into their philanthropic priorities and reasons why they choose to support, or might choose not to support, their alma mater, the importance of supporting the LGBTQ communities became very clear. Understanding this unconscious motivation for giving within the LGBTQ communities exposed the importance of campus climate for nonmajority communities.

While identity-based philanthropy is an emerging field of study within higher education, it is still very limited and often based in practice rather than strong theoretical foundations. The identity-based philanthropy literature shows that minority donors' identities are a factor in their decisions to give and how those gifts are manifested (Drezner, 2013b). Though there is limited research on racial and ethnic minority philanthropy, it is the largest body of identity-based philanthropy work in higher education.

Outside of higher education and within a different understanding of identity, J. Mize Smith (2013) explored how a person's work identity influences philanthropic giving. In her case study, she found that work environment and workplace interactions strengthened employees' philanthropic values and influenced increased giving and volunteering along with shaping decisions about where to give of their time and money.

AVENUES FOR FUTURE RESEARCH

Each donor and volunteer brings pieces of themselves to their prosocial actions. Social identity theory and the accompanying self-categorization theory are a strong foundation to explain how those identities are formed, and the identity-based motivation model can be used to explain how social identity and philanthropic motivations interact. The scholarship around identity-based philanthropy is in a nascent phase; while gaining ground, there is still a lot of room for additional research on how identity affects prosocial behaviors.

The scholarship around giving and volunteering in higher education has historically been devoid of identity, thereby focusing on White, heterosexual men, often wealthy donors. Within higher education, as within the larger philanthropic studies field, scholars who have explored the importance of identity within prosocial behaviors have focused most of their research on gender, race, and ethnicity. There has been some investigation of sexual orientation, religion, and ability. However, these identities have virtually not been explored. To date, there has been no research on giving and volunteering of non-normative gender identities, with cisgender being focus of all prior research. Therefore, it is unclear how the existing models of donor motivation fit outside majority identities. As identity-based philanthropy is further explored, researchers should test existing theories and advance new theories where appropriate.

NOTE

1 Hir is a gender-neutral third-person singular object pronoun, which coordinates with *him* and *her.*

7

CONCLUSION

A Call to Advance the Field of Advancement Research

A LOOK BACK IN ORDER TO LOOK FORWARD

American higher education and fundraising are nearly synonymous. The need for external funding for American higher education has existed since its inception through today. As such, fundraising has played an important role throughout the history of American higher education. Fundraising for colleges in America began during the colonial era. In 1640, Henry Dunster, the first president of Harvard College, sent the first fundraising brochure, *New England's First Fruits*, back to the motherland asking for support, and these appeals have continued relentlessly ever since (Cook & Lasher, 1996). Educational advancement has evolved over the past four centuries with different leaders taking on fundraising roles, including local clergy, presidents, financial agents, trustees, senior faculty, treasurers, alumni secretaries, and development directors (Cook & Lasher, 1996; Curti & Nash, 1965; Cutlip, 1965; Stover, 1930). Fundraising at colleges and universities became more organized at the beginning of the 20th century with the launch of the first organized capital campaign. After World War I, professional fundraising consultants began to advise and in some cases run entire campus fundraising campaigns (Cutlip, 1965; Drezner, 2011; Gasman & Drezner, 2008, 2009, 2010). In the 1920s, campus-based fundraisers, whose sole responsibility was fundraising, first emerged (Flack, 1932). And in the 1930s the first vice presidents for fundraising arrived on campus at a handful of private institutions (Jacobson, 1990).

At the conclusion of World War II campuses expanded, mostly due to the GI Bill, and many more colleges and universities began to employ their own fundraising staffs (Thelin, 2011). And thus, calls for ways to professionalize higher education fundraising began. In 1958 over 70 presidents, trustees, fundraisers, and representatives from professional fundraising and public relations organizations held a meeting at the Greenbrier Hotel in West Virginia. The conference was funded by the Ford Foundation and cosponsored by the American Alumni Council and the American College Public Relations Association.

The resulting "Greenbrier Report" recommended the creation of a vice president with status equal to other chief administrators on campus that oversaw the functions of public relations, fundraising, and alumni affairs. This integration began the discussions around the concept of institutional advancement (Reck, 1976). In 1974 the American Alumni Council and the American College Public Relations Association joined forces to form the Council for Advancement and Support of Education (CASE). CASE serves as the primary professional society for all areas of institutional advancement. Around the creation of CASE, although unrelated, fundraising programs in public higher education first began to appear in a more concerted fashion. In the last 35 years, fundraising staffs, budgets, and expectations have expanded exponentially, with the largest private and public institutions successfully closing multibillion-dollar campaigns.

WHERE INSTITUTIONAL ADVANCEMENT IS TODAY

The dollars that are raised through philanthropic giving provide support for nearly every aspect of our institutions, from keeping the lights on, to constructing new buildings, to supporting students, to allowing new lines of research. According to the Council for Aid to Education, unrestricted annual giving programs make up more than 10 percent of current operations at the nation's colleges and universities. However, when combined with restricted gifts and interest from endowments—a result of prior philanthropy—the percentage of annual budgets stemming from giving increases dramatically. Private and public colleges would not be able to reach their fiscal obligations or curricular goals without the voluntary dollars that donors provide to supplement tuition and other sources of institutional income. The importance of philanthropic giving is especially heightened by the decrease in external support of higher education from state governments and the increased dependency in tuition. As such, in the past few decades, comprehensive campaigns and other more specific, targeted campaigns have become more frequent, elaborate, and sophisticated. They are longer in duration and are often endless; as one campaign closes, the next one begins its silent phase. Yet, for such an important aspect of American higher education, philanthropy, fundraising, and the rest of institutional advancement have seen limited scholarship or critical interest.

THE STATE OF THE PEER REVIEW PUBLICATIONS

Institutional advancement and all of its components are complex phenomena that are of central importance to higher education. However, they have lacked rigorous academic inquiry, resulting in an enormous body of atheoretical literature authored by some scholars, practitioners, consultants, and even the media (Drezner, 2011). In 1991, Kathleen Kelly found that "there are few, if any studies on basic research or theory building" (p. 114) within the greater fundraising and public relations literature. Within the field of higher education, Brittingham et al. (1990) similarly found that the institutional advancement literature was fragmented. Building on these discussions, Caboni and Proper (2007) argue that higher education fundraising has made slow "progresses toward professional status [because of] the lack of inquiry into the fund raising function within the college and university environment" (p. 6).

When reviewing the number of peer-reviewed journal articles published on institutional advancement topics in the past 20 years (1993–2012), the nascent aspects of this field become clear. When searching the Education Resource Information Center (ERIC) database for unique peer-reviewed articles over 20 years, we only found 139 articles that had the keywords of alumni/alumnae, fund raising/fundraising, philanthropy, trustee, or institutional advancement in the abstract of the article. These articles spanned all publications in journals within the higher education field and journals situated in the traditional discipline and allied fields. Figure 7.1 shows the growth in the number of peer-reviewed articles over the past two decades. The number of peer-reviewed articles on these topics began to increase dramatically beginning in 2000 with the creation of the *International Journal of Educational Advancement* (originally known as the *CASE International Journal of Educational Advancement*). As we move forward, we can expect a decrease in growth in peer-reviewed articles being disseminated with the closure in 2011 of the only journal devoted to institutional advancement. Besides the *International Journal of Educational Advancement*, there was a short period where there was a second peer-reviewed journal,

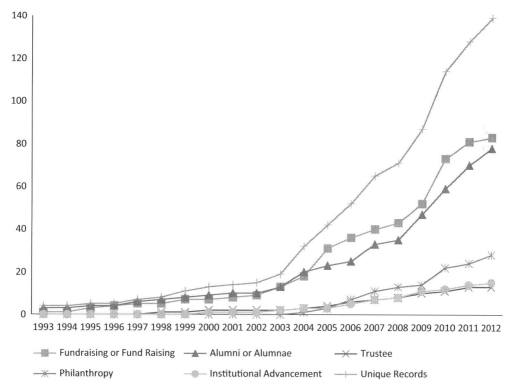

Figure 7.1 Number of citations of peer-reviewed journal articles from 1993–2012 by keyword and unique records

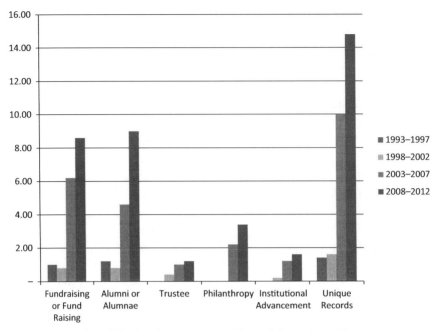

Figure 7.2 Average number of citations in peer-reviewed journals by topic and the average total number of unique journal records from 1993–2012

New Directions in Philanthropic Fundraising (1993–2005); however, *New Directions* did not focus on giving toward education nor was it theory-based research; it mostly focused on best practices. As noted in the preface, there are a number of journals in the field of nonprofit management and philanthropy that provide outlets for theoretically sound research. However, these too are not focused on higher education.

When looking at Figure 7.2, we can see more clearly the impact of these journals. Figure 7.2 examines the growth in the field more closely by topic within five-year averages. In the last five years, 15 articles, on average, were published each year in all of the peer-reviewed journals indexed by ERIC. This is substantial growth from 1993 through 2002, when on average there were less than two articles published per year. More specifically, the peer-reviewed research looking at fundraising and alumni accounts for most of the growth in publications in the last decade (2003–2012). This low number of peer-reviewed publications is partially a recognition of the small number of faculty and researchers that are looking at these topics—a concerning fact. However, it is even more concerning when we look at the number of dissertations that are written on these topics yet never make it to publication.

THE NEED TO PUBLISH DISSERTATION RESEARCH

Caboni and Proper (2007) did a comprehensive analysis of the fundraising dissertations (both Ph.D. and Ed.D.) published between 1991 and 2006. They found that of the 246 fundraising dissertations in their analysis, only 10 percent were published in a journal, with 19 (76%) being published in the *International Journal of Educational Advancement*, 3 (12%) published in the *Community College Journal of Research and Practice*, and 1 (4%) each in the *Journal of Black Studies* and the *Journal of Higher Education*. Their finding correlates nicely with their additional finding that only 9 percent of the dissertation authors in their sample have become full-time faculty at research institutions.

In Appendix B we tabulated all of the dissertations written between 1993 and 2013 that were indexed by ProQuest Dissertations and Theses. Building on Caboni and Proper's (2007) work, we cataloged all dissertations beyond fundraising, to include the other topics in institutional advancement (alumni, governance, leadership, and marketing). The discrepancy in the number of dissertations (129 vs. 246) in our analysis and Caboni and Proper's (2007) is explained by the topics of dissertations that were reviewed. In their study, Caboni and Proper included dissertations on public relations, international institutions, history of fundraising, and a category called "institutional types and causes" that our searches did not include.

Other than indicating methodology, theoretical framework, and whether the dissertation was republished elsewhere, this data has not been formally analyzed. It serves primarily to point to a significant but untapped body of information about higher education. Of the 129 dissertations we indexed, only 12 were published in peer-reviewed journals. Figure 7.3, like Figure 7.1, shows the growth in the dissertation research over the past 20 years.

Caboni and Proper (2007) and our findings around institutional advancement dissertations begs the question of what is going on with the remaining dissertations that

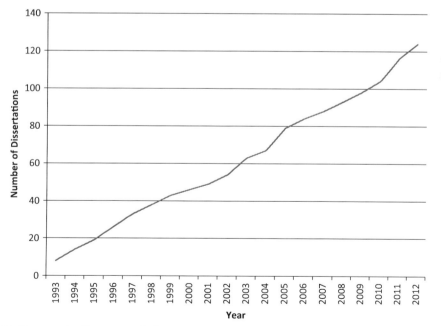

Figure 7.3 The growth of institutional advancement dissertations from 1993–2012

are being completed annually on these topics. Given that approximately 90 percent of all Ph.D. and Ed.D. recipients that research advancement for their dissertations do not go into faculty positions, we can assume that they are going into (or were remaining in) positions of practice. Practitioners have little reason to publish their dissertations, unlike faculty, who have the obligations of the academy.

When dissertations are not published, not only are important findings lost, but there is also a great potential for replication of work and the stagnation of the field. This stagnation does not only apply to practice but to the testing and building of theory as well. As we pointed out, there is a need to ground more of the advancement literature in theory. However, in our review of the dissertations, theory is being used and enhanced, even if it is not published. Therefore, there is a need to encourage newly minted Ph.D. and Ed.D. recipients, even scholar-practitioners, to publish their findings.

THE NEED TO BRIDGE THEORY AND PRACTICE

Scholar-practitioners have the ability to more easily bridge theory and practice than most professors and researchers. Most calls for bridging of theory and practice are focused on researchers writing in more clear and less academic language that is more accessible to practitioners. While this is very important, and we join our voices to this call, it is equally important that practitioners increase their interaction with scholars and theorists. The top professional organization in the field, CASE, has nearly shut out scholarship from their conferences and publications, opting to discuss 'best practices' that might not translate across campuses and often are not theoretically based but rather developed through trial and error, calling into question whether it is actually best practice. CASE and other professional organizations should partner with academics and scholar-practitioners to create a forum for the exchange of ideas across theory and practice. This will strengthen both fundraising and alumni engagement as well as scholarship and theory development. Too often academics build and test theory through experimentation and predictive models, rather than in real-life situations.

THE NEED FOR MORE PUBLISHING OPPORTUNITIES

One way that we can increase the conversation across theory and practice is by increasing the number of publication venues for institutional advancement-related work. With the closure of both *New Directions for Philanthropic Fundraising* and the *International Journal of Educational Advancement*, the number of journal pages available for articles has greatly decreased. However, as demonstrated in Figures 7.1 and 7.2, the field is increasing and therefore warrants a venue for publication and the creation of a new journal and space in existing journals. Any journal that is created should have a strong commitment to both theory and practice. This venue should be receptive to the publication of articles stemming from dissertations often written by scholar-practitioners and publish articles that have strong implications for practice sections, so that the scholarship is easily translated and used in the field. In addition, scholars and practitioners should investigate publishing theory-based work in nonprofit- and philanthropy-focused journals.

AVENUES FOR FUTURE RESEARCH

As noted, much of the literature on institutional advancement is atheoretical or at best weakly uses theory and theoretical frameworks. The majority of the work published at the intersection of higher education and philanthropic studies reviews the literature of this small field. Graduate students, practitioners, and scholars alike often fail to explore the theories from a disciplinary perspective.

In order for our work, as a field, to be stronger, the search for theory must go beyond the immediate topic and explore the disciplines and allied fields (Drezner, 2011; De Sawal & Maxwell, 2014). Throughout this book, we have attempted to explore the existing theories and theoretical frameworks within multiple disciplines that have been or can be used to understand the different functions of institutional advancement. It is our hope that this book provides a coherent starting point for all researchers, whether they are students, scholars, or practitioners, to better understand the theories that can be used to explore these topics and therefore be able to better incorporate theory into their work.

As with all work, due to the limits of space, time, and our own perspectives from which we write, this book is not and could never be an exhaustive review of the literature and theories. Rather, we hope that by reading this book we encouraged you to explore and delve further into the different disciplines when engaging your own research questions. By more strongly using theoretical constructs in our field's research and engaging practitioners in our work, not only will our research and publications will be stronger, fundraising will be more successful and, ultimately, higher education will be stronger.

APPENDIX A

Philanthropic Research Resources

There are a growing number of academic centers that are focused on the study of philanthropy and the nonprofit sector. These include Boston College's Social Welfare Research Institute, Case Western Reserve University's Mandel Center for Nonprofit Organizations, City University of New York's Center on Philanthropy and Civil Society, Duke University's Center for the Study of Philanthropy and Voluntarism, Grand Valley State University's Dorothy A. Johnson Center for Philanthropy and Nonprofit Leadership, Harvard University's Hauser Center for Nonprofit Institutions, and the University of Maryland's Center for Philanthropy and Nonprofit Leadership. The Nonprofit Academic Centers Council (http://nonprofit-academic-centers-council.org/) supports the work of the research centers. A current list of academic centers can be found on their site.

Seton Hall University (http://academic.shu.edu/npo/) maintains a database of higher education institutions offering coursework in philanthropy and nonprofit management. In 2013 the Center on Philanthropy at Indiana University became the world's first school of philanthropy, named for its biggest benefactor, the Lilly family. Additionally, Indiana University recently established the first bachelor's and Ph.D. programs in philanthropic studies.

ASSOCIATIONS AND ORGANIZATIONS

Aspen Institute

The Aspen Institute's Nonprofit Sector and Philanthropy Program seeks to expand knowledge of the nonprofit sector and philanthropy through research and dialogue focused on public policy management and other important issues affecting the sector. www.aspeninstitute.org

Association for Research on Nonprofit Organizations and Voluntary Action (ARNOVA)

Founded in 1971 as the Association of Voluntary Action Scholars, ARNOVA is a neutral, open forum committed to strengthening the research community in the emerging field of nonprofit and philanthropic studies. ARNOVA brings together both theoretical and applied interests, helping scholars gain insight into the day-to-day concerns of third-sector organizations, while providing nonprofit professionals with research they can use to improve the quality of life for citizens and communities. Principal activities include an annual conference, publications, electronic discussions, and special interest groups.

www.arnova.org

Association of Fundraising Professionals (AFP)

The Association of Fundraising Professionals (AFP) represents more than 30,000 members in 213 chapters throughout the world, working to advance philanthropy through advocacy, research, education, and certification programs. The association fosters development and growth of fundraising professionals and promotes high ethical standards in the fundraising profession.

www.afpnet.org

Boston College Center on Wealth and Philanthropy

The Center on Wealth and Philanthropy (CWP) is a multidisciplinary research center specializing in the study of spirituality, wealth, philanthropy, and other aspects of cultural life in an age of affluence.

www.bc.edu/swri

Center for Civil Society Studies

As part of the Johns Hopkins Institute for Health and Social Policy, the center is a source for research about the nonprofit sector, social investment, and public policy.

http://ccss.jhu.ed/

Center for Effective Philanthropy

The center pursues its mission through data collection and research that fuel the creation of assessment tools, publications, and programming and recognition. Since receiving initial funding in 2001, the center has produced widely referenced research reports on foundation performance assessment, foundation governance, and foundation-grantee relationships.

www.effectivephilanthropy.org

City University of New York Center on Philanthropy and Civil Society

The Center on Philanthropy and Civil Society is committed to strengthening civil society through education, research, and leadership training.
www.philanthropy.org

Council for Advancement and Support of Education (CASE)

CASE helps its members build stronger relationships with their alumni and donors, raise funds for campus projects, produce recruitment materials, market their institutions to prospective students, diversify the profession, and foster public support of education.
www.case.org

Council for Aid to Education (CAE)

CAE is a national nonprofit organization established to advance corporate support of education and to conduct policy research on higher education; today CAE is also focused on improving quality and access in higher education. CAE also is the nation's sole source of empirical data on private giving to education, through the annual Voluntary Support of Education (VSE) survey and its Data Miner interactive database.
www.cae.org

Foundation Center

Established in 1956 and today supported by close to 550 foundations, the Foundation Center is the leading source of information about foundation philanthropy world-wide. Through data, analysis, and training, it connects people who want to change the world to the resources they need to succeed. The center maintains the most comprehensive database on U.S. and, increasingly, global grant makers and their grants—a robust, accessible knowledge bank for the sector. It also operates research, education, and training programs designed to advance knowledge of philanthropy at every level. Thousands of people visit the center's website each day and are served in its five regional library/learning centers and its network of 450 funding information centers located in public libraries, community foundations, and educational institutions nationwide and beyond.
www.foundationcenter.org

The Giving Institute (formerly the American Association of Fundraising Counsel)

Giving USA, the annual report on philanthropy, is published by Giving USA Foundation, a public service initiative of the institute. The study is researched and written at the Lilly Family School of Philanthropy at Indiana University.
http://givinginstitute.org

Independent Sector

Independent Sector is committed to strengthening, empowering, and partnering with nonprofit and philanthropic organizations in their work on behalf of the public good.
www.independentsector.org

International Society for Third-Sector Research

Membership organization that promotes global scholarship on civil society, the nonprofit sector, and philanthropy.
www.istr.org

Lilly Family School of Philanthropy at Indiana University

The School of Philanthropy is dedicated to improving philanthropy by training and empowering students and practitioners to be innovators and leaders who create positive and lasting change in the world. The first such school in the world is partnered with colleagues the IU School of Liberal Arts at Indiana University-Purdue University Indianapolis (IUPUI), the School of Public and Environmental Affairs at IUPUI and IU Bloomington, and colleagues in this field across Indiana University and around the world to strengthen philanthropy.
www.philanthropy.iupui.edu

National Association of College and University Business Officers (NACUBO)

NACUBO represents chief administrative and financial officers through a collaboration of knowledge and professional development, advocacy, and community. The organization publishes the annual NACUBO-Commonfund Study of Endowments.
www.nacubo.org

National Center for Charitable Statistics

The National Center for Charitable Statistics is the national clearinghouse of data on the nonprofit sector in the United States. NCCS is a program of the Center on Nonprofits and Philanthropy (CNP) at the Urban Institute.
www.nccs.urban.org

New York University School of Law National Center on Philanthropy and the Law

The NCPL was established at New York University School of Law to explore a broad range of legal issues affecting the nation's nonprofit sector and to provide an integrated examination of the legal doctrines related to the activities of charitable organizations.
www.law.nyu.edu/ncpl

Partnership for Philanthropic Planning

The Partnership for Philanthropic Planning helps maximize the value of charitable giving for nonprofit organizations and donors by helping fundraising professionals provide the most meaningful charitable giving experience for donors, helping financial planning professionals provide their clients with excellent advice on charitable giving and estate planning, and helping nonprofit managers and trustees better accomplish the missions of their organizations through meaningful philanthropic planning.
www.pppnet.org

Planned Giving Design Center

A national network of hosting organizations that proudly provide members with timely, objective content on the subjects of charitable taxation and planned giving; an engaging community; and a collection of services aimed at facilitating charitable gifts.
www.pgdc.com/usa

University of Southern California Center on Philanthropy and Public Policy

The Center on Philanthropy and Public Policy promotes more effective philanthropy and strengthens the nonprofit sector through research that informs philanthropic decision making and public policy to advance public problem solving.
www.usc.edu/schools/sppd/philanthropy

PEER-REVIEWED JOURNALS

Foundation Review

Published quarterly by the Johnson Center for Philanthropy at Grand Valley State University. The focus is research by and for foundation staff, boards, and those who work to implement foundation programs.
http://scholarworks.gvsu.edu/tfr/

International Journal of Educational Advancement

The *International Journal of Educational Advancement* publishes new ideas, shares examples of best practices, and develops a body of knowledge in educational advancement. The journal includes thought-provoking, topical articles from academic researchers and advancement professionals working in schools, colleges, and universities, thus providing a forum for the equally important aspects of alumni relations, fundraising, communications, public relations, and marketing. Its contents acknowledge the increasingly complex management of advancement, with articles that provide in-depth and cutting-edge analysis of new concepts and applications.
www.palgrave-journals.com/ijea/index.html

International Journal of Nonprofit and Voluntary Sector Marketing

Published quarterly by Wiley. Focus is international in scope, with emphasis on practice. Content is peer-reviewed research on marketing.

Nonprofit and Voluntary Sector Quarterly

Nonprofit and Voluntary Sector Quarterly (*NVSQ*), peer-reviewed and published bimonthly, is an international, interdisciplinary journal for nonprofit sector research dedicated to enhancing our knowledge of nonprofit organizations, philanthropy, and voluntarism by providing cutting-edge research, discussion, and analysis of the field. *NVSQ* provides a forum for researchers from around the world to publish timely articles from a variety of disciplinary perspectives. *NVSQ* is sponsored by the Association for Research on Non-profit Organizations and Voluntary Action (ARNOVA).
http://nvs.sagepub.com

Nonprofit Management and Leadership

Published quarterly in sponsorship with the Jack, Joseph and Morton Mandel School of Applied Social Sciences at Case Western Reserve University. The content focuses on high-quality scholarship in all aspects of nonprofit management. Currently published by Wiley.

Voluntas: International Journal of Voluntary and Nonprofit Organizations

The journal of the International Society for Third-Sector Research (ISTR), a major international association promoting research and education in the fields of civil society, philanthropy, and the nonprofit sector. ISTR is an organization committed to building a global community of scholars and interested others dedicated to the creation, discussion, and advancement of knowledge pertaining to the third sector and its impact on human and planetary well-being and development internationally.
www.istr.org and www.springerlink.com/content/0957–8765

OTHER PUBLICATIONS

Chronicle of Philanthropy

www.philanthropy.com

Fundraising Success Magazine

www.fundraisingsuccessmag.com

NonProfit Times

www.nptimes.com

Philanthropy Journal

www.philanthropyjournal.org

Philanthropy News Digest

www.fdncenter.org/pnd

Philanthropy Roundtable

www.philanthropyroundtable.org

Planned Giving Today

www.pgtoday.com

DATABASES

Catalog of Nonprofit Literature

The Catalog of Nonprofit Literature is a searchable database of the literature of philanthropy. It incorporates the unique contents of the Foundation Center's five libraries and contains approximately 28,000 full bibliographic citations, of which nearly 20,000 have descriptive abstracts. It is updated daily. The catalog was formerly known as Literature of the Nonprofit Sector (LNPS).

cnl.foundationcenter.org

Philanthropic Studies Index

Philanthropic Studies Index (PSI) is a tool to locate information on voluntarism, nonprofit organizations, fundraising, and charitable giving. The bulk of citations currently indexed are from academic journals, dated 1940 to the present. There are some dissertations, working papers, websites, and other information sources in the database.

http://cheever.ulib.iupui.edu/psipublicsearch

Philanthropy Central

The Center for Strategic Philanthropy and Civil Society at the Duke University Sanford School of Public Policy sponsors a growing database of case studies for teaching about philanthropy and nonprofit management.

http://cspcs.sanford.duke.edu/casenotes

Voluntary Support of Education Survey

The Council for Aid to Education's Voluntary Support of Education (VSE) survey is the authoritative national source of information on private giving to higher education and

private K–12, consistently capturing about 85 percent of the total voluntary support to colleges and universities in the United States. CAE has managed the survey as a public service for over 50 years.
www.cae.org/content/pro_data_trends.htm

OTHER USEFUL RESOURCES

Association of Fundraising Professional's Standards of Professional Practice

The Association of Fundraising Professionals (AFP) exists to foster the development and growth of fundraising professionals and the profession, to promote high ethical standards in the fundraising profession, and to preserve and enhance philanthropy and volunteerism.
www.afpnet.org/Ethics

Council for Advancement and Support of Education (CASE) Management and Reporting Standards

The CASE Management and Reporting Standards provide a common set of definitions and procedures for managing and reporting the results of fundraising activities at educational institutions.
www.case.org
Additional resources can be found on the website of the **Joseph and Matthew Payton Philanthropic Studies Library** at Indiana University-Purdue University Indianapolis.
www.ulib.iupui.edu/collections/special/psl

APPENDIX B

**Institutional Advancement
Related Dissertations, 1993–2013**

Citation	Purpose	Methodology	Theories Used	Published (Y/N)
Apsey, G. R. (1993). Marketing strategies by higher education for corporation fund-raising (Ph.D.). Michigan State University, United States—Michigan.	The researcher's purpose in this study was to determine whether Michigan public and private four-year colleges and universities use marketing strategies and techniques to raise funds from corporations.	Three-part mixed methods: qualitative questionnaires, interviews, and content analysis		No
Flores, F. C. (1993). Academic leadership in advancement activities: A dimension of the dean's role in American higher education (Ph.D.). The Claremont Graduate University, United States—California.	This study addresses the problem of how American schools of dentistry may organize and manage their fundraising programs to maximize voluntary financial support: ideal development programs, fundraising for schools of dentistry, role of the dean, sources of financial support, and best fundraising techniques.	Questionnaires, interviews, and comparative analysis		No
Grunig, S. D. (1993). A model of donor behavior for law school alumni (Ph.D.). The University of Arizona, United States—Arizona.	The purpose of this study was to create an aggregate model of donor behavior for alumni of colleges of law.	Surveys with factor analysis of other data	Paton's donor behavior model	No
Howard, G. D. (1993). Analysis of what constitutes productive case statements for higher education capital campaigns (Ph.D.). Indiana University, United States—Indiana.	This study reveals elements that may distinguish these case statements and how the case statements were developed and used.	Qualitative research case study	Communications theory	No

Citation	Description	Method	Theory	
Royce, L. G. (1993). The responsibilities and effectiveness of trustees at church-related colleges and universities (Ed.D.). Peabody College for Teachers of Vanderbilt University, United States—Tennessee.	This study examines the responsibilities and effectiveness of trustees at selected church-related colleges and universities. Research also focuses on factors that facilitate and impede trustee effectiveness in carrying out trustee responsibilities.	Qualitative study: personal interviews		No
Sinisi, C. S. (1993). The origins of volunteerism: Socialization antecedents and personal variables (Ph.D.). Kansas State University, United States—Kansas.	The purpose of the present research was to assess the ability of various parenting and personality variables to predict volunteering.	Qualitative questionnaires	The joy hypothesis, negative-mood relief, empathy-altruism hypothesis	No
Smith, D. R. (1993). Effects of perceived goal congruency upon fund-raising at selected church-related colleges (Ed.D.). Peabody College for Teachers of Vanderbilt University, United States—Tennessee.	This study investigates the impact of perceived goal agreement upon fundraising efficiency at three church-related colleges and the effects of goal congruency upon denominational funding at church-related colleges.	Document analysis	Organizational behavioral theory	No
Cook, W. B. (1994). Courting philanthropy: The role of university presidents and chancellors in fund raising (Ph.D.). The University of Texas at Austin, United States—Texas.	This study sought to describe and explain fundraising by university presidents.	Qualitative embedded case study	Role theory, prestige maximization, social exchange theory, and grounded theory	Yes
Heyns, E. P. (1994). Fund raising in publicly supported academic libraries of institutions belonging to the National Association of State Universities and Land-Grant Colleges (Ph.D.). Indiana University, United States—Indiana.	This study developed and tested a fundraising model identifying organizational practices that contribute to fundraising effectiveness in publicly supported academic libraries.	Qualitative questionnaire		No

(continued)

Citation	Purpose	Methodology	Theories Used	Published (Y/N)
Janney, S. R. P. (1994). The college president and fund raising effectiveness (Ed.D.). Temple University, United States—Pennsylvania.	This dissertation examined the relationship of open administrative style and commitment to the field of higher education with dollars raised per student by the institution.	Surveys and questionnaires; regression analysis		No
Miller, L. G. (1994). Patterns of philanthropic giving in American community colleges (Ph.D.). The University of Texas at Austin, United States—Texas.	Over the past two decades, two-year institutions have increased activity in the quest for support to programs and endowments. This research adds to the understanding of philanthropy directed toward these colleges.	Survey		No
Thompson, T. M. (1994). Who gives? A study of variables at graduation and their predictive value for alumni fund raisers (Ph.D.). University of Missouri–Kansas City, United States—Missouri.	This study was designed to identify significant demographic and psychographic variables, which could be used to identify potential donors at graduation.	Quantitative study with survey		No
Wasmer, D. J. (1994). The influence of organizational culture, size, and mission on the implementation of the marketing concept (D.B.A.). Southern Illinois University at Carbondale, United States—Illinois.	The purpose of this study was to empirically test a number of propositions regarding the antecedents of a marketing orientation.	Qualitative surveys	Organizational theory	No
Ashcraft, R. F. (1995). An analysis of alumni donation and non-donation related to selected personal, involvement and outcome factors (Ph.D.). Arizona State University, United States—Arizona.	The purpose of this study was to gain greater understanding of differences between alumni donors and alumni non-donors at Arizona State University.	Survey questionnaire	Student involvement theory developed by C. Robert Pace.	No

Citation	Purpose	Method	Theory	
Cockup, J.B. (1995). A study of strategic marketing in Liberal Arts II Colleges (Ed.D.). Ball State University, United States—Indiana.	The purpose of this quantitative study was to survey Liberal Arts II colleges nationally to determine the strategic marketing orientation adopted by these small, private colleges.	Regression analysis	Exchange theory	No
Gristle, K.M. (1995). Alumni reactions to the use of prospect research in institutional fund raising (Ph.D.). State University of New York at Buffalo, United States—New York.	The purpose of this research was to assist fundraisers with resolving the dilemmas created by the use of prospect research by clarifying the issue from an alumni perspective.	Mixed method qualitative and quantitative: questionnaires		No
McIntosh, C.J. (1995). An analysis of the use of gift annuity agreements at selected United States colleges and universities for the period 1988–1993 (Ed.D.). University of North Texas, United States—Texas.	The objective of this research was to describe the extent to which Gift Annuity Agreements were used by U.S. higher education institutions in raising private philanthropic support during the period 1988–93.	Surveys		No
Mel, C.L. (1995). Demographic and attitudinal characteristics of alumni and non-alumni planned giving contributions to the University of Akron (Ed.D.). The University of Akron, United States—Ohio.	The study's purpose was to test the ability of demographic and attitudinal variables to differentiate between planned-giving donors and non-donors for two groups: alumni and non-alumni of the University of Akron.	Quantitative study: questionnaires with chi-square and ANOVA analyses		No
Abbe, S.E. (1996). Roles and responsibilities of governing boards from three different institutional settings offering nursing education programs (Ph.D.). The University of Connecticut, United States—Connecticut.	The purpose of the study was to determine if the perceived roles and responsibilities of boards of trustees differ among the three institutional settings and to ascertain the actual involvement of these governing boards on selected issues.	Analysis of variance (ANOVA)		No

(continued)

Citation	Purpose	Methodology	Theories Used	Published (Y/N)
Baker, M. K. (1996). A student advancement program model for a multicultural nontraditional institution of higher education (Ed.D.). Pepperdine University, United States—California.	This study developed a model approach for a student advancement program at a multicultural nontraditional institution of higher education.	Delphi process		No
Melton, D.O. (1996). A study of institutional advancement in selected Southern Baptist colleges and universities (Ph.D.). University of North Texas, United States—Texas.	The purpose of this project was to study women who have broken the glass ceiling and determine the leadership styles they shared that had been most beneficial to their success in achieving upper-level leadership positions in higher education.	Qualitative study with grounded theory approach	Grounded theory, social role congruity theory	No
Mulnix, M. W. (1996). The focus and scope of marketing in higher education: Key indicators of organizational structure (Ph.D.). University of Maryland College Park, United States—Maryland.	The purpose of this dissertation was to build a coherent theory of marketing, one that is consistent with, and an integral part of, existing theories of public relations.	Historical and critical research study	Systems theory, public relations theory	No
Nelson, F.E. (1996). Feminist administration in higher education: A Heideggerian hermeneutical analysis (Ph.D.). The University of Wisconsin–Madison, United States—Wisconsin.	The purpose of this dissertation was to find the meaning of feminist administration for women administrators in higher education.	Phenomenology, Heideggerian hermeneutical methods	Feminist theory and Heideggerian theory	No

Citation	Purpose	Methodology	Framework	
Pearson, W.E. (1996). A study of donor predictability among graduates of a school of education within a Research I, public university (Ph.D.). University of Virginia, United States—Virginia.	The purpose of this study was to increase the knowledge regarding the donating behavior of alumni at a school of education within a Research I, public university.	Quantitative study: questionnaires and discriminant function analysis		No
Piovane, M.F. (1996). An analysis of major gift programs and the development of a strategic plan for major gift cultivation at Kutztown University (Ed.D.). Nova Southeastern University, United States—Florida.	The purpose of this study was to analyze major gift programs at 77 public, four-year institutions that are members of the Middle Atlantic region of CASE and to develop a strategic plan to cultivate major gift donors at Kutztown University.	Evaluation and development problem-solving		No
Drummond, M.B. (1997). The power of money: Colleges and universities bank on the boundary-spanning roles of development officers (Ed.D.). Oklahoma State University, United States—Oklahoma.	The purpose of this study was to examine the roles of development officers in public higher education fundraising: perception of role in fundraising process, role ambiguities or role conflicts created by internal versus external goal differences, relationship management of external versus internal stakeholders, and the relationship of resources to boundary-spanning activities of the development officer.	Qualitative research	Boundary spanning	No
Jenkins, L.W. (1997). Inception, growth, and development of a community college foundation: A case study (Ed.D.). North Carolina State University, United States—North Carolina.	This case study sought to contribute to the research by examining one community college foundation. How and why was the foundation established? What influenced the development of the foundation?	Case study		Yes

(continued)

Citation	Purpose	Methodology	Theories Used	Published (Y/N)
Kajcienski, C. D. (1997). The utilization of selected marketing elements by higher education institutions (Ed.D.). University of Nevada, Las Vegas, United States—Nevada.	The purpose of this study was to determine the utilization of selected marketing elements by higher education institutions enrolling 5,000 or more students.	Quantitative study: surveys	Marketing concept of exchange	No
Porter, G. A. (1997). Patterns of giving to urban public higher education among corporate foundations in Virginia and select others which have a significant presence in Virginia (Ph.D.). Old Dominion University, United States—Virginia.	This study was undertaken to examine corporate foundations in Virginia and certain others that have a notable presence in Virginia with respect to trends in giving, motivation for giving, and amount given.	ANOVA and correlation matrix, and factor analysis	Altruism, profit maximization, mutual collective action	No
Rhinehart, P.T. (1997). Effects of involvement, expectations, attitudes, and selected demographics on policy-making intentions among presidents and advancement officers of selected institutions (Ph.D.). The University of Southern Mississippi, United States—Mississippi.	The general purpose of this study was to determine the relationship between the criterion variable of intention to perform a specific higher education policy-making behavior and the predictor variables of attitude, expectations, involvement, and selected demographics, among presidents and advancement officials at selected institutions.	Survey and structural equation modeling (LISREL), ANOVAs, and Pearson correlations	Cognitive motivation theory, theory of planned behavior, expectancy-value theory, situational communication theory	No
Ryan, R. R. (1997). Impact of donor motivations and characteristics on giving to higher education (Ph.D.). The University of Oklahoma, United States—Oklahoma.	This research was an endeavor to gain an understanding of the factors that influenced donors to make contributions to higher education institutions.	Questionnaires with chi-square and discriminant analysis	Resource theory, marketing theory, Silberg's philanthropic chain of response theory	No

Reference	Purpose	Methodology	Theory	
Baker, P. C. (1998). The relationship of selected characteristics and attitudes of professional school alumni to financial support within a public research university (Ph.D.). State University of New York at Buffalo, United States—New York.	The general purpose of this study was to investigate the feasibility of identifying donor indicators among alumni of a select number of professional schools at a public research university.	Qualitative questionnaire and analysis	Student involvement theory (Robert Pact, 1984)	No
Gerke-Newman, C. M. (1998). An evaluation of marketing positioning in four year colleges and universities (Ph.D.). University of Pennsylvania, United States—Pennsylvania.	The main goal of the study was to produce information that would facilitate an assessment of the extent to which the elements and purposes of positioning, as prescribed by the marketing literature, are present among these institutions.	Case study, ethnographic methodology		No
Mathis, H. R. (1998). Leadership strategies of effective presidents in fund raising programs at small, private colleges (Ph.D.). The Union Institute, United States—Ohio.	It was the specific purpose of this study to discover the key leadership factors that effective fundraising presidents employ in their roles as fundraisers for their respective institutions.	Quantitative study: surveys with multiple regression analysis		No
McNamara, L. A. M. (1998). Communication used in institutional advancement efforts with international alumni from United States institutions of higher education (Ph.D.). Southern Illinois University at Carbondale, United States—Illinois.	The purpose of this study was to investigate the nature of institutional advancement communication with international alumni of selected U.S. higher education institutions.	Quantitative survey	Organizational theories: resource dependence theory and institutional theory	No

(continued)

Citation	Purpose	Methodology	Theories Used	Published (Y/N)
Eldredge, R. G. (1999). The advancement president in higher education (Ed.D.). Johnson & Wales University, United States—Rhode Island.	The aim of this action research project was to garner new insights in how some college presidents are more successful leaders than others in marketing their institutions. Also, to ascertain if the transformational theory of leadership is the most effective approach for higher education chief executive officers to utilize in their interaction with their own institutions and the fundraising foundations with respect to unrestricted use of revenue and autonomy of relationship.	Qualitative study: questionnaires and interviews	Transformational leadership theory	No
Oliver, F. H. (1999). Fellow beggars: The history of fund raising campaigning in United States higher education (Ed.D.). Columbia University Teachers College, United States—New York.	This project traces the history of fundraising campaigns in American higher education.	Historical research		No
Schanning, K. F. (1999). Doing good deeds: A multi-dimensional model of volunteerism (Ph.D.). University of Virginia, United States—Virginia.	This study constructs and tests a multidimensional model of volunteerism. The goal of this project was to devise and test a multifaceted model that can be used to explain why some people volunteer and others do not.	Questionnaires with logistic regression	Exchange theory	No

Citation	Purpose	Methodology	Theory	
Till, J. M. (1999). Correlates of fund-raising effectiveness in public four-year institutions of higher education (Ed.D.). University of Minnesota, United States—Minnesota.	The purpose of this research was to identify a set of peer institutions using a procedure developed by Loessin, Duronio, and Borton (1988), and to apply Hombaker's model in order to identify institutional characteristics that explain fundraising effectiveness.	Quantitative study with regression analysis		No
Townsend, R. L. (1999). An assessment of professional consultants' perceptions about institutional advancement organizations within higher education (Ph.D.). Southern Illinois University at Carbondale, United States—Illinois.	The purpose of this study was to describe the perspectives of professional institutional advancement consultants regarding organizational issues being addressed by institutional advancement organizations as they attempt to promote public understanding and support for the institution.	Qualitative research: interviews and questionnaires		No
Cash, S. G. (2000). Private, voluntary support of public research universities in the United States: 1785–1958 (Ed.D.). University of Georgia, United States—Georgia.	This study explores the history of private, voluntary support of public research universities in the United States.	Historical research		Yes
Hanson, S. K. (2000). Alumni characteristics that predict promoting and donating to alma mater: Implications for alumni relations (Ph.D.). The University of North Dakota, United States—North Dakota.	The purpose of this study was to determine the relationship of selected student demographics, student academic involvement, student social involvement, alumni demographics, alumni social involvement, and alumni attitudinal measures with alumni supportive behaviors.	Canonical correlation analysis and logistic regression	Relationship marketing theory; student involvement theory	No

(continued)

Citation	Purpose	Methodology	Theories Used	Published (Y/N)
Schmidt, B. C. (2000). The service sojourn: Conceptualizing the college student volunteer experience (Ph.D.). The University of Utah, United States—Utah.	The purpose of this study was to conceptualize the student volunteer experience with a model that could generally describe what was happening to students.	Ethnography	Interpretivist social theory, symbolic interactionism	No
Briechle, P. (2001). Alumnae supporting higher education (Ph.D.). State University of New York at Buffalo, United States—New York.	The purpose of this study was to determine if there are differences among alumnae who have donated at least $500 as a single gift in the past five years.	Quantitative study: survey and chi-square (test of association) analysis		Yes
Grant, A. S. C. (2001). Major gift donor stewardship in higher education (Ph.D.). Washington State University, United States—Washington.	The overall purpose of this study was to find out what major gift donors expect and experience after giving a major gift to an institution.	Online interviews and focus groups	Communications and marketing theories: social exchange theory, norm of reciprocity, attribution and equity theories	No
Melching, S. F. (2001). Resource development at the University of Alabama: Practices and perceptions of executive administrators and development professionals (Ed.D.). The University of Alabama, United States—Alabama.	The purpose of this study was to examine the perceptions of executive-level administrators and development professionals regarding the practices to enhance resource development at the University of Alabama.	Case study		No

Campbell, J. M. (2002). The use of relationship marketing techniques in higher education: A case study (Ph.D.). University of Colorado at Denver, United States—Colorado.	The purpose of this research was to investigate the use of relationship marketing by public institutions of higher education in Colorado as a tool for retention.	Exploratory case study	No
Durand, B. R. (2002). Demographic, institutional and leadership characteristics affecting fund raising performance: A study of public colleges in New York State (Ph.D.). State University of New York at Buffalo, United States—New York.	The purpose of this study was to examine the fundraising performance of the comprehensive colleges in the State University of New York (SUNY) system.	Descriptive study with inferential techniques	Fundraising theories of Loessin and Duronio	No
Hudec, S. M. (2002). Inducing volunteer community service in undergraduates: The relative contributions of prior experience, coursework, and the dispositions of empathy and moral development (Ph.D.). New York University, United States—New York.	This study examined the effects of on-site faculty mentorship, empathy levels, and levels of postconventional moral development on the decision to continue in voluntary prosocial behavior of undergraduate students.	Qualitative study: questionnaires	Moral development theories	No
Pierson, C. T. (2002). Volunteerism in college: Impacts on cognitive outcomes, learning orientations, and educational aspirations (Ph.D.). The University of Iowa, United States—Iowa.	The major purpose of this study was to extend previous research on the effects of volunteerism in college by studying how and to what extent students change in cognitive skills, learning orientations, and educational aspirations as a result of volunteer work.	Regression analyses	Tinto's theory of student development, Astin's theory of student involvement, Pascarella's model of the college influences on student learning	No

(continued)

Citation	Purpose	Methodology	Theories Used	Published (Y/N)
Vogel, A. (2002). The redistribution arena: On the professionalization of fund raising and the rationalization of gift giving in the late welfare state (Ph.D.). University of Washington, United States—Washington.	The relationship between the long rise of the fundraising profession and the stable patterns of philanthropic wealth redistribution in the United States is analyzed, taking on as case the higher education development office.	Literature review and analysis	New institutionalism, social worlds/arenas theory, public sphere theory	No
Filardo, C. E. (2003). Alumni student-athletes' attitudes towards educational philanthropy (Ed.D.). University of Southern California, United States—California.	The purpose of this study was to better understand the financial giving behavior of former collegiate student-athletes.	Mixed methods, qualitative and quantitative: questionnaires with chi-square analysis		No
Friedmann, A.S. (2003). Building communities of participation through student advancement programs: A first step toward relationship fund raising (Ph.D.). The College of William and Mary, United States—Virginia.	The purpose of this study was to examine if and how student advancement programs influence prosocial behavior and how institutions' fundraising processes encourage this behavior, as evidenced by increased alumni giving.	Mixed methods, qualitative and quantitative: questionnaires, interviews, and data analysis	Social psychology theories of prosocial behavior	No
Gonzalez, S. A. (2003). Latino alumni giving at a major southwestern university (Ph.D.). The University of Texas at Austin, United States—Texas.	The purpose of this study was to uncover the factors that influence Latino alumni giving.	Qualitative questionnaires with follow-up interviews.		No
McGuire, J.P. (2003). Integrating fund raising with academic planning and budgeting: Toward an understanding of strategic fund raising (Ph.D.). University of Pennsylvania, United States—Pennsylvania.	This study explored strategic fundraising and many issues, challenges, and concerns associated with integrating fundraising with academic planning and budgeting.	Qualitative study: interviews and document analysis	Organizational and culture theories: social exchange theory	No

Citation	Purpose	Methodology	Theory	
Morris, L. M. (2003). Integrated marketing: The process and challenge of implementing this evolving concept at three private universities (Ed.D.). Texas Tech University, United States—Texas.	The study sought to discover how private universities were defining, developing, organizing, implementing, and assessing integrated marketing.	Multi-site case study: interviews		No
Rosenthal, G. (2003). A name by any other name: Responding to the increasing role of marketing in higher education (Ed.D.). University of Pennsylvania, United States—Pennsylvania.	The purpose of this inquiry was to explore a fundamental change in marketing structure and philosophy.	Case study		No
Rosynsky, M. O. (2003). The experience of women college presidents: An oral history (Ed.D.). Rutgers, The State University of New Jersey–New Brunswick, United States—New Jersey.	The purpose of this study was to document the experiences of women college presidents by drawing on individual oral histories of four women.	Oral history	Leadership theory	No
White, J. L. (2003). An analysis of the effects of fund raising investment and practices on fund raising production: A case study of Auburn University's College of Business fund raising program from 1991 to 2001 (Ed.D.). Auburn University, United States—Alabama.	This study analyzes the fundraising investment patterns and correlating returns, in the form of private contributions, of Auburn University.	Mixed-method: interviews and regression analysis		No
Meisenbach, R. J. (2004). Framing fund raising: A poststructuralist analysis of higher education fund raisers' work and identities (Ph.D.). Purdue University, United States—Indiana.	This project analyzes how higher education fundraisers engage in processes of identity negotiation.	Qualitative study and grounded theory approach		Yes

(continued)

Citation	Purpose	Methodology	Theories Used	Published (Y/N)
Muller, H. S. (2004). The contribution of organizational identification and induced reciprocity to institutional support and philanthropy by expatriate alumni of an American university abroad: An exploratory theoretical model (Ph.D.). New York University, United States—New York.	The purpose of this study was to examine the conditions for maintaining and enhancing alumni support for their alma mater among the alumni of an American university abroad.	Questionnaires with descriptive statistics analysis. Also, factor analyses, analyses of variance, and correlation and regression analysis	Social identity theory	No
Pumerantz, R. K. (2004). Alumni-in-training: Institutional factors associated with greater alumni giving at public comprehensive colleges and universities (Ph.D.). The Claremont Graduate University, United States—California.	The purpose of this study is to explore the most relevant indicators of alumni giving at public comprehensive colleges and universities.	Mixed methods, qualitative and quantitative: surveys, review, interviews, and correlation matrix analysis of data	Alumni-in-training theory	Yes
Arriola, R. S. (2005). The utilization of a market-driven strategy for fund raising at a Hispanic serving university (Ed.D.). University of Pennsylvania, United States—Pennsylvania.	The purpose of this study was to learn why and how University of Texas-Pan American UTPA developed a market-driven strategy for corporate fundraising and how successful the program has been in strengthening relationships and increasing corporate support.	Mixed qualitative case study: interviews, field notes, and content analysis	Comparative advantage theory of competition (Hunt & Morgan, 1995)	No
Chung-Hoon, T. L. (2005). Beyond give and take: A donor/organization integration model for enduring donor relations in public higher education fund raising (Ph.D.). Brigham Young University, United States—Utah.	The research sought to explore and describe the internal organizational structure and relational processes in higher education fundraising activity.	Mixed methods	Post-positivism, grounded theory	Yes

Citation	Purpose	Methodology	Theory	
Dent, N. B. (2005). The philanthropic motivations of female donors to institutions of higher education: A study of a woman's organization in two southwestern cities (Ph.D.). New Mexico State University, United States—New Mexico.	The purpose of the study was to examine the motivations of female donors to give to institutions of higher education by surveying a women's organization in two southwestern cities: Las Cruces, NM, and San Antonio, TX.	Nonparametric data, contingency analysis		No
Germany, C. D. (2005). African American women in educational leadership: An examination of their characteristics, attitudes, leadership styles, self-images, and perceptions (Ph.D.). Capella University, United States—Minnesota.	The purpose of this study was to expose the barriers, influences, leadership styles, and self-images of five African American women in educational administration.	Case study		No
Johnsen, L. L. (2005). Understanding deliberative conflicts that confront academic fund raisers: A grounded theory study (Ed.D.). Arizona State University, United States—Arizona.	The specific purpose of the study was to provide a contextual understanding of dilemmas that confront academic fundraisers during the process of cultivating, soliciting, and stewarding donors.	Phenomenology	Grounded theory	No
Joyce, P. M. (2005). Regional branding by colleges, universities and their community partners: Expectations and sustainability of a marketing consortium (Ed.D.). University of Pennsylvania, United States—Pennsylvania.	This study was about a consortium of colleges and universities and their community partners that have banded together to promote the benefits of living and studying in their region.	Constructivist case study		No
King, D. A. (2005). A qualitative analysis of major donor decisions in higher education (Ed.D.). Temple University, United States—Pennsylvania.	The purpose of this study was to identify the institutional factors, donor characteristics, and environmental conditions that contribute to the decisions made by major donors.	Qualitative study: interviews	Adult development theory; self-actualization theory	No

(continued)

Citation	Purpose	Methodology	Theories Used	Published (Y/N)
Marek, M. W. (2005). Portrayal of the mission of higher education in the media: A national baseline (Ed.D.). University of South Dakota, United States—South Dakota.	This descriptive study investigated images (metaphors or other descriptions, representations, or conceptualizations) portraying the mission of higher education in the U.S. news media.	Qualitative case study with descriptive analysis	Brand theory, systems theory	No
McWherter, L. C. (2005). The development, design, and implementation of a community college institutional advancement program (Ed.D.). Peabody College for Teachers of Vanderbilt University, United States—Tennessee.	The purpose of the study was to distill a useable, scalable tool or model of success by which other community college advancement and/or development professionals, presidents, and boards of trustees are enabled to better analyze the effectiveness of their current operations.	Qualitative study: interactive method, research and documentation		No
Ryder, J. A. (2005). College student volunteerism: A quantitative analysis of psychological benefits gained through time spent in service to others (Ph.D.). The University of Kansas, United States—Kansas.	The purpose of this project was to investigate the role of the average amount of time spent in volunteer activities in a predictive model to evaluate a number of different aspects of psychological well-being in a population of college students.	Field study: surveys with correlation and hierarchical regression analysis	Psychological theories: hope theory	No
Schoenecke, M. (2005). A description of successful fundraising programs in student affairs divisions (Ph.D.). The University of Oklahoma, United States—Oklahoma.	This study examined the development practices among student affairs divisions that currently have a full-time student affairs development officer in decentralized development divisions at public research institutions.	Case study	Organizational theory, donor motivation theories	No

Citation	Purpose	Method	Theoretical framework	
Sturgis, R. L. (2005). Team relationships within institutional advancement: Board of trustees, president, and vice president of institutional advancement (Ed.D.). The George Washington University, United States—District of Columbia.	The primary purpose of this study was to determine the perceived team relationship among the board of trustees, the president, and the vice president for institutional advancement at private baccalaureate I liberal arts colleges.	Quantitative study: questionnaires	Organizational theory and behavior	Yes
Brower, D. R. (2006). Factors that relate to alumni giving at public master's colleges and universities (Ph.D.). University of Virginia, United States—Virginia.	The purpose of this study was to determine what factors relate to alumni giving at public master's colleges and universities.	Multiple regression analysis		No
Fraser, G. E. (2006). Institutionally-related foundation boards: Processes and perceptions of performance (Ed.D.). University of Pennsylvania, United States—Pennsylvania.	This dissertation explored what factors contribute to the fundraising performance of institutionally related foundation boards of public master's colleges and universities.	Case study		No
Lasater, W. D. (2006). A descriptive study of select higher education fund raising programs: Centralized, hybrid and decentralized (Ph.D.). Indiana University, United States—Indiana.	The purpose was to obtain a comprehensive understanding of how college and university development operations are structured.	Quantitative study: surveys and analysis	Organizational theories	No
Prescott, D. A. (2006). The characteristics of donors and non-donors among alumni of Mississippi State University: A descriptive study (Ph.D.). Mississippi State University, United States—Mississippi.	The purpose of this study was to examine the characteristics of graduates of Mississippi State University to develop a profile of donors and non-donors.	Quantitative study with descriptive and inferential research		No

(continued)

Citation	Purpose	Methodology	Theories Used	Published (Y/N)
Troppe, P. A. (2006). Private funding for public education: A local response to state actions? (Ph.D.). The George Washington University, United States—District of Columbia.	This dissertation explores the relationship between private funding and the degree of education, while controlling for other factors such as district wealth, state charitable contribution provisions, district charitable giving patterns, and local support of public education.	Mixed method: qualitative and quantitative	Public choice theory	No
Dean, M. S. (2007). Perceptions of chief development officers about factors that influence alumni major giving (Ph.D.). Southern Illinois University at Carbondale, United States—Illinois.	The purpose of this study was to investigate the perceptions of chief development officers about the influence of sociodemographic, alumni involvement, and student experience factors of alumni on major giving to higher education institutions.	Descriptive research study	Resource dependence theory	No
Edmiston-Strasser, D. M. (2007). An examination of integrated marketing communication in U.S. public institutions of higher education (D.Mgt.). University of Maryland University College, United States—Maryland.	This study examines common marketing language and its progressive development in the field of higher education marketing and its effective integration of marketing communications processes.	Mixed method research: quantitative survey and analysis with additional qualitative interviews	Open systems theory	Yes
Horrigan, D. W. (2007). Integrated marketing communications in higher education (Ph.D.). University of Connecticut, United States—Connecticut.	The purpose of this study was to assess a private research university integrated marketing communications (IMC) effort in building a brand that represented the university's attempt to reposition itself in the higher education marketplace.	Case study	Integrated marketing communications development model	No

Citation	Purpose	Methodology	Theory	Empirical
Nehls, K. K. (2007). Presidential transitions during capital campaigns: Perspectives of chief development officers (Ph.D.). University of Nevada, Las Vegas, United States—Nevada.	This study analyzed the impact of a presidential transition during a capital campaign from the perspective of the chief development officer (CDO).	Multiple-site, descriptive case study	Theory of transition	No
Black, T.L. (2008). An organizational history of the University of Mississippi Foundation: 1973–2005 (Ph.D.). The University of Mississippi, United States—Mississippi.	The purpose of this study was to record the organizational history of the University of Mississippi Foundation from its inception in 1973 to 2005.	Historical research		No
Drezner, N.D. (2008). Cultivating a culture of giving: An exploration of institutional strategies to enhance African American young alumni giving (Ph.D.). University of Pennsylvania, United States—Pennsylvania.	The purpose of this study was to explore the United Negro College Fund's National Pre-Alumni Council as a model of socialization and how it involves and teaches the next generation of alumni donors the importance of supporting their alma mater and the UNCF.	Organizational case study	Prosocial behavior theory, organizational development theory, and relationship marketing theory	Yes
Eubanks, A. C. (2008). To what extent is it altruism? An examination of how dimensions of religiosity predict volunteer motivation amongst college students (Ph.D.). Southern Illinois University at Carbondale, United States—Illinois.	This dissertation addressed to what extent altruism mediates the relationship between religiosity and volunteer motivation.	Questionnaires and self-reported scales	Human capital theory; exchange theory, social resources theory	No

(continued)

Citation	Purpose	Methodology	Theories Used	Published (Y/N)
Fox, D.J. (2008). A multiple case study of community college presidents: Perceptions of leadership demands and competencies (Ph.D.). University of Idaho, United States—Idaho.	The purpose of this study was to examine community college presidents' perceptions of the demands and competencies of leadership at the community college presidential level.	Multi-site case study	Leadership theories: resiliency theory, transactional theory, transformational leadership theory	No
Kotti, W.P. (2008). Leadership orientations and demographic characteristics of chief development officers at doctoral/research universities in the United States (Ph.D.). University of South Carolina, United States—South Carolina.	The purpose of this study was to create a demographic profile of chief development officers (CDOs) at doctoral/research universities, and to identify the CDOs' predominant leadership orientations.	Quantitative study: survey and analysis	Leadership frame theory (main), general leadership theories	No
Broussard, S.L. (2009). Source-message-receiver in integrated marketing communication: A study of U.S. institutional advancement (Ph.D.). The University of Southern Mississippi, United States—Mississippi.	This study attempted to assess whether the Lee and Park dimensions of integrated marketing communication are evident in institutional advancement and whether organizational complexity and practitioner engagement interrelate with the process model	Exploratory and descriptive study	Communication theory: source-message-receiver	Yes
Dickerson, F.C. (2009). Writing the voice of philanthropy: How to raise money with words (Ph.D.). The Claremont Graduate University, United States—California.	Linguistic analysis of an extensive body of fundraising literature was analyzed to determine if the style of writing effectively serves the purposes of fundraising discourse.	Quantitative and qualitative study: surveys and linguistic/MD analysis		No

Citation	Purpose	Methodology		
Harris-Vasser, D. G. (2003). A comparative analysis of the aspects of alumni giving at public and private historically Black colleges and universities (Ed.D.). Tennessee State University, United States—Tennessee.	The purpose of this study was to investigate alumni giving patterns at HBCUs and the relationship of those patterns with variables that predict gift giving to provide a comparative analysis of the descriptive aspects of alumni giving at public and private HBCUs, and to reveal strategies that are deemed most effective for securing donations from HBCU alumni.	Quantitative research through survey research		No
Hauenstein, D. R. (2009). Development of strategic fund-raising theory for small, 2-year public colleges (Ed.D.). Nova Southeastern University, United States—Florida.	The purpose of this study was to determine how incorporating organized and consistent fundraising into a small, two-year public college's strategic planning results in positive and sustainable revenues that will supplement a college's annual operating budget.	Interviews and survey analysis		No
Lineberger, J. D. (2009). The DBU brand: A case study over the process of branding at Dallas Baptist University (Ed.D.). The University of Alabama, United States—Alabama.	The purpose of this study sought to uncover some of the key factors behind creating a new brand at Dallas Baptist University.	Case study	Brand equity	No
Suh, E. K. (2009). Helping across continents: A holistic understanding of six undergraduate students' experiences as international volunteers (Ed.D.). Teachers College, Columbia University, United States—New York.	The purpose of the study was to understand the international volunteer experiences of six American undergraduate college students from their own perspectives, focusing on why they volunteered and the meaning the experience had for them and how they believe it might inform prospective undergraduate volunteers.	Qualitative study with interviews and the critical incident technique	Holism	No

(continued)

Citation	Purpose	Methodology	Theories Used	Published (Y/N)
Dunick, J. (2010). Teaching altruism: Essays examining the impact of education on volunteerism among young adults (Ph.D.). University of Illinois at Urbana-Champaign, United States—Illinois.	This dissertation sought to understand the impact of secondary and postsecondary education on the future civic behavior of individuals.	Quantitative study with instrumental variables and difference-in-difference equation analyses.	Investment model	No
Gardner, B.J. (2010). The role of institutional relations with alumni major donors in evangelical higher education (Ph.D.). Loyola University Chicago, United States—Illinois.	The purpose of this study was to explore the nature of the relationship that evangelical Christian institutions of higher education maintain with selected alumni who are major donors to their alma mater.	Case study	Kelly's four models of fund raising; the situational theory of publics; social identity theory	No
Hurvitz, L. A. (2010). Building a culture of student philanthropy: A study of the Ivy-Plus institutions' philanthropy education initiatives (Ed.D.). University of Pennsylvania, United States—Pennsylvania.	The research explored how colleges and universities educate their entire student body about the importance of sustained philanthropic support for the institution and how the changes incorporating the philosophies into the environment influence the campus culture as they became instituted.	Case study	Student development theory	Yes
Marks, L. (2010). Visioning civic identity: The intersection of student engagement, civic engagement, and financial scholarships (Ph.D.). The University of Wisconsin–Milwaukee, United States—Wisconsin.	The purpose of this research was to explore the experiences of low-income college students who participate in community service scholarship programs.	Constant comparative analysis	Citizen capital and civic identity development theory	No

Citation	Purpose	Method	Theory	
Terry, L. (2010). Alumni attitudes study: A secondary analysis of Auburn University alumni attitudes (Ed.D.). Auburn University, United States—Alabama.	The purpose of the Alumni Attitudes Study was to determine the influence of measured variables on alumni attitudes and perception toward Auburn University and the Auburn Alumni Association.	Quantitative study and analysis	Identity theory	No
Thompson, L. A. (2010). Data mining for higher education advancement: A study of eight North American colleges and universities (Ph.D.). North Dakota State University, United States—North Dakota.	The purpose of the study was to examine alumni advancement databases at eight public and private higher education institutions in North America to uncover variables that predict the overall likelihood of alumni giving.	Multiple regression analysis	Social exchange theory, equity theory, theory of games and economic behavior, organizational identity theory, social identity theory, supply and demand theory	No
Alkhas, A. B. (2011). An examination of internet social media marketing in higher education institutions (Ed.D.). California State University, Stanislaus, United States—California.	The main purpose of this study was to explore how integrated marketing communications professionals at higher education institutions are using social media as a marketing, communications, and branding tool.	Three-part mixed methods design: interviews, qualitative methods (survey), and content analysis	Agenda setting theory, paradigm shift, and chaos theory	No
Boal, J. R. (2011). Influencing factors of alumni giving in religious institutions of higher education (D.Sc.). Robert Morris University, United States—Pennsylvania.	This study examined how Grace College and Seminary created the motivation for alumni to give.	Case study	Altruism, self-interest models of giving	No

(continued)

Citation	Purpose	Methodology	Theories Used	Published (Y/N)
Cates, D. W. (2011). Undergraduate alumni giving: A study of six institutions and their efforts related to donor participation (Ed.D.). University of Pennsylvania, United States—Pennsylvania.	This project explores the factors that explain how university development and alumni relations professionals view undergraduate participation.	Case study	Circular cumulative causation	No
Foster, D. H. (2011). The fiber of South Carolina higher education philanthropy: A historical case analysis of James C. Self and the Self Family Foundation (Ph.D.). University of South Carolina, United States—South Carolina.	The purpose of this study was to document the benevolent efforts of one family to support South Carolina higher education.	Case study	Seven donor personalities	No
Greentree, V.W. (2011). Choosing to serve: Modeling antecedents of public service motivation in undergraduate students (Ph.D.). Old Dominion University, United States—Virginia.	The purpose of this survey study was to advance the understanding of the dimensions of public service motivation by exploring its development and effect upon student public service motivation levels.	Qualitative cross-sectional survey and analysis	Public service motivation (PSM)	No
Holquist, G. W. (2011). Identifying key determinants that influence athletic alumni intent to give financially to intercollegiate athletic department fundraising campaigns (Ed.D.). University of Minnesota, United States—Minnesota.	The purpose of this study was to identify key determinants that influence athletic alumni intent to give financially to intercollegiate athletic department fundraising campaigns.	ANOVA and chi-square analysis	Social exchange theory	No

Reference	Purpose	Methodology	Theory	
Kelleher, L. A. (2011). Alumni participation: An investigation using relationship marketing principles (Ph.D.). University of Nevada, Las Vegas, United States—Nevada.	The purpose of this study was to determine if, and in what ways, relationship marketing was used to strengthen the ties between alumni and their alma maters.	Case study	Relationship marketing	No
Lamboy, J. V. (2011). Implications of branding initiatives in higher education among trademarked institutions in California (Ed.D.). University of San Francisco, United States—California.	The purpose of this study was to examine the ascribed importance and perceived impact of branding initiatives in higher education in California.	Quantitative study: online survey and analysis	Organizational culture theory	No
Lozano, R. (2011). The relationship between community service involvement and student outcomes in Mexican higher learning institutions (Ph.D.). Andrews University, United States—Michigan.	The purpose of this study was to understand the characteristics of community service experiences that occur in selected Adventist higher learning institutions in Mexico.	Mixed methods, qualitative and quantitative: case study, survey with ANOVA/Pearson coefficient and multiple regression analyses	Social psychology theories of prosocial behavior	No
Proper, E. (2011). The outcomes of board involvement in fundraising at independent, four-year colleges: An organization theory perspective (Ph.D.). Vanderbilt University, United States—Tennessee.	This dissertation examined the effects of board involvement in fundraising at private, four-year colleges.	Quantitative analysis followed by qualitative case studies	Organizational theories: principal-agent theory, grounded theory	No
Saichaie, K. (2011). Representation on college and university websites: An approach using critical discourse analysis (Ph.D.). The University of Iowa, United States—Iowa.	The purpose of this study is to understand how colleges and universities use language to represent themselves on their institutional websites.	Critical discourse analysis		No

(continued)

Citation	Purpose	Methodology	Theories Used	Published (Y/N)
Williams, J. M. (2011). Reverend Robert Draper Swanson: Funding a Christian liberal arts ethos at Alma College (Ph.D.). Indiana University, United States—Indiana.	This study examines the fundraising leadership of Reverend Robert Draper Swanson, the president of Alma College from 1956 to 1980.	Historical case study		No
Balram, A. (2012). Female college presidents: Characteristics to become and remain chief executive officer of a college (Ed.D.). Dowling College, United States—New York.	The purpose of this study was to examine the perceptions of six female college presidents regarding the factors that contributed to the attainment of their position and their potential longevity.	Ethnographic case study		No
Bent, L. G. (2012). Young alumni giving: An exploration of institutional strategies (Ed.D.). Johnson & Wales University, United States—Rhode Island.	The purpose of this study was to explore strategies that colleges and universities utilize to promote young alumni giving.	Case study	Sense of community theory	No
Hammond, R. E. (2012). Exploring the why of volunteer and philanthropic commitment at one community college: Case study of a capital campaign (Ed.D.). Fielding Graduate University, United States—California.	The study explored the perceptions and understanding of why selected stakeholders made significant commitments of volunteerism and philanthropy to a capital campaign at one public community college, and what influenced their decisions.	Case study	Communities of participation, frameworks of consciousness, models and experiences from one's youth	No
Johnson, K. (2012). From beliefs to virtuous behaviors: The influence of God-concepts on intentions to volunteer (Ph.D.). Arizona State University, United States—Arizona.	The purpose of the research was to test the effects of God-concepts and beliefs about the self and the world on volunteer motivations and intentions to volunteer.	Qualitative study: questionnaires and analysis	God-concepts	No

Citation	Purpose	Methodology	Theory	Column
Lawson-Graves, W.E. (2012). Leadership styles and creativity: An examination of the four female Ivy League presidents (Ed.D.). Fielding Graduate University, United States—California.	The purpose of this study was to identify the factors that influenced the career advancement of the four Ivy League female college presidents and their leadership.	Case study	Theory of transformational leadership, liberal feminist theory, generativity theory	No
Linares, R. T. (2012). An examination of relationship marketing as a determinant of commitment and loyalty in college and university students (D.B.A.). Nova Southeastern University, United States—Florida.	The purpose of this research was to conceptualize and measure the concept "student loyalty," to analyze the effect of commitment on student loyalty, and to identify and measure some of the more significant determinants of both student commitment and student loyalty.	Non-experiential research study: surveys and analysis	Organizational theory, commitment concepts	No
Schanz, J.M. (2012). Differences in university fundraising: The role of university practices and organization (Ph.D.). State University of New York at Albany, United States—New York.	This dissertation explored the differences in annual giving at four-year public universities what factors explain fundraising success and what types of institutional arrangements or practices exist at these universities that make them successful or unsuccessful.	Case study		No
Smith, L. (2012). Women of color in higher education administration: An exploration of barriers to advancement (Ph.D.). Capella University, United States—Minnesota.	The purpose of this study was to explore commonly reported barriers to promotion delineated by personal, cultural, and structural reasons among a cohort of women of color administrators in higher education.	Case study	Critical race theory, third-wave feminism	No

(continued)

Citation	Purpose	Methodology	Theories Used	Published (Y/N)
Bourgeois, S. A. (2013). The relationship between alumni presence on the governing board and institutional support (Ph.D.). The Claremont Graduate University, United States—California.	The purpose of this study was to gain information about the factors that may influence alumni to provide voluntary financial support to their alma maters.	Mixed method: stepwise linear regression and qualitative analysis.	Social identity theory and organizational identification theory	No
Collins, A. J. (2013). The partnership between private university presidents and governing boards in effective governance (Ed.D.). Pepperdine University, United States—California.	This study examined the role of presidents at private colleges and universities in fostering a partnership with governing boards as a mechanism for facilitating greater efficacy in university governance.	Case study		No
Davis, S. R. (2013). Terry L. Fairfield: A portraiture of nonprofit leadership in educational fundraising (Ph.D.). The University of Nebraska–Lincoln, United States—Nebraska.	The purpose of this research is to explore the leadership challenges, victories, and life events of former University of Nebraska Foundation president and chief executive officer, Terry Fairfield.	Portraiture methodology	Trait theory of leadership	No
Galligan, C. J. (2013). Alumni of varying eras: An examination of the differences in factors that influence feelings of connectivity and reasons for giving (Ed.D.). University of Hartford, United States—Connecticut.	The purpose of this study was to examine differences in factors that influence feelings of connectivity and reasons for giving of alumni of varying eras at a public, regional, comprehensive university.	Sequential mixed-methods research design: descriptive and inferential analyses	The AIDA sales model	No

Citation	Purpose	Method	Theory	
Horn, A. S. (2013). Educative conditions for prosocial value development during college (Ph.D.). University of Minnesota, United States—Minnesota.	The purpose of this study was to provide an analysis of potential focal points for intervention by examining the associations among prosocial values and related constructs, including empathy, existential engagement, prosocial expectancies, and understanding of social problems. The second purpose was to examine the direct and indirect associations among prosocial values and four facets of the undergraduate experience: academic major, diversity, community service, and a prosocial ethos.	Longitudinal data from surveys and multiple regression analysis	Prosocial behavior theory	No
Johnson, E. A. M. (2013). Factors associated with non-traditional and traditional undergraduate alumni giving to alma maters (Ph.D.). Mercer University, United States—Georgia.	The purpose of the study was to uncover motivating factors influencing alumni gift-giving behaviors by nontraditional (25+ years of age) and traditional (21–24 years of age) undergraduate alumni.	Quantitative survey study with multiple cross-tabulations	Maslow's hierarchy of needs theory and social exchange theory	No
King, A. L. (2013). Integrated marketing communications (IMC) variables that influence perceived return on investment (ROI) in higher education: Chief marketing officers' perceptions (Ed.D.). West Virginia University, United States—West Virginia.	This study examines the relationship of the level of integrated marketing communications (IMC) implementation, level of open systems, and change in state appropriations on perceived return on investment (ROI) in U.S. public higher education institutions (HEIs).	Multiple regression analysis	Systems theory, integrative marketing communication	No

(continued)

Citation	Purpose	Methodology	Theories Used	Published (Y/N)
Littana, P. P. (2013). Success factors of minority academic leadership in American higher education (Ph.D.). Capella University, United States—Minnesota.	The purpose of this study was to determine how factors such as demographics, leadership skills, intrinsic motivation and attitudes, and life experiences contribute to the success of minority academic leaders in the American higher education system.	Phenomenology		No
Tolbert, D. (2013). An exploration of the use of branding to shape institutional image in the marketing activities of faith-based higher education institutions (Ed.D.). Union University, United States—Tennessee.	The purpose of this study was to quantify how strongly a college or university portrays the faith portion of its institutional brand in the materials it creates for recruiting and general marketing and to determine whether that measure is predictive of external perception of that institution as measured by three factors: alumni giving rate, peer assessment score, and U.S. News ranking.	Quantitative study		No

BIBLIOGRAPHY

Aaker, J. L. (1997). Dimensions of brand personality. *Journal of Marketing Research, 34*(3), 347–356.

Aaker, J. L., & Akutsu, S. (2009). Why do people give? The role of identity in giving. *Journal of Consumer Psychology, 19*(3), 267–270.

Aaker, J. L., Akutsu, S., & Liu, W. (2009). *The psychology of giving* (Working Paper) (pp. 1–41). Stanford University.

Achen, C. H. (2002). Parental socialization and rational party identification. *Political Behavior, 24*(2), 151–170.

Agard, K. (Ed.) (2011). *Leadership in nonprofit organizations: A reference handbook.* Thousand Oaks, CA: SAGE Publications.

Ahammer, I. M., & Murray, J. P. (1979). Kindness in the kindergarten: The relative influence of role playing and prosocial television in facilitating altruism. *International Journal of Behavioral Development, 2*(2), 133–157.

Ahmed, A. M. (2007). Group identity, social distance and intergroup bias. *Journal of Economic Psychology, 28*(3), 324–337.

Akerlof, G. A., & Kranton, R. E. (2000). Economics and identity. *The Quarterly Journal of Economics, 115*(3), 715–753.

Akerlof, G. A., & Kranton, R. E. (2005). Identity and the economics of organizations. *Journal of Economic Perspectives, 19*(1), 9–32.

Akerlof, G. A., & Kranton, R. E. (2010). *Identity economics: How our identities shape our work, wages, and well-being.* Princeton: Princeton University Press.

Albert, S., & Whetten, D. A. (1985). Organizational identity. In L. L. Cummings and B. M. Straw (Eds.), *Research in organizational behavior* (Vol. 7, pp. 263–295). Greenwich, CT: JAI Press.

Aldersley, S. (1995). "Upward drift" is alive and well: Research/doctoral model still attractive to institutions. *Change, 27*(5), 50–56.

Allen, N. J., & Rushton, J. P. (1983). Personality characteristics of community mental health volunteers: A review. *Nonprofit and Voluntary Sector Quarterly, 12*(1), 36–49.

Altizer, A. W. (1992). *Seeking major gifts: How 57 institutions do it.* Washington, DC: Council for Advancement and Support of Education.

Alvesson, M. (1994). Talking in organizations: Managing identity and impressions in an advertising agency. *Organization Studies (Walter de Gruyter GmbH & Co. KG.), 15*(4), 535–563.

Alwin, D. F., Cohen, R. L., & Newcomb, T. M. (1991). *Political attitudes over the life span: The Bennington women after fifty years.* Madison: University of Wisconsin Press.

Anderson, J. D. (1988). *The education of Blacks in the South, 1860–1935*. Chapel Hill: University of North Carolina Press.

Andreoni, J. (1988). Why free ride? Strategies and learning in public goods experiments. *Journal of Public Economics, 37*(3), 291–304.

Andreoni, J. (1989). Giving with impure altruism: Applications to charity and Ricardian equivalence. *Journal of Political Economy, 97*(6), 1447–58.

Andreoni, J. (1990). Impure altruism and donations to public goods: A theory of warm-glow giving. *The Economic Journal, 100*(401), 464.

Andreoni, J. (1998). Toward a theory of charitable fund-raising. *Journal of Political Economy, 106*(6), 1186.

Andreoni, J., & Vesterlund, L. (2001). Which is the fair sex? Gender differences in altruism. *Quarterly Journal of Economics, 116*(1), 293–312.

Anheier, H. K. (2005). *Nonprofit organizations: Theory, management, policy*. London and New York: Routledge.

Aries, E., Olver, R. R., Blount, K., Christaldi, K., Fredman, S., & Lee, T. (1998). Race and gender as components of the working self-concept. *Journal of Social Psychology, 138*(3), 277–290.

Ashbrook, W. (1932). The board of trustees. *Journal of Higher Education, 13*(1), 8–10.

Ashforth, B. E., & Mael, F. (1989). Social identity theory and the organization. *Academy of Management Review, 14*(1), 20–39.

Association for Research on Nonprofit Organizations and Voluntary Action. (1989). *Nonprofit and voluntary sector quarterly*. San Francisco: Jossey-Bass.

Astin, A. W., Gardner, J. N., & Sax, L. J. (1998). *The changing American college student: Implications for the freshman year and beyond*. University of South Carolina, Distance Education and Instructional Support.

Astin, A. W., & Sax, L. J. (1998). How undergraduates are affected by service participation. *Journal of College Student Development, 39*(3), 251–263.

Atchley, R. C. (1989). A continuity theory of normal aging. *The Gerontologist, 29*(2), 183–190.

Avalos, J., Sax, L. J., & Astin, A. W. (1999). Long-term effects of volunteerism during the undergraduate years. *The Review of Higher Education, 22*(2), 187–202.

Avolio, B. J., Walumbwa, F. O., & Weber, T. J. (2009). Leadership: Current theories, research, and future directions. *Annual Review of Psychology, 60*, 421–429.

Bar-Tal, D. (1976). *Prosocial behavior: Theory and research*. Washington: Hemisphere Publishing Corporation.

Bar-Tal, D. (1982). Sequential development of helping behavior: A cognitive-learning approach. *Developmental Review, 2*(2), 101–124.

Bass, B. M. (1990). *Bass & Stogdill's handbook of leadership: Theory, research, and managerial applications* (3rd ed.). New York: The Free Press.

Bass, B. M. (1997). Does the transactional-transformational leadership paradigm transcend organizational and national borders? *American Psychologist, 52*(2), 130–139.

Bass, B. M. (1998). *Transformational leadership: Industrial, military, and educational impact*. Mahwah, NJ: Erlbaum.

Becker, G. S. (1974). A theory of social interactions. *Journal of Political Economy, 82*(6), 1063–93.

Becker, G. S. (1976). *The economic approach to human behavior*. Chicago: University of Chicago Press.

Bekkers, R. (2003). Trust, accreditation, and philanthropy in the Netherlands. *Nonprofit and Voluntary Sector Quarterly, 32*(4), 596–615.

Bekkers, R. (2004a). *Giving & volunteering in the Netherlands: sociological and psychological perspectives*. Utrecht: Interuniversity Center for Social Science Theory and Methodology.

Bekkers, R. (2004b). *Volunteering from one generation to the next: Modeling effects or confounding variables?* Mimeo, Utrecht University.

Bekkers, R. (2005). *Charity begins at home: How socialization experiences influence giving and volunteering*. Presented at the Association for Research on Nonprofit Organizations and Voluntary Action, Washington, DC.

Bekkers, R., & De Graaf, N. D. (2002). Verschuivende achtergronden van verenigingsparticipatie in Nederland. *Mens & Maatschappij, 77*(4), 338.

Bell, D. C. (2009). *Constructing social theory*. Lanham, MD: Rowman & Littlefield Publishers.

Bem, S. L. (1974). The measurement of psychological androgyny. *Journal of Consulting and Clinical Psychology, 42*(2), 155–162.

Ben-Ner, A., Kong, F., & Putterman, L. (2004). Share and share alike? Gender-pairing, personality, and cognitive ability as determinants of giving. *Journal of Economic Psychology, 25*(5), 581–589.

Bensimon, E. M., & Neumann, A. (1993). *Redesigning collegiate leadership: Teams and teamwork in higher education.* Baltimore: Johns Hopkins University Press.

Bentley, R. J., & Nissan, L. (1996). *The roots of giving and serving: A literature review studying how school-age children learn the philanthropic tradition.* Indianapolis: Indiana University Center on Philanthropy.

Berger, P. D., & Smith, G. E. (1997). The effect of direct mail framing strategies and segmentation variables on university fundraising performance. *Journal of Interactive Marketing, 11*(1), 30–43.

Bergstrom, T., Blume, L., & Varian, H. (1986). On the private provision of public goods. *Journal of Public Economics, 29*(1), 25–49.

Berry, M. L., & Chao, J. (2001). *Engaging diverse communities for and through philanthropy.* Arlington, VA: Forum of Regional Association of Grantmakers.

Best, S. (2003). *A beginner's guide to social theory.* London and Thousand Oaks, CA: SAGE.

Beutel, A. M., & Johnson, M. K. (2004). Gender and prosocial values during adolescence: A research note. *Sociological Quarterly, 45*(2), 379–393.

Bjorhovde, P. O. (2002a). *Teaching philanthropy to children: A comprehensive study of philanthropy curricula.* Winona: St. Mary's University of Minnesota.

Bjorhovde, P. O. (2002b). Teaching philanthropy to children: Why, how, and what. In P. O. Bjorhovde (Ed.), *Creating tomorrow's philanthropists: Curriculum development for youth.* (pp. 7–19). San Francisco: Jossey-Bass.

Blau, P. M. (1964). *Exchange and power in social life.* New York: John Wiley.

Blau, P. M. (1992). *Exchange and power in social life: With a new introduction by the author.* New Brunswick, NJ: Transaction Publishers.

Boardman, W. (1993). An effective model of a principal gift program. In R. Muir & J. May (Eds.), *Developing an effective major gift program* (pp. 79–83). Washington, DC: Council for Advancement and Support of Education.

Bong, M., & Clark, R. E. (1999). Comparison between self-concept and self-efficacy in academic motivation research. *Educational Psychologist, 34*(3), 139–153.

Boote, D. N., & Beile, P. (2005). Scholars before researchers: On the centrality of the dissertation literature review in research preparation. *Educational Researcher, 34*(6), 3–15.

Boraas, S. (2003). Volunteerism in the United States. *Monthly Labor Review, 126*, 3.

Bornstein, R. (1989). The capital campaign: Benefits and hazards. In J. Fisher & G. Quehl (Eds.), *The president and fund raising* (pp. 202–211). New York: American Council on Education.

Boverini, L. (2006). When venture philanthropy rocks the ivory tower. *International Journal of Educational Advancement, 6*(2), 84–106.

Brady, H., Schlozman, K., & Verba, S. (1999). Prospecting for participants: Rational expectations and the recruitment of political activists. *APSR, 93*(1), 153–168.

Brawley, J. P. (1981). *Oral history.* Columbia University Oral History Collection, New York.

Bremner, R. H. (1994). *Giving: Charity and philanthropy in history.* New Brunswick, NJ: Transaction Publishers.

Brewer, M. B. (1979). In-group bias in the minimal intergroup situation: A cognitive-motivational analysis. *Psychological Bulletin, 86*(2), 307–324.

Brittingham, B. E., ERIC Clearinghouse on Higher Education, Association for the Study of Higher Education, & Council for Advancement and Support of Education. (1990). *The campus green: Fund raising in higher education.* Washington, DC: George Washington University.

Brittingham, B. E., & Pezzullo, T. R. (1989). *Fund raising in higher education: What we know, what we need to know.* Presented at the Annual Meeting of the Association of Higher Education, Atlanta.

Brown, E. (1999). Patterns and purposes of philanthropic giving. In C. Clotfelter & T. Erlich (Eds.), *Philanthropy and the nonprofit sector in a changing America* (pp. 212–230). Bloomington: Indiana University Press.

Brown, R. (1988). The presidential role in financial development. In D. Dagley (Ed.), *Courage in mission: Presidential leadership in the church-related college* (pp. 45–55). Washington, DC: Council for Advancement and Support of Education.

Brown, W. A. (2005). Exploring the association between board and organizational performance in nonprofit organizations. *Nonprofit Management and Leadership, 15*, 317–339.

Brown, W. A., & Guo, C. (2010). Exploring the key roles for nonprofit boards. *Nonprofit and Voluntary Sector Quarterly, 39*, 536–546.

Bruggink, T. H., & Siddiqui, K. (1995). An econometric model of alumni giving: A case study for a liberal arts college. *American Economist, 39*(2), 1995.

Bulotaite, N. (2003). University heritage—an institutional tool for branding and marketing. *Higher Education in Europe, 28*(4), 449–454.

Burnett, K. (2002). *Relationship fundraising: A donor-based approach to the business of raising money* (2nd ed.). San Francisco: Jossey-Bass.

Burnett, K., & International Fund Raising Group (London). (1992). *Relationship fundraising: A donor-based approach to the business of raising money.* London: White Lion Press.

Burns, J. M. (1978). *Leadership.* New York: Harper Collins.

Buttle, F. (1996). Relationship marketing. In F. Buttle (Ed.), *Relationship marketing: Theory and practice* (pp. 1–16). London: Paul Chapman Publishing.

Byrne, B. M. (1984). The general/academic self-concept nomological network: A review of construct validation research. *Review of Educational Research, 54*(3), 427–456.

Byrne, B. M., & Gavin, D. A. W. (1996). The Shavelson model revisited: Testing for the structure of academic self-concept across pre-, early, and late adolescents. *Journal of Educational Psychology, 88*(2), 215–228.

Caboni, T., & Proper, E. (2007). *Dissertations related to fundraising and their implications for higher education.* Presented at the Association for the Study of Higher Education, Louisville, KY.

Cabrales, J. A. (2011). *Conceptualizing Latina/o philanthropy in higher education: A study of Latina/o undergraduate alumni from a predominantly white Jesuit institution.* Iowa State University, Ames.

Cabrales, J. A. (2013). An approach to engaging Latina/o alumni in giving initiatives: Madrinas y Padrinos. In N. Drezner (Ed.), *Expanding the donor base in higher education: Engaging non-traditional donors* (pp. 26–39). New York: Routledge.

Caers, R., Du Bois, C., Jegers, M., De Gieter, S., Schepers, C., & Pepermans, R. (2006). Principal-agent relationships on the stewardship-agency axis. *Nonprofit Management and Leadership, 17*(1), 25–47.

Campoamor, D., Díaz, W. A., & Ramos, H. (1999). *Nuevos senderos: Reflections on Hispanics and philanthropy.* Houston: Arte Público Press.

Capanna, C., Steca, P., & Imbimbo, A. (2002). Un'indagine sulla motivazione al volontariato. (A motivational study among volunteers). *Rassegna Di Psicologia, 19*, 73–90.

Carbone, R. F. (1986). *An agenda for research on fund raising.* College Park, MD: Clearinghouse for Research on Fund Raising.

Carlo, G., Eisenberg, N., & Knight, G. P. (1992). An objective measure of adolescents' prosocial moral reasoning. *Journal of Research on Adolescence, 2*(4), 331–349.

Carlo, G., Fabes, R. A., Laible, D., & Kupanoff, K. (1999). Early adolescence and prosocial/moral behavior II: The role of social and contextual influences. *The Journal of Early Adolescence, 19*(2), 133–147.

Carlo, G., & Randall, B. A. (2001). Are all prosocial behaviors equal? A socioecological developmental conception of prosocial behavior. In F. Columbus (Ed.), *Advances in psychology research* (Vol. 2, pp. 151–170). New York: Nova Science.

Carlo, G., & Randall, B. A. (2002). The development of a measure of prosocial behaviors for late adolescents. *Journal of Youth and Adolescence, 31*(1), 31–44.

Carson, E. D. (1987a). *Black philanthropic activity past and present: A 200 year tradition continues.* Washington, DC: Joint Center for Political Studies.

Carson, E. D. (1987b). The charitable activities of Black Americans: A portrait of self-help? *Review of Black Political Economy, 15*(3), 100–111.

Carson, E. D. (1987c). *Pulling yourself up by your bootstraps: The evolution of black philanthropic activity.* Washington, DC: Joint Center for Political Studies.

Carson, E. D. (1989a). Black philanthropy: Shaping tomorrow's nonprofit sector. *The Journal: Contemporary Issues in Fund Raising, (1989, Summer),* 23–31.

Carson, E. D. (1989b). *The charitable appeals fact book: How Black and White Americans respond to different types of fund-raising efforts.* Washington, DC: Joint Center for Political Studies.

Carson, E. D. (1990a). *Black volunteers as givers and fundraisers.* New York: Center for the Study of Philanthropy, City University of New York.

Carson, E. D. (1990b). Patterns of giving in black churches. In V. A. Hodgkinson & R. Wuthnow (Eds.), *Faith and philanthropy in America: Exploring the role of religion in America's voluntary sector*. San Francisco: Jossey-Bass.

Carson, E. D. (2001). Giving strength: Understanding philanthropy in the Black community. *Philanthropy Matters, 2*, 4.

Carson, E. (2005). Black philanthropy's past, present, and future. *New Directions for Philanthropic Fundraising, 48*, 5–12.

Cascione, G. L. (2003). *Philanthropists in higher education: Institutional, biographical, and religious motivations for giving*. New York: RoutledgeFalmer.

Chacon, F., & Vecina, M. L. (2000). Motivation and burnout in voluntarism. *Psychology in Spain, 4*, 75–81.

Chait, T., Holland, T., & Taylor, B. (1991). *The effective board of trustees*. New York: Macmillan.

Chait, T., Holland, T., & Taylor, B. (1996). *Improving the performance of governing boards*. Phoenix: Oryx Press.

Chambers, M. (1938). The good trustee. *Journal of Higher Education, 9*(3), 127–132.

Chao, J. (1999). Asian American philanthropy: Expanding circles of participation. In *Cultures of caring* (pp. 189–254). Washington, DC: Council on Foundations.

Chao, J. (2001). Asian American philanthropy: Acculturation and charitable vehicles. In Association for Research on Nonprofit Organizations and Voluntary Action, *Philanthropy in communities of color: Traditions and challenges* (pp. 57–79). Indianapolis: Association for Research on Nonprofit Organizations and Voluntary Action.

Chao, J. (2002/2008). What is Chinese American philanthropy? In A. Walton et al. (Eds.), *Philanthropy, volunteerism, and fundraising in higher education* (pp. 816–818). Boston: Pearson.

Cheng, K.-M. (2011). Fund-raising as institutional advancement. In P. G. Altbach (Ed.), *Leadership for world-class universities: Challenges for developing countries* (pp. 159–175). New York: Routledge.

Chewning, P. G. (1993). The ultimate goal: Installing the volunteer and philanthropic ethic. In B. Tipsord Todd (Ed.), *Student advancement programs: Shaping tomorrow's leaders today*. Washington, DC: Council for Advancement and Support of Education.

Child Trend Databank. (2003). *Volunteering*. Retrieved from http://childtrendsdatabank.org

Cialdini, R. B., & Kenrick, D. T. (1976). Altruism as hedonism: A social development perspective on the relationship of negative mood state and helping. *Journal of Personality and Social Psychology, 34*(5), 907–914.

Clark, M. S. (1992). Research on communal and exchange relationships viewed from a functionalist perspective. In D. A. Owens & M. Wagner (Eds.), *Progress in modern psychology: The legacy of American functionalism* (pp. 241–258). Westport, CT: Praeger.

Clary, E. G., & Miller, J. (1986). Socialization and situational influences on sustained altruism. *Child Development, 57*(6), 1358–1369.

Clary, E. G., & Snyder, M. (1990). *A functional analysis of volunteers' motivations*. Presented at the Spring Research Forum, Boston.

Clary, E. G., Snyder, M., Ridge, R. D., Copeland, J., Stukas, A. A., Haugen, J., & Miene, P. (1998). Understanding and assessing the motivations of volunteers: A functional approach. *Journal of Personality and Social Psychology, 74*(6), 1516–1530.

Clotfelter, C. T. (2003). Alumni giving to elite private colleges and universities. *Economics of Education Review, 22*(2), 109–120.

Coleman, J. S. (1988). Social capital in the creation of human capital. *American Journal of Sociology, 94*(Supplement), S95–S120.

Conley, D. (2000). The racial wealth gap: Origins and implications for philanthropy in the African American community. *Nonprofit and Voluntary Sector Quarterly, 29*(4), 530–540.

Connolly, M. S., & Blanchette, R. (1986). Understanding and predicting alumni giving behavior. In J. A. Dunn (Ed.), *New directions for institutional research: Enhancing the management of fund raising* (pp. 69–89). San Francisco: Jossey-Bass.

Conrad, D., & Hedin, D. (1982). The impact of experiential education on adolescent development. In D. Conrad & D. Hedin (Eds.), *Youth participation and experiential education* (pp. 57–76). New York: Haworth.

Cook, W. (1997). Fund raising and the college presidency in an era of uncertainty: From 1975 to the present. *The Journal of Higher Education, 68*(1), 53–86.

Cook, W., & Lasher, W. (1996). Toward a theory of fund raising in higher education. *Review of Higher Education, 20*(1), 33–51.

Cornes, R., & Sandler, T. (1984). Easy riders, joint production, and public goods. *Economic Journal, 94*(375), 580–598.

Cortés, M. (1999). Do Hispanic nonprofits foster Hispanic philanthropy? *New Directions for Philanthropic Fundraising, 1999*(24), 31–40.

Council for Advancement and Support of Education. (2000). *The CASE International Journal of Educational Advancement.* Washington, DC: Council for Advancement and Support of Education; London: Henry Stewart Publications.

Council for Advancement and Support of Education. (2004). *International Journal of Educational Advancement.* London: Henry Stewart Publications.

Council of Michigan Foundations. (2014). Michigan Community Foundations' YOUTH Project. Retrieved from https://www.michiganfoundations.org/youth

Cowley, W. (1980). *Presidents, professors, and trustees.* San Francisco: Jossey-Bass.

Croson, R., Handy, F., & Shang, J. (2009). Keeping up with the Joneses: The relationship of perceived descriptive social norms, social information, and charitable giving. *Nonprofit Management & Leadership, 19*(4), 467–489.

Crutchfield, L., & Grant, H. M. (2008). *Forces for good: The six practices of high-impact nonprofits.* San Francisco: Jossey-Bass.

Curry, J., Rodin, S., & Carlson, N. (2012). Fundraising in difficult economic times: Best practices. *Christian Higher Education, 11*(4), 241–252.

Curti, M., & Nash, R. F. (1965). *Philanthropy in the shaping of American higher education.* New Brunswick, NJ: Rutgers University Press.

Cutlip, S. M. (1965). *Fund raising in the United States.* New Brunswick, NJ: Rutgers University Press.

Daloz, L. A., & Indiana University Center on Philanthropy. (1998). *Can generosity be taught?* Indianapolis: Indiana University Center on Philanthropy.

Dana, E. H. (1947). Why college trustees? *Journal of Higher Education, 18*(5), 259–262, 279–280.

Dawes, R., Van de Kragt, J. C. A., & Orbell, J. M. (1990). Cooperation for the benefit of us—not me or my conscience. In J. J. Mansbridge (Ed.), *Beyond self-interest* (pp. 97–110). Chicago: University of Chicago Press.

Deaux, K., & Martin, D. (2003). Interpersonal networks and social categories: Specifying levels of context in identity processes. *Social Psychology Quarterly, 66*(2), 101–117.

De Graaf, N. D., De Graaf, P. M., & Kraaykamp, G. (2000). Parental cultural capital and educational attainment in the Netherlands: A refinement of the cultural capital perspective. *Sociology of Education, 73*(2), 92–111.

Dekker, P., & De Hart, J. (2002). Het zout der aarde: Een analyse van de samenhang tussen godsdienstigheid en sociaal kapitaal in Nederland. *Sociale Wetenschappen, 45*(1), 45–61.

De Sawal, D. M. and Maxwell, D. (2014). Fundraising and philanthropy in college unions. *New Directions for Student Services,* 49–55. doi: 10.1002/ss.20079

de Tocqueville, A. (1835). *Democracy in America.* London: Saunders and Otley.

Dewey, J. (1910). *How we think.* Boston: D.C. Heath.

Diamond, W. D., & Kashyap, R. K. (1997). Extending models of prosocial behavior to explain university alumni contributions. *Journal of Applied Social Psychology, 27*(10), 915–928.

Dichev, I. (2001). News or noise? Estimating the noise in the *U.S. News* university rankings. *Research in Higher Education, 42,* 237–266.

DiMaggio, P. T., & Powell, W. W. (1983). The iron cage revisited: Institutional isomorphism and collective rationality in organizational fields. *American Sociological Review, 48*(2), 147–160.

Dowden, G. (1990). Presidents: Effective fund raising leadership. In W. Willmer (Ed.), *Friends, funds, and freshmen* (pp. 21–37). Washington, DC: Christian College Coalition.

Drake, S. C., & Cayton, H. R. (1945/1993). *Black metropolis: A study of Negro life in a northern city.* Chicago: University of Chicago Press.

Drezner, N. D. (2005). Advancing Gallaudet: Alumni support for the nation's university for the deaf and hard-of-hearing and its similarities to Black colleges and universities. *International Journal of Educational Advancement, 5*(4), 301–316.

Drezner, N. D. (2008). For alma mater and the fund: The United Negro College Fund's National Pre-Alumni Council and the creation of the next generation of donors. In M. Gasman & C. Tudico (Eds.), *Historically Black colleges and universities: Triumphs, troubles, and taboos* (pp. 15–26). New York: Palgrave Macmillan.

Drezner, N. D. (2009). Why give? Exploring social exchange and organization identification theories in the promotion of philanthropic behaviors of African-American millennials at private-HBCUs. *International Journal of Educational Advancement, 9*(3), 147–165.

Drezner, N. D. (2010). Private Black colleges' encouragement of student giving and volunteerism: An examination of prosocial behavior development. *International Journal of Educational Advancement, 10*(3), 126–147.

Drezner, N. D. (2011). *Philanthropy and fundraising in American higher education.* San Francisco: Jossey-Bass.

Drezner, N. D. (2013a). The Black church and millennial philanthropy: Influences on college student prosocial behaviors at a church-affiliated Black college. *Christian Higher Education, 12*(5), 363–382.

Drezner, N. D. (Ed.). (2013b). *Expanding the donor base in higher education engaging non-traditional donors.* New York: Routledge.

Drezner, N. D., & Garvey, J. C. (Forthcoming). (Un)Conscious queer identity and influence on philanthropy towards higher education. *Nonprofit and Voluntary Sector Quarterly.*

Drucker, P. F. (1990). *Managing the non-profit organization: Practices and principles* (1st ed.). New York: HarperCollins.

Dufwenberg, M., & Muren, A. (2006). Generosity, anonymity, gender. *Journal of Economic Behavior and Organization, 61*(1), 42–49.

Duncan, B. (2004). A theory of impact philanthropy. *Journal of Public Economics, 88*(9–10), 2159–2180.

Durkheim, É. (1897/1930). *Le suicide: étude de sociologie* (Nouv. éd.). Paris: F. Alcan.

Dvorak, T., & Toubman, S. R. (2013). Are women more generous than men? Evidence from alumni donations. *Eastern Economic Journal, 39*(1), 121–131.

Ebener, D. R., & O'Connell, D. J. (2010). How might servant leadership work? *Nonprofit Management and Leadership, 20*(3), 315–335.

Eckel, C. C., & Grossman, P. J. (2001). Chivalry and solidarity in ultimatum games. *Economic Inquiry, 39*(2), 171–188.

Ehrenberg, R. (2003). Reaching for the brass ring: The *U.S. News and World Report* rankings and competition. *Review of Higher Education, 26*(2), 145–162.

Eisenberg, N. (Ed.). (1982). *The development of prosocial behavior.* New York: Academic Press.

Eisenberg, N., & Fabes, R. A. (1998). Prosocial development. In W. Damon & N. Eisenberg (Eds.), *Handbook of child psychology* (5th ed., Vol. 3, pp. 701–778). New York: Wiley.

Eisenberg, N., & Lennon, R. (1983). Sex differences in empathy and related capacities. *Psychological Bulletin, 94*(1), 100–131.

Eisenberg, N., & Mussen, P. H. (1989). *The roots of prosocial behavior in children.* Cambridge and New York: Cambridge University Press.

Ellemers, N., & Barreto, M. (2001). The impact of relative group status: Affective, perceptual and behavioural consequences. In R. Brown & S. L. Gaertner (Eds.), *Intergroup processes* (pp. 324–343). Malden, MA: Blackwell.

Ellison, C. G., & Sherkat, D. E. (1995). The "semi-involuntary institution" revisited: Regional variations in church participation among Black Americans. *Social Forces, 73*(4), 1415–1437.

Erdle, S., Sansom, M., Cole, M. R., & Heapy, N. (1992). Sex differences in personality correlates of helping behavior. *Personality and Individual Differences, 13*(8), 931–936.

Erikson, E. H. (1963). *Childhood and society* (2nd ed., rev. and enl.). New York: Norton.

Essex, G., & Ansbach, C. (1993). Fundraising in a changing economy: Notes for presidents and trustees. *Foundation Development Abstracts, 3*(2).

Fischer, L. R., & Schaffer, K. B. (1993). *Older volunteers: A guide to research and practice.* Newbury Park, CA: SAGE Publications.

Fisher, J. (1985). Role of the public college or university president in fund raising. In M. J. Worth (Ed.), *Public college and university development* (pp. 49–56). Washington, DC: Council for Advancement and Support of Education.

Fisher, J. (1989). The historical importance of major gifts. In J. Fisher & G. Quehl (Eds.), *The president and fund raising* (pp. 212–220). New York: American Council on Education/Macmillan.

Flack, H. (1932). History of early fund raising. In *An alumni fund survey* (pp. 1–9). Ithaca, NY: American Alumni Council.

Flanagan, C. A., Bowes, J. M., Jonsson, B., Csapo, B., & Sheblanova, E. (1998). Ties that bind. *Journal of Social Issues, 54*(3), 457–475.

Flawn, P. (1990). *A primer for university presidents: Managing the modern university.* Austin: University of Texas Press.

Fletcher, A. C., Elder, G. H., Jr., & Mekos, D. (2000). Parental influences on adolescent involvement in community activities. *Journal of Research on Adolescence, 10*(1), 29–48.

Flor, D. L., & Knapp, N. F. (2001). Transmission and transaction: Predicting adolescents' internalization of parental religious values. *Journal of Family Psychology, 15*(4), 627–645.

Foote, E., II. (1986). The president's role in a capital campaign. In H. Quigg (Ed.), *The successful capital campaign* (pp. 73–80). Washington, DC: Council for Advancement and Support of Education.

Francis, N. (1975). The president's management role in development. In *The president's role in development* (pp. 2–5). Washington, DC: Association of American Colleges.

Fredette, C., & Bradshaw, P. (2012). Social capital and nonprofit governance effectiveness. *Nonprofit Management and Leadership, 22*(4), 391–409.

Gächter, S., Fehr, E., & Kment, C. (1996). Does social exchange increase voluntary cooperation? *Kyklos, 49*(4), 541–554.

Gaier, S. (2005). Alumni satisfaction with their undergraduate academic experience and the impact on alumni giving and participation. *International Journal of Educational Advancement, 5*(4), 279–288.

Gaines, K. K. (1996). *Uplifting the race: Black leadership, politics, and culture in the twentieth century.* Chapel Hill: University of North Carolina Press.

Gallo, P. J., & Hubschman, B. (2003). *The Relationships between alumni participation and motivation on financial giving.* Paper presented at the Annual Meeting of the American Educational Research Association, Chicago, IL, April 21–25, 2003.

Gallup Organization, Independent Sector (Firm). (1992). *Giving and volunteering in the United States.* Washington, DC: Independent Sector.

Gallup Organization, Independent Sector (Firm). (1996). *Giving and volunteering in the United States.* Washington, DC: Independent Sector.

Gamble, P. R., Stone, M., Woodcock, N., & Foss, B. (1999). *Up close and personal? Customer relationship marketing @ work.* London and Dover, NH: Kogan Page.

Garbarino, E., & Johnson, M. S. (1999). The different roles of satisfaction, trust, and commitment in customer relationships. *Journal of Marketing, 63*(2), 70–87.

Garvey, J. C., & Drezner, N. D. (2013a). Advancement staff and alumni advocates: Cultivating LGBTQ alumni by promoting individual and community uplift. *Journal of Diversity in Higher Education, 6*(3), 199–218.

Garvey, J. C., & Drezner, N. D. (2013b). Alumni giving in the LGBTQ communities. In N. D. Drezner (Ed.), *Expanding the donor base in higher education: Engaging non-traditional donors* (pp. 74–86). Florence, KY: Routledge.

Gasman, M. (2002). An untapped resource: Bringing African Americans into the college and university giving process. *CASE International Journal of Educational Advancement, 2*(3), 280–292.

Gasman, M., & Anderson-Thompkins, S. (2003). *Fund raising from Black-college alumni: Successful strategies for supporting alma mater.* Washington, DC: Council for Advancement and Support of Education.

Gasman, M., & Bowman, N. (2013). *Engaging diverse college alumni: The essential guide to fundraising.* New York: Routledge.

Gasman, M., & Drezner, N. (2008). White corporate philanthropy and its support of private Black colleges in the 1960s and 70s. *International Journal of Educational Advancement, 8*(2), 79–92.

Gasman, M., & Drezner, N. (2009). A maverick in the field: The Oram Group and fundraising for change in the Black college community during the 1970s. *History of Education Quarterly, 49*(4), 465–506.

Gasman, M., & Drezner, N. (2010). Fundraising for Black colleges during the 1960s and 1970s: The case of Hampton Institute. *Nonprofit and Voluntary Sector Quarterly, 39*(2), 321–342.

Gasman, M., Drezner, N. D., Epstein, E., Freeman, T., & Avery, V. L. (2011). *Race, gender, and leadership in nonprofit organizations*. New York: Palgrave Macmillan.

George, B. (2003). *Authentic leadership*. San Francisco: Jossey-Bass.

Gergen, K. J. (1991). *The saturated self: Dilemmas of identity in contemporary life*. New York: Basic Books.

Giannakakis, A. E., & Fritsche, I. (2011). Social identities, group norms, and threat: On the malleability of ingroup bias. *Personality and Social Psychology Bulletin, 37*(1), 82–93.

Gidron, B. (1985). Predictors of retention and turnover among service volunteer workers. *Journal of Social Service Research, 8*(1), 1–16.

Ginsberg, A., & Gasman, M. (Eds.) (2007). *Gender and educational philanthropy: New perspectives on funding, collaboration and assessment*. New York: Palgrave Macmillan.

Glenn, N. D. (1964). Negro religion and Negro status in the United States. In L. Schneider (Ed.), *Religion, culture, and society* (pp. 623–629). New York: Wiley.

Glier, J. (2004). *Higher education leadership and fundraising*. Presented at the Council for Industry and Higher Education, London.

Godley, A. J. (2003). Literacy learning as gendered identity work. *Communication Education, 52*(3–4), 273–285.

Gouldner, A. W. (1960). The norm of reciprocity: A preliminary statement. *American Sociological Review, 25*(2), 161–178.

Graen, G., & Uhl-Bien, M. (1995). Relationship-based approach to leadership: Development of leader-member exchange (LMX) theory of leadership over 25 years: Applying a multi-level, multi-domain perspective. *Leadership Quarterly, 6*(2), 219–247.

Greenleaf, R. (1991). *The servant leader*. Indianapolis: Robert K. Greenleaf Center.

Grezenbach, Glier, & Associates. (2013). *Capital campaigns in higher education with billion-dollar+ goals*. Chicago: Grezenbach, Glier, & Associates.

Grimm, R., Jr., Dietz, N., Spring, K. A., & Foster-Bey, J. (2005). *Building active citizens: The role of social institutions in teen volunteering*. Washington, DC: Corporation for National and Community Service.

Grolnick, W. S., & Slowiaczek, M. L. (1994). Parents' involvement in children's schooling: A multidimensional conceptualization and motivational model. *Child Development, 65*(1), 237–252.

Grusec, J. E. (1982). Socialization of altruism. In N. Eisenberg (Ed.), *The development of prosocial behavior* (pp. 139–166). New York: Academic Press.

Grusec, J. E. (1991). Socialization of empathy. In M. S. Clark (Ed.), *Review of personality and social psychology* (Vol. 12, pp. 9–33). Newbury Park, CA: Sage.

Grusec, J. E., & Hastings, P. D. (Eds.). (2007, 2008). *Handbook of socialization: Theory and research*. New York: Guilford Press.

Grusec, J. E., & Kuczynski, L. (Eds.). (1997). *Parenting and children's internalization of values: A handbook of contemporary theory*. New York: John Wiley.

Gumport, P. J., & Snydman, S. K. (2006). Higher education: Evolving forms and emerging markets. In W. W. Powell & R. Steinberg (Eds.), *The nonprofit sector: A research handbook* (2nd ed., pp. 462–484). New Haven: Yale University Press.

Guo, C. (2007). When government becomes the principal philanthropist: The effects of public funding on patterns of nonprofit governance. *Public Administration Review, 67*(3), 458–473.

Hall, D. T. (1986). *Career development in organizations* (1st ed.). San Francisco: Jossey-Bass.

Hankinson, P. (2001). Brand orientation in the charity sector: A framework for discussion and research. *International Journal of Nonprofit and Voluntary Sector Marketing, 6*(3), 231–242.

Hanks, M. (1981). Youth, voluntary associations and political socialization. *Social Forces, 60*(1), 211–223.

Hanks, M., & Eckland, B. K. (1978). Adult voluntary associations and adolescent socialization. *The Sociological Quarterly, 19*(3), 481–490.

Harbaugh, W. (1998). The prestige motive for making charitable transfers. *American Economic Review, 88*(2), 277–282.

Hardin, P. (1984). How I learned to love fund raising. *Currents (Washington, DC), 10*(1), 14–18.

Harlan, S., & Saidel, J. (1994). Board members' influence on the government-nonprofit relationship. *Nonprofit Management and Leadership, 5*, 173–196.

Harrison, W. B. (1995). College relations and fund-raising expenditures: Influencing the probability of alumni giving to higher education. *Economics of Education Review, 14*(1), 73–84.

Hart, D., Atkins, R., & Ford, D. (1998). Urban America as a context for the development of moral identity in adolescence. *Journal of Social Issues, 54*(3), 513–530.

Hart, D., & Fegley, S. (1995). Prosocial behavior and caring in adolescence: Relations to self-understanding and social judgment. *Child Development, 66*(5), 1346–1359.

Hartley, M., & Morphew, C. (2008). What's being sold and to what end? A content analysis of college viewbooks. *Journal of Higher Education, 79*(6), 671–691.

Haslam, S. A. (1997). Stereotyping and social influence: Foundations of stereotype consensus. In R. Spears, P. Oakes, & N. Ellemers (Eds.), *The social psychology of stereotyping and group life* (pp. 119–143). Oxford: Blackwell.

Haslam, S. A. (2001). *Psychology in organizations: The social identity approach.* London and Thousand Oaks, CA: Sage.

Haslam, S. A., Oakes, P., Turner, J., & McGarty, C. (1996). Social identity, self-categorization, and the perceived homogeneity of ingroups and outgroups: The interaction between social motivation and cognition. In R. Sorrentino & E. Higgins (Eds.), *Handbook of motivation and cognition: The interpersonal context* (Vol. 3, pp. 182–222). New York: Guilford Press.

Hecht, M. L., Jackson, R. L., & Ribeau, S. A. (2003). *African American communication: Exploring identity and culture* (2nd ed.). Mahwah, NJ: L. Erlbaum Associates.

Hesburgh, T. (1988). Academic leadership. In J. Fisher & M. Tack (Eds.), *Leaders on leadership: The college presidency* (pp. 5–8). San Francisco: Jossey-Bass.

Ho, J. C., & W. K. Kellogg Foundation. (2003). *Youth and community: Engaging young people in philanthropy and service.* Battle Creek, MI: W. K. Kellogg Foundation.

Hoffman, M. L. (1977). Sex differences in empathy and related behaviors. *Psychological Bulletin, 84*(4), 712–722.

Hoffman, R. M. (2004). Conceptualizing heterosexual identity development: Issues and challenges. *Journal of Counseling & Development, 82*(3), 375–380.

Hoffman, R. M., Hattie, J. A., & Borders, L. D. (2005). Personal definitions of masculinity and femininity as an aspect of gender self-concept. *Journal of Humanistic Counseling, Education and Development, 44*(1), 66–83.

Hogg, M. A. (1987). Social identity and group cohesiveness. In J. C. Turner (Ed.), *Rediscovering the social group: A self-categorization theory* (pp. 89–116). Oxford: Basil Blackwell.

Hogg, M. A., Terry, D. J., & White, K. M. (1995). A tale of two theories: A critical comparison of identity theory with social identity theory. *Social Psychology Quarterly, 58*(4), 255–269.

Hogg, M. A., & Turner, J. C. (1987). Intergroup behaviour, self-stereotyping and the salience of social categories. *British Journal of Social Psychology, 26*(4), 325–340.

Hollander, H. (1990). A social exchange approach to voluntary cooperation. *American Economic Review, 80*(5), 1157–1167.

Homans, G. C. (1958). Social behavior as exchange. *American Journal of Sociology, 63*(6), 597–606.

Hopt, K. J., & Von Hippel, T. (2010). *Comparative corporate governance of non-profit organizations.* Cambridge, UK, and New York: Cambridge University Press.

Horn, L., & Berktold, J. (1998). *Profile of undergraduates in US post-secondary education institutions: 1995–6.* Washington, DC: Corporation for National and Community Service.

Horn, L., Peter, K., & Rooney, K. (2002). *Profile of undergraduates in US post-secondary education institutions: 1999–2000.* Washington, DC: Corporation for National and Community Service.

Howe, F. (1991). *The board member's guide to fund raising: What every trustee needs to know about raising money.* San Francisco: Jossey-Bass.

Hunt, M. M. (1990). *The compassionate beast: What science is discovering about the humane side of humankind* (1st ed.). New York: Morrow.

Hunt, P. (2012). *Development for academic leaders: A practical guide for fundraising success.* San Francisco: Jossey-Bass.

Hunt, S. D., & Morgan, R. M. (1995). The comparative advantage theory of competition. *Journal of Marketing, 59*(April), 1–15.

Hunter, C. S., Jones, E. B., & Boger, C. (1999). A study of the relationship between alumni giving and selected characteristics of alumni donors of Livingstone College, NC. *Journal of Black Studies, 29*(4), 523.

Independent Sector. (2000). *Childhood events and philanthropic behavior.* Washington, DC: Independent Sector. Retrieved from www.independentsector.org/gandv/s_chil.htm

Independent Sector. (2002). *Faith & philanthropy: The connection between charitable behavior and giving to religion.* Washington, DC: Independent Sector.

International Journal of Nonprofit and Voluntary Sector Marketing. (1999). London and Birmingham: Henry Stewart Publications.

International Society for Third-Sector Research. (n.d.). *Voluntas: International Journal of Voluntary and Nonprofit Organizations.* New York: Kluwer Academic/Plenum Publishers.

Irving, J. A. (2005). Exploring the relationship between servant leadership and team effectiveness: Findings from the nonprofit sector. In *Proceedings.* Regent University. Retrieved from www.regent.edu/acad/global/publications/sl_proceedings/home.cfm

Israel, A. C. (1978). Some thoughts on correspondence between saying and doing. *Journal of Applied Behavior Analysis, 11*(2), 271–276.

Jackson, E. F., Bachmeier, M. D., Wood, J. R., & Craft, E. A. (1995). Volunteering and charitable giving: Do religious and associational ties promote helping behavior? *Nonprofit and Voluntary Sector Quarterly, 24*(1), 59–78.

Jacobson, C. K., Heaton, T. B., & Dennis, R. M. (1990). Black-White differences in religiosity: Item analyses and a formal structural test. *Sociology of Religion, 51*(3), 257–270.

Jacobson, H. K. (1990). *The evolution of institutional advancement on American campuses, 1636–1989.* Oshkosh: Journalism Research Bureau, University of Wisconsin Oshkosh.

Janoski, T., & Wilson, J. (1995). Pathways to voluntarism: Family socialization and status transmission models. *Social Forces, 74*(1), 271–292.

Jaskyte, K. (2012). Boards of directors and innovation in nonprofit organizations. *Nonprofit Management & Leadership, 22*(4), 439–459.

Johnson, M. K., Beebe, T., Mortimer, J. T., & Snyder, M. (1998). Volunteerism in adolescence: A process perspective. *Journal of Research on Adolescence, 8*(3), 309–332.

Kasper, G., Ramos, H. A. J., & Walker, C. J. (1999). Making the case for diversity in philanthropy. *Foundation News & Commentary, 45*(6), 26–35.

Kaufman, B. (2004). Juggling act. *University Business, 7*(7), 50–52.

Keeter, S., & Center for Information and Research in Civic Learning & Engagement. (2002). *The civic and political health of the nation: A generational portrait.* College Park, MD: CIRCLE.

Kelly, K. S. (1991). *Fund raising and public relations: A critical analysis.* Hillsdale, NJ: L. Erlbaum Associates.

Kelly, K. S. (1998). *Effective fund-raising management.* Mahwah, NJ: Lawrence Erlbaum Associates.

Kelly, K. S. (2002). The state of fund-raising theory and research. In M. J. Worth (Ed.), *New strategies for educational fundraising* (pp. 39–55). Westport, CT: American Council on Education/Praeger.

Kemp, E., Kennett-Hensel, P. A., & Kees, J. (2013). Pulling on the heartstrings: Examining the effects of emotions and gender in persuasive appeals. *Journal of Advertising, 42*(1), 69–79.

Kerns, J. R. (1986). *Two-year college alumni programs into the 1990s.* Presented at the National Workshop on Two-Year College Programs, Junior and Community College Institute, Washington, DC.

King, M., Walder, L. O., & Pavey, S. (1970). Personality change as a function of volunteer experience in a psychiatric hospital. *Journal of Consulting and Clinical Psychology, 35*(3), 423–425.

Kohlberg, L. (1984). *The psychology of moral development: The nature and validity of moral stages.* San Francisco: Harper & Row.

Kohr, R. V. (1977). Capital campaigning. In A. Rowland (Ed.), *Handbook of institutional advancement* (pp. 236–264). San Francisco: Jossey-Bass.

Kotler, P. (1975). *Marketing for nonprofit organizations.* Englewood Cliffs, NJ, and London: Prentice-Hall.

Kotler, P. (1997). *Marketing management: Analysis, planning, implementation, and control.* Upper Saddle River, NJ: Prentice Hall.

Kotler, P., & Fox, K. F. A. (1995). *Strategic marketing for educational institutions.* Englewood Cliffs, NJ: Prentice-Hall.

Kotler, P., & Levy, S. J. (1969). Broadening the concept of marketing. *Journal of Marketing, 33*(1), 10–15.

Kottasz, R. (2004). Differences in the donor behavior characteristics of young affluent males and females: Empirical evidence from Britain. *Voluntas: International Journal of Voluntary and Nonprofit Organizations, 15*(2), 181–203.

Kraaykamp, G. (1996). Ontwikkelingen in de sociale segmentering van vrijetijdsbesteding; toenemende exclusiviteit of evenredige participatie? In H. B. G. Ganzeboom & W. Ultee (Eds.), *De sociale segmentatie van Nederland in 2015* (pp. 171–203). Den Haag: Sdu Uitgevers.

Krachenberg, A. R. (1972). Bringing the concept of marketing to higher education. *The Journal of Higher Education, 43*(5), 369–380.

Kravis-deRoulet Leadership Conference. (2004). *Improving leadership in nonprofit organizations* (1st ed.). San Francisco: Jossey-Bass.

Krumm, A. J., & Corning, A. F. (2008). Who believes us when we try to conceal our prejudices? The effectiveness of moral credentials with in-groups versus out-groups. *The Journal of Social Psychology, 148*(6), 689–710.

Lake Snell Perry and Associates & The Tarrance Group, Inc. (2002). *Short-term impacts, long-term opportunities: The political and civic engagement of young adults in America.* Washington, DC: The Center for Information and Research in Civic Learning & Engagement (CIRCLE), The Center for Democracy & Citizenship, The Partnership for Trust in Government at the Council for Excellence in Government. Available at: http://www.gwu.edu/~ccps/Natlsurvey.pdf

Larson, E. E. (1994). *Recruiting: Help and hope for finding volunteers.* Cincinnati: Standard Pub.

Lawler, E. J. (2001). An affect theory of social exchange. *American Journal of Sociology, 107*(2), 321–352.

Lee, L. (1997). *Change of self-concept in the first year of college life: The effect of gender and community involvement.* (Unpublished doctoral dissertation). University of Wisconsin, Madison, Madison, WI.

Lerner, M. J. (1975). The justice motive in social behavior: Introduction. *Journal of Social Issues, 31*(3), 1–19.

Leslie, L. L., & Ramey, G. (1988). Donor behavior and voluntary support for higher education institutions. *The Journal of Higher Education, 59*(2), 115.

Levi-Strauss, C. (1957/1996). The principle of reciprocity. In A. E. Komter (Ed.), *The gift: An interdisciplinary perspective* (pp. 18–25). Amsterdam: Amsterdam University Press.

Levy, D. C. (1987). A comparison of private and public educational organizations. In W. W. Powell (Ed.), *The nonprofit sector: A research handbook* (1st ed., pp. 258–276). New Haven: Yale University Press.

Levy, N. (2006). Against philanthropy, individual and corporate. In *The kindness of strangers: Philanthropy and higher education* (pp. 159–170). Lanham, MD: Rowman & Littlefield Publishers.

Liao, M.-N. (2008). Applying the marketing concept in higher education. In A. Sargeant & W. Wymer (Eds.), *Routledge companion to nonprofit marketing* (pp. 255–266). London and New York: Routledge.

Liao, M.-N., Foreman, S., & Sargeant, A. (2001). Market versus societal orientation in the nonprofit context. *International Journal of Nonprofit and Voluntary Sector Marketing, 6*(3), 254–268.

Lin, N. (2001). *Social capital: A theory of social structure and action.* London and New York: Cambridge University Press.

Lindahl, W. E., & Winship, C. (1992). Predictive models for annual fundraising and major gift fundraising. *Nonprofit Management and Leadership, 3*(1), 43–64.

Ling, K., Beenen, G., Ludford, P., Wang, X., Chang, K., Li, X., . . . Kraut, R. (2005). Using social psychology to motivate contributions to online communities. *Journal of Computer-Mediated Communication, 10*(4).

Loesssin, B., Duronio, M., Borton, G. (1988). Finding peer institutions for fund-raising comparisons. *Currents, 14*, 37–40.

Logan, R. D. (1985). Youth volunteerism and instrumentality: A commentary, rationale, and proposal. *Nonprofit and Voluntary Sector Quarterly, 14*(1), 45–48.

Lovitts, B. E. (2001). *Leaving the ivory tower: The causes and consequences of departure from doctoral study.* Lanham, MD: Rowman & Littlefield Publishers.

Luthans, F., & Avolio, B. J. (2003). Authentic leadership: A positive developmental approach. In K. Cameron, J. Dutton, & R. Quinn (Eds.), *Positive organizational scholarship: Foundations of a new discipline* (pp. 241–256). San Francisco: Berrett-Koehler.

Madden, C. C. (2008). The promise of marketing in higher education: Where we have been, where we are and where we are going. In A. Sargeant & W. Wymer (Eds.), *Routledge companion to nonprofit marketing* (pp. 280–296). London and New York: Routledge.

Mael, F., & Ashforth, B. E. (1992). Alumni and their alma mater: A partial test of the reformulated model of organizational identification. *Journal of Organizational Behavior, 13*(2), 103–123.

Malinowski, B. (1922/1996). The principle of give and take. In A. E. Komter (Ed.), *The gift: An interdisciplinary perspective* (pp. 15–17). Amsterdam: University of Amsterdam Press.

Mandel Center for Nonprofit Organizations, & Centre for Voluntary Organisation (London School of Economics and Political Science). (1990). *Nonprofit management & leadership.* San Francisco: Jossey-Bass.

Marta, E., & Scabini, E. (2003). *Giovani volontari. (Young volunteers).* Firenze: Giunti.

Martin, M. W. (1994). *Virtuous giving: Philanthropy, voluntary service, and caring.* Bloomington: Indiana University Press.

Maxwell, J. A. (2006). Literature reviews of, and for, educational research: A commentary on Boote and Beile's "Scholars before Researchers." *Educational Researcher, 35*(9), 28–31.

McAlexander, J. H., Koenig, H. F., & Schouten, J. W. (2006). Building relationships of brand community in higher education: A strategic framework for university advancement. *International Journal of Educational Advancement, 6*(2), 107–118.

McGoldrick, W. (1989). Details you should know. In *The president and fund raising* (pp. 160–169). New York: American Council on Education/Macmillan.

McKenna, R. (1991). *Relationship marketing: Successful strategies for the age of the customer.* Reading, MA: Addison-Wesley Pub. Co.

McMurray, A. J., Islam, M., Sarros, J. A., & Pirola-Merlo, A. (2012). The impact of leadership on workgroup climate and performance in a non-profit organization. *Leadership & Organization Development Journal, 33*(6), 522–549.

McMurray, A. J., Pirola-Merlo, A., Sarros, J. A., & Islam, M. (2010). Leadership, climate, psychological capital, commitment, and wellbeing in a non-profit organization. *Leadership & Organization Development Journal, 31*(5), 436–457.

Meer, J. (2008). *The habit of giving.* (Working Paper). Stanford University, Palo Alto, CA.

Meier, A. (1963). *Negro thought in America, 1880–1915: Racial ideologies in the age of Booker T. Washington.* Ann Arbor: University of Michigan Press.

Meredith, M. (2004). Why do universities compete in the ratings game? An empirical analysis of the effects of the *U.S. News and World Report* college rankings. *Research in Higher Education, 45*(5), 443–461.

Merriam, S. B. (2009). *Qualitative research: A guide to design and implementation.* San Francisco: Jossey-Bass.

Meuth, E. (1992). *Corporate philanthropy in American higher education: An investigation of attitudes towards giving* (Doctoral dissertation). University of Akron, Akron, OH.

Middleton, M. (1987). Nonprofit boards of directors: Beyond the governance function. In W. W. Powell (Ed.), *The nonprofit sector: A research handbook* (pp. 141–153). New Haven: Yale University Press.

Midlarsky, E. (1971). Aiding under stress: The effects of competence, dependency, visibility, and fatalism. *Journal of Personality, 39*(1), 132–149.

Milem, J. F., Berger, J. B., & Dey, E. L. (2000). Faculty time allocation: A study of change over twenty years. *The Journal of Higher Education, 71*(4), 454–475.

Miley, W. (1980). Self-awareness and altruism. *Psychological Record, 30*, 3–8.

Miller, D. T. (1977). Personal deserving versus justice for others: An exploration of the justice motive. *Journal of Experimental Social Psychology, 13*(1), 1–13.

Miller, M. (1991). *The college president's role in fund raising.* ERIC (ED337099).

Miller, M. T., & Casebeer, A. L. (1990). *Donor Characteristics of College of Education Alumni: Examining Undergraduate Involvement.* Retrieved from http://eric.ed.gov/?id=ED323836

Miller-Millesen, J. L. (2003). Understanding the behavior of nonprofit boards of directors: A theory-based approach. *Nonprofit and Voluntary Sector Quarterly, 32*, 521–546.

Minor, J. T. (2008). The relationship between selection processes of public trustees and state higher education performance. *Educational Policy, 22*(6), 830–853.

Molm, L. D. (1997). *Coercive power in social exchange*. Cambridge, UK, and New York: Cambridge University Press.

Money, K., Money, A., Downing, S., & Hillebrand, C. (2008). Relationship marketing and the not-for-profit sector: An extension and application of the commitment-trust theory. In A. Sargeant & W. Wymer (Eds.), *Routledge companion to nonprofit marketing* (pp. 28–48). London and New York: Routledge.

Monks, J. (2003). Patterns of giving to one's alma mater among young graduates from selective institutions. *Economics of Education Review, 22*(2), 121–130.

Moore, B. S., & Eisenberg, N. (1984). The development of altruism. In G. Whitehurst (Ed.), *Annals of child development* (pp. 107–174). Greenwich, CT: JAI Press.

Morgan, R. M., & Hunt, S. D. (1994). The commitment-trust theory of relationship marketing. *Journal of Marketing, 58*(3), 20–38.

Morphew, C. (2002). A rose by any other name: Which colleges became universities. *Review of Higher Education, 25*(2), 207–224.

Mortimer, J. T., Finch, M. D., & Kumka, D. (1982). Persistence and change in development: The multidimensional self-concept. *Life-Span Development and Behavior.* Retrieved from http://agris.fao.org/agris-search/search.do?recordID=US201301454576

Mortimer, J. T., Pimentel, E. E., Ryu, S., Nash, K., & Lee, C. (1996). Part-time work and occupational value formation in adolescence. *Social Forces, 74*(4), 1405–1418.

Mosser, J. W. (1993). *Predicting alumni/ae gift-giving behavior: A structural equation model approach* (Ph.D.). Ann Arbor: University of Michigan.

Mount, J. (1996). Why donors give. *Nonprofit Management and Leadership, 7*(1), 3–14.

Muniz, A., Muniz, J., & O'Guinn, T. C. (2001). Brand community. *Journal of Consumer Research, 27*(4), 412–432.

Musick, M. A., & Wilson, J. (2008). *Volunteers: A social profile*. Bloomington: Indiana University Press.

Nakada, L. H. (1993). Student interns: Cultivating the next generation of advancement professionals. In B. Tipsord Todd (Ed.), *Student advancement programs: Shaping tomorrow's leaders today* (pp. 141–146). Washington, DC: Council for Advancement and Support of Education.

Nayman, R. L., Gianneschi, H. R., & Mandel, J. M. (1993). Turning students into alumni donors. In M. C. Terrell & J. A. Gold (Eds.), *New Roles in Educational Fundraising and Institutional Advancement* (pp. 85–94). San Francisco: Jossey-Bass.

Nealon, J. T., & Giroux, S. S. (2012). *The theory toolbox: Critical concepts for the humanities, arts, and social sciences* (2nd ed.). Lanham, MD: Rowman & Littlefield.

Nehls, K. (2008). Presidential transitions during capital campaigns. *International Journal of Educational Advancement, 8*(4), 198–218.

Nettles, M. T., & Millett, C. M. (2006). *Three magic letters: Getting to Ph.D.* Baltimore: Johns Hopkins University Press.

Nicholson, W. D., II. (2007). Leading where it counts: An investigation of the leadership styles and behaviors that define college and university presidents as successful fundraisers. *International Journal of Educational Advancement, 7*(4), 256–270.

Nixon, J. (2004). What is theory? *Educar, 34*, 27–37.

Oakes, P. J., Haslam, S. A., & Turner, J. C. (1994). *Stereotyping and social reality*. Oxford, UK, and Cambridge, MA: Blackwell Publishers.

Oates, B. (2005). *Unleashing youth potential understanding and growing youth participation in philanthropy and volunteerism*. Montreal: McGill University; Saint-Lazare, Quebec: Gibson Library Connections.

Oda, N. (1991). Motives of volunteer works: Self and other oriented motives. *Tohoku Psychologica Folia, 50*, 55–61.

Okunade, A. A. (1996). Graduate school alumni donations to academic funds: Micro-data evidence. *American Journal of Economics and Sociology, 55*(2), 213–229.

Okunade, A. A., & Justice, S. (1991). Micropanel estimates of the life-cycle hypothesis with respect to alumni donations. In *Proceedings of the business and economics statistical section of the American Statistical Association* (pp. 298–305). Alexandria, VA: American Statistical Association.

Okunade, A. A., Wunnava, P. V., & Walsh, R., Jr. (1994). Charitable giving of alumni: Micro-data evidence from a large public university. *American Journal of Economics and Sociology, 53*(1), 73–84.

O'Meara, K. (2007). Striving for what? Exploring the pursuit of prestige. In J. Smart (Ed.), *Higher education: Handbook of theory and research* (Vol. 22, pp. 121–179). New York: Springer.

Omoto, A. M., & Snyder, M. (1990). Basic research in action volunteerism and society's response to AIDS. *Personality and Social Psychology Bulletin, 16*(1), 152–165.

Omoto, A. M., & Snyder, M. (2000). Doing good for self and society: Volunteerism and the psychology of citizen participation. In M. Van Vougt, M. Snyder, T. Tyber, & A. Biel (Eds.), *Cooperation in modern society* (pp. 127–141). London: Modern Society.

Oyserman, D. (2007). Social identity and self-regulation. In A. W. Kruglanski & E. T. Higgins (Eds.), *Social psychology: Handbook of basic principles* (2nd ed., pp. 432–453). New York: Guilford Press.

Oyserman, D. (2008). Racial-ethnic self-schemas: Multidimensional identity-based motivation. *Journal of Research in Personality, 42*(5), 1186–1198.

Oyserman, D. (2009a). Identity-based motivation and consumer behavior. *Journal of Consumer Psychology, 19*(3), 276–279.

Oyserman, D. (2009b). Identity-based motivation: Implications for action-readiness, procedural-readiness, and consumer behavior. *Journal of Consumer Psychology, 19*(3), 250–260.

Oyserman, D., & Destin, M. (2010). Identity-based motivation: implications for intervention. *The Counseling Psychologist, 38*(7), 1001–1043.

Oyserman, D., & Markus, H. R. (1998). Self as social representation. In U. Flick (Ed.), *The psychology of the social* (pp. 107–125). New York: Cambridge University Press.

Palfrey, T. R., & Prisbrey, J. E. (1996). Altruism, reputation and noise in linear public goods experiments. *Journal of Public Economics, 61*(3), 409–427.

Palfrey, T. R., & Prisbrey, J. E. (1997). Anomalous behavior in public goods experiments: How much and why? *American Economic Review, 87*(5), 829–846.

Panas, J. (1984). *Mega gifts: Who gives them, who gets them.* Chicago: Pluribus Press.

Pancer, S. M., & Pratt, M. W. (1999). Social and family determinants of community service involvement in Canadian youth. In M. Yates & J. Youniss (Eds.), *Roots of civic identity: International perspectives on community service and activism in youth* (pp. 32–55). New York: Cambridge University Press.

Pancer, S. M., Pratt, M. W., & Hunsberger, B. (1998). *Community and political involvement in adolescence. What distinguishes the activist from the uninvolved?* Presented at the Seventh Biennial Meeting of the Society for Research in Adolescence, San Diego.

Parsons, Talcott. (1951). *The social system.* Glencoe, IL: Free Press.

Paton, G. J. (1986). Microeconomic perspectives applied to development planning and management. In J. A. Dunn (Ed.), *New directions for institutional research: Enhancing the management of fund raising* (Vol. 51, pp. 17–37). San Francisco: Jossey-Bass.

Pearson, J. (1999). Comprehensive research on alumni relationships: Four years of market research at Stanford University. *New Directions for Institutional Research, 1999*(101), 5–21.

Perkins, L. M. (1981a). *Black Feminism and "Race Uplift," 1890–1900.* Working Paper. Retrieved from http://eric.ed.gov/?id=ED221445

Perkins, L. M. (1981b). Black women and racial "uplift" prior to emancipation. In F. C. Steady (Ed.), *The black woman cross-culturally* (pp. 317–334). Cambridge, MA: Schenkman Publishing.

Pezzullo, T. T., & Brittingham, B. E. (1993). Characteristics of donors. In J. M. Worth (Ed.), *Educational fund raising: Principles and practice* (pp. 31–38). Phoenix: Oryx Press.

Pfeffer, J. (1972). Size, composition, and function of corporate boards of directors: The organization and its environment. *Administrative Science Quarterly, 17*, 218–228.

Pfeffer, J. (1973). Size, composition, and function of hospital boards of directors: A study of organization-environment linkage. *Administrative Science Quarterly, 18*, 349–364.

Pfeffer, J., & Salancik, G. (1978). *The external control of organizations: A resource dependence perspective.* New York: Harper & Row.

Pickett, W. L. (1986). Fund raising effectiveness and donor motivation. In W. A. Rowland (Ed.), *Handbook of institutional advancement* (pp. 231–239). San Francisco: Jossey-Bass.

Piliavin, J. A., & Charng, H. (1990). Altruism: A review of recent theory and research. *Annual Review of Sociology, 16*, 27–65.

Piliavin, J. A., Dovidio, J. F., Gaertner, S. L., & Clark, R. D., III. (1981). *Emergency intervention*. New York: Academic Press.

Piliavin, J. A., Grube, J. A., & Callero, P. L. (2002). Role as resource for action in public service. *Journal of Social Issues, 58*(3), 469–485.

Powell, W. W. (Ed.). (1987). *The nonprofit sector: A research handbook*. New Haven: Yale University Press.

Powell, W. W., & Steinberg, R. (Eds.). (2006). *The nonprofit sector: A research handbook* (2nd ed.). New Haven: Yale University Press.

Primavera, J. (1999). The unintended consequences of volunteerism. *Journal of Prevention & Intervention in the Community, 18*(1–2), 125–140.

Proper, E. (2011). *The outcomes of board involvement in fundraising at independent, four-year colleges: An organization theory perspective* (Doctoral dissertation). Vanderbilt University, Nashville, TN.

Purpura, M. (1980). Building the alumni habit. In V. Carter & P. A. Alberger (Eds.), *Building your alumni programs: The best of CASE Currents*. Washington, DC: Council for Advancement and Support of Education.

Putnam, R. D. (2000). *Bowling alone: The collapse and revival of American community*. New York: Simon & Schuster.

Ramos, H. A. (1999). Latina/o philanthropy: Expanding U.S. models of giving and civic participation. In *Cultures of caring* (pp. 147–187). Washington, DC: Council on Foundations.

Ramos, H. A., & Kasper, G. (2000). *Building a tradition of Latino philanthropy: Hispanics as donors, grantees, grant makers, and volunteers*. Los Angeles: Center on Philanthropy and Public Policy, University of Southern California.

Randolph, J. J. (2009). A guide to writing the dissertation literature review. *Practical Assessment, Research & Evaluation, 14*(13), 1–13.

Reck, W. E. (1976). *The changing world of college relations: History and philosophy, 1917–1975*. Washington: Council for Advancement and Support of Education.

Ribar, D. C., & Wilhelm, M. O. (2002). Altruistic and joy-of-giving motivations in charitable behavior. *Journal of Political Economy, 110*(2), 425–457.

Riesman, D. (1956). *Constraint and variety in American education*. Lincoln: University of Nebraska Press.

Riggio, R. E., Bass, B. M., & Orr, S. S. (2004). Transformational leadership in nonprofit organizations. In R. E. Riggio & S. S. Orr (Eds.), *Improving leadership in nonprofit organizations* (pp. 49–62). San Francisco: Jossey-Bass.

Rivas-Vásquez, A. G. (1999). New pools of Latino wealth: A case study of donors and potential donors in U.S. Hispanic/Latino communities. In W. A. Diaz & H. A. J. Ramos (Eds.), *Nuevos senderos: Reflections on Hispanics and philanthropy* (pp. 115–138). Houston: Arte Público Press.

Roberts, R. D. (1984). A positive model of private charity and public transfers. *Journal of Political Economy, 92*(1), 136–148.

Rocco, T. S., & Plakhotnik, M. S. (2009). Literature reviews, conceptual frameworks, and theoretical frameworks: Terms, functions, and distinctions. *Human Resource Development Review, 8*(1), 120–130.

Rodriguez, C. (1991). *Alumni and the president: Presidential leadership behavior affecting alumni giving at small private liberal arts colleges* (Doctoral dissertation). Union Institute, Cincinnati, OH.

Ronquillo, J. C. (2011). Servant, transformational, and transactional leadership. In K. A. Agard (Ed.), *Leadership in nonprofit organizations: A reference handbook* (pp. 345–353). Thousand Oaks, CA: Sage.

Roof, W. C., & McKinney, W. (1987). *American mainline religion: Its changing shape and future*. New Brunswick, NJ: Rutgers University Press.

Rooney, P., Brown, E., & Mesch, D. (2007). Who decides in giving to education? A study of charitable giving by married couples. *International Journal of Educational Advancement, 7*(3), 229–242.

Rosenhan, D. L. (1970). The natural socialization of altruistic autonomy. In J. Macauley & L. Berkowitz (Eds.), *Altruism and helping behavior*, (pp. 251–268). New York: Academic Press.

Rosenhan, D. L. (1973). The natural socialization of altruistic autonomy. In J. Macauley & L. Berkowitz (Eds.), *Altruism and help behavior* (pp. 98–120). New York: Academic Press.

Rosenhan, D. L. (1978). Toward resolving the altruism paradox: Affect self-reinforcement and cognition. In L. Wispe (Ed.), *Altruism, sympathy, and helping* (pp. 101–113). New York: Academic Press.

Rushton, J. P. (1975). Generosity in children: Immediate and long-term effects of modeling, preaching, and moral judgment. *Journal of Personality and Social Psychology, 31*(3), 459–466.

Rushton, J. P. (1982). Social learning theory and the development of prosocial behavior. In N. Eisenberg (Ed.), *The development of prosocial behavior* (pp. 77–108). New York: Academic Press.

Sargeant, A., Ford, J. B., & Hudson, J. (2008). Charity brand personality: The relationship with giving behavior. *Nonprofit and Voluntary Sector Quarterly, 37*(3), 468–491.

Sargeant, A., Ford, J. B., & West, D. C. (2006). Perceptual determinants of nonprofit giving behavior. *Journal of Business Research, 59*(2), 155–165.

Sargeant, A., Hudson, J., & West, D. C. (2008). Conceptualizing brand values in the charity sector: The relationship between sector, cause and organization. *The Service Industries Journal, 28*(5), 615–632.

Sargeant, A., & Lee, S. (2002). Individual and contextual antecedents of donor trust in the voluntary sector. *Journal of Marketing Management, 18*(7–8), 779–802.

Sargeant, A., & Lee, S. (2004a). Donor trust and relationship commitment in the U.K. charity sector: The impact on behavior. *Nonprofit and Voluntary Sector Quarterly, 33*(2), 185–202.

Sargeant, A., & Lee, S. (2004b). Trust and relationship commitment in the United Kingdom voluntary sector: Determinants of donor behavior. *Psychology and Marketing, 21*(8), 613–635.

Sargeant, A., & McKenzie, J. (1998). *A lifetime of giving: An analysis of donor lifetime value.* (Research Report No. 4). Kings Hill, Kent, England: Charities Aid Foundation.

Sargeant, A., & Woodliffe, L. (2005). The antecedents of donor commitment to voluntary organizations. *Nonprofit Management and Leadership, 16*(1), 61–78.

Satterwhite, C. (2004). *The function of university presidents and CEOs in fundraising: A study of public universities with capital campaigns less than $100 million* (Doctoral dissertation). Texas Tech University, Lubbock, TX.

Scabini, E., & Rossi, G., Università Cattolica del Sacro Cuore, & Centro Studi e Ricerche Sulla Famiglia. (1997). *Giovani in famiglia tra autonomia e nuove dipendenze / Rossi, Giovanna.* Milano: Vita e pensiero.

Schervish, P. G. (1993). Taking giving seriously. In P. Dean (Ed.), *Taking giving seriously* (pp. 11–42). Indianapolis: Indiana University Center on Philanthropy.

Schervish, P. G. (1995). Passing it on: The transmission of wealth and financial care. In P. G. Schervish & V. A. Hodgkinson (Eds.), *Care and community in modern society: Passing on the tradition of service to future generations* (pp. 109–133). San Francisco: Jossey-Bass.

Schervish, P. G. (2003). *Inclination, obligation, and association: What we know and what we need to learn about donor motivations.* Presented at the Association for the Study of Higher Education, Boston.

Schervish, P. G., & Havens, J. J. (1997). Social participation and charitable giving: A multivariate analysis. *Voluntas: International Journal of Voluntary and Nonprofit Organizations, 8*(3), 235–260.

Schroeder, D. A., Penner, L. A., Dovidio, J. F., & Piliavin, J. A. (1995). *The psychology of helping and altruism: Problems and puzzles.* New York: McGraw-Hill.

Schwartz, S., & Ben David, A. (1976). Responsibility and helping in an emergency: Effects of blame, ability and denial of responsibility. *Sociometry, 39*(4), 406.

Schwarz, N. (2007). Attitude construction: Evaluation in context. *Social Cognition, 25*(5), 638–656.

Schwarz, N. (2010). Meaning in context: Meta-cognitive experiences. In L. F. Barrett, B. Mesquita, & E. Smith (Eds.), *The mind in context* (pp. 105–125). New York: Guilford Press.

Seashore, S. (1983). A framework for an integrated model of organizational effectiveness. In K. Cameron & D. Whetten (Eds.), *Organizational effectiveness: A comparison of multiple models* (pp. 55–70). Orlando, FL: Academic Press.

Segal, L. M. (1993). *Four essays on the supply of volunteer labor and econometrics* (Ph.D.). Northwestern University, Evanston, IL.

Shang, J., Reed, A., & Croson, R. (2008). Identity congruency effects on donations. *Journal of Marketing Research, 45*, 351–361.

Shanley, M. G. (1985). Student, faculty and staff involvement in institutional advancement: University of South Carolina. *Carolina View, 1*, 40–43.

Shapiro, S. L., & Ridinger, L. L. (2011). An analysis of donor involvement, gender, and giving in college athletics. *Sport Marketing Quarterly, 20*(1), 22–32.

Shavelson, R. J., & Bolus, R. (1982). Self-concept: The interplay of theory and methods. *Journal of Educational Psychology, 74*(1), 3–17.

Shavelson, R. J., Hubner, J. J., & Stanton, G. C. (1976). Self-concept: Validation of construct interpretations. *Review of Educational Research, 46*(3), 407–441.

Siddiq, K., Meyer, E., & Ashleigh, M. (2013). What is the impact of authentic leadership on leader accountability in a non-profit context? In *Proceedings of the International Conference on Management, Leadership, & Governance*. Kidmore End: Academic Conferences International Limited.

Simmel, G. (1908/1996). Faithfulness and gratitude. In A. E. Komter (Ed.), *The gift: An interdisciplinary perspective* (pp. 39–48). Amsterdam: University of Amsterdam Press.

Simmons, R. G. (1991). Presidential address on altruism and sociology. *Sociological Quarterly, 32*(1), 1–22.

Skelly, M. (1991). College presidents as fund raisers. *School and College*, (August), 28–29.

Slinker, J. (1988). *The role of the college or university president in institutional advancement* (Doctoral dissertation). Northern Arizona University, Flagstaff, AZ.

Smart, J. C. (2007). *Higher education: Handbook of theory and research*. Dordrecht: Springer.

Smith, B., Shue, S., Vest, J. L., & Villarreal, J. (1999). *Philanthropy in communities of color*. Bloomington: Indiana University Press.

Smith, B. M. M., & Nelson, L. (1975). Personality correlates of helping behavior. *Psychological Reports, 37*, 307–310.

Smith, C. L., Gelfand, D. M., Hartmann, D. P., & Partlow, M. E. Y. (1979). Children's causal attributions regarding help giving. *Child Development, 50*(1), 203–210.

Smith, D. H. (1975). Voluntary action and voluntary groups. *Annual Review of Sociology, 1*, 247–270.

Smith, D. H., & Baldwin, B. R. (1974). Parental socialization, socioeconomic status, and volunteer organization participation. *Nonprofit and Voluntary Sector Quarterly, 3*(3–4), 59–66.

Smith, E. R, & Semin, G. (2004). Socially situated cognition: Cognition in its social context. *Advances in Experimental Social Psychology, 36*, 53–117.

Smith, E. R., & Semin, G. R. (2007). Situated social cognition. *Current Directions in Psychological Science, 16*(3), 132–135.

Smith, G. (1986). The chief executive and advancement. In A. Rowland (Ed.), *Handbook of institutional advancement* (2nd ed., pp. 697–705). San Francisco: Jossey-Bass.

Smith, J. M. (2013). Philanthropic identity at work: Employer influences on the charitable giving attitudes and behaviors of employees. *Journal of Business Communication, 50*(2), 128–151.

Spaeth, J. L., & Greeley, A. M. (1970). *Recent alumni and higher education: A survey of college graduates*. New York: McGraw-Hill.

Spears, L. C. (2010). Practicing servant-leadership. In J. L. Perry (Ed.), *The Jossey-Bass reader on nonprofit and public leadership* (pp. 116–123). San Francisco: Jossey-Bass.

Steinberg, R., & Wilhelm, M. (2003a). *Giving: The Next Generation—Parental Effects on Donations*. Working Paper No. CPNS 21. Indianapolis: Center on Philanthropy at Indiana University. Retrieved from http://eprints.qut.edu.au/49980/

Steinberg, R., & Wilhelm, M. (2003b). Tracking giving across generations. *New Directions for Philanthropic Fundraising, 2003*(42), 71–82.

Steinberg, R. S. (1987). Voluntary donations and public expenditures in a federal system. *American Economic Review, 77*(1), 24–36.

Steinberg, R. S. (2010). Principal–agent theory and nonprofit accountability. In K. Hopt & T. Von Hippel (Eds.), *Comparative corporate governance of non-profit organizations* (pp. 73–125). Cambridge, UK: Cambridge University Press.

Stensaker, B., & Norgård, J. D. (2001). Innovation and isomorphism: A case study of university identity struggle 1969–1999. *Higher Education, 42*, 473–492.

Stover, W. S. (1930). *Alumni stimulation by the American college president*. New York: Teachers College, Columbia University.

Sturgis, R. (2006). Presidential leadership in institutional advancement: From the perspective of the president and vice president of institutional advancement. *International Journal of Educational Advancement, 6*(3), 221–231.

Sugden, R. (1982). On the economics of philanthropy. *Economic Journal, 92*(366), 341–350.

Sugden, R. (1984). Reciprocity: The supply of public goods through voluntary contributions. *Economic Journal, 94*(376), 772–787.

Sun, X., Hoffman, S. C., & Grady, M. L. (2007). A multivariate causal model of alumni giving: Implications for alumni fundraisers. *International Journal of Educational Advancement, 7*(4), 307–332.

Sundeen, R. A., & Raskoff, S. A. (1994). Volunteering among teenagers in the United States. *Nonprofit and Voluntary Sector Quarterly, 23*(4), 383–403.

Tajfel, H. (1970). Experiments in intergroup discrimination. *Scientific American, 223*(5), 96–102.

Tajfel, H. (Ed.). (1978). *Differentiation between social groups: Studies in the social psychology of intergroup relations.* Oxford: Academic Press.

Tajfel, H., & Turner, J. C. (1979). An integrative theory of intergroup conflict. In S. Worchel & W. G. Austin (Eds.), *The social psychology of intergroup relations* (pp. 33–47). Monterey, CA: Brooks/Cole.

Tajfel, H., & Turner, J. C. (1986). The social identity theory of intergroup behavior. In S. Worchel & W. G. Austin (Eds.), *The psychology of intergroup relations* (pp. 7–24). Chicago: Nelson-Hall.

Taylor, A. L., & Martin, J. C., Jr. (1993). *Predicting alumni giving at a public research university.* Presented at the Annual Forum of the Association for Institutional Research, Chicago.

Taylor, J. S., & Machado, M. (2008). Governing boards in public higher education institutions: A perspective from the United States. *Tertiary Education and Management, 14*(3), 243–260.

Thelin, J. R. (2011). *A history of American higher education.* Baltimore: Johns Hopkins University Press.

Tierney, J. P., & Branch, A. Y. (1992). *College students as mentors for at-risk youth: A study of six campus partners in learning programs.* Philadelphia: Public/Private Ventures.

Triandis, H. C. (1989). The self and social behavior in differing cultural contexts. *Psychological Review, 96*(3), 506–520.

Triandis, H. C. (1995). *Individualism & collectivism* (Vol. xv). Boulder, CO: Westview Press.

Truell, A. D. (2001). Marketing. In B. S. Kaliski (Ed.), *Encyclopedia of business and finance.* New York: Macmillan Reference USA.

Trulear, H. D. (2009). Philanthropy and religion. In R. M. Jackson (Ed.), *A philanthropic covenant with Black America.* Hoboken, NY: John Wiley & Sons.

Tsiotsou, R. (2006). Investigating differences between female and male athletic donors: A comparative study. *International Journal of Nonprofit and Voluntary Sector Marketing, 11*(3), 209–223.

Tsunoda, K. (2010). Asian American giving to US higher education. *International Journal of Educational Advancement, 10*(1), 2–23.

Tsunoda, K. (2011). *Unraveling the myths of Chinese American giving: Exploring donor motivations and effective fundraising strategies for U.S. higher education* (Ph.D.). University of Maryland, College Park.

Tsunoda, K. (2013). Chinese American philanthropy: Cultural contexts behind major gifts in higher education. In N. Drezner (Ed.), *Expanding the donor base in higher education: Engaging non-traditional donors* (pp. 40–58). New York: Routledge.

Turner, J. C. (1978). Social categorization and social discrimination in the minimal group paradigm. In H. Tajfel (Ed.), *Differentiation between social groups* (pp. 101–140). New York: Academic Press.

Turner, J. C. (1987). *Rediscovering the social group: Self-categorization theory.* Oxford and New York: Blackwell.

Turner, J. C. (1999). Some current issues in research on social identity and self-categorization theories. In N. Ellemers, R. Spears, & B. Doosje (Eds.), *Social identity* (pp. 6–34). Oxford: Blackwell.

Turner, J. C., & Oakes, P. J. (1986). The significance of the social identity concept for social psychology with reference to individualism, interactionism and social influence. *British Journal of Social Psychology, 25*(3), 237–252.

Turner, J. C., & Reynolds, K. J. (2010). The story of social identity. In T. Postmes & N. Branscombe (Eds.), *Rediscovering social identity: Key readings* (pp. 13–32). New York: Psychology Press.

Uslaner, E. M. (2002). *The moral foundations of trust.* Cambridge and New York: Cambridge University Press.

Van Nostrand, I. (1999). Young alumni programming. In J. A. Feudo (Ed.), *Alumni relations: A newcomer's guide to success* (pp. 127–136). Washington, DC: Council for Advancement and Support of Education.

Van Puyvelde, S., Caers, R., Du Bois, C., & Jegers, M. (2011). The governance of nonprofit organizations: Integrating agency theory with stakeholder and stewardship theories. *Nonprofit and Voluntary Sector Quarterly, 41*, 431–451.

Venable, B. T., Rose, G. M., Bush, V. D., & Gilbert, F. W. (2005). The role of brand personality in charitable giving: An assessment and validation. *Academy of Marketing Science Journal, 33*(3), 295–312.

Vesterlund, L. (2004). Why do people give? In W. W. Powell & R. Steinberg (Eds.), *The nonprofit sector: A research handbook* (2nd ed., pp. 568–590). New Haven: Yale University Press.

Wade, J. C. (1998). Male reference group identity dependence: A theory of male identity. *The Counseling Psychologist, 26*(3), 349–383.

Walton, A. (Ed.). (2005). *Women and philanthropy in education.* Bloomington: Indiana University Press.

Warr, P. G. (1982). Pareto optimal redistribution and private charity. *Journal of Public Economics, 19*(1), 131–138.

Warr, P. G. (1983). The private provision of a public good is independent of the distribution of income. *Economics Letters, 13*(2–3), 207–211.

Warren, P. E., & Walker, I. (1991). Empathy, effectiveness and donations to charity: Social psychology's contribution. *British Journal of Social Psychology, 30*(4), 325–337.

Weidner, D. (2008). Fundraising tips for deans with intermediate development programs. *University of Toledo Law Review, 39*(2), 393–398.

West, D. (1983). The presidency of a small college. In A. Falander & J. Merson (Eds.), *Management techniques for small and specialized institutions* (pp. 11–24). San Francisco: Jossey-Bass.

Weyant, J. M., & Smith, S. L. (1987). Getting more by asking for less: The effects of request size on donations of charity. *Journal of Applied Social Psychology, 17*(4), 392–400.

Wicklund, R. A., & Gollwitzer, P. M. (1981). Symbolic self-completion, attempted influence, and self-deprecation. *Basic and Applied Social Psychology, 2*(2), 89–114.

Wilhelm, M. O., Brown, E., Rooney, P. M., & Steinberg, R. (2008). The intergenerational transmission of generosity. *Journal of Public Economics, 92*(10–11), 2146–2156.

Willmer, W. (1993). Blueprint for a small college: Ten building blocks for strong advancement in challenging times. *Currents (Washington, DC), 19*(9), 36–40.

Wilson, E. O. (1975). *Sociobiology: The new synthesis.* Cambridge, MA: Belknap Press of Harvard University Press.

Wilson, J., & Musick, M. (1997). Who cares? Toward an integrated theory of volunteer work. *American Sociological Review, 62*(5), 694–713.

Wilson, J., & Musick, M. (1998). The contribution of social resources to volunteering. *Social Science Quarterly, 79*(4), 799–814.

Winfree, W., III. (1989). *The role of persons other than professional development staff in the solicitation of major gifts from private individuals for senior colleges and universities* (Doctoral dissertation). University of North Texas, Denton.

Winniford, J. C., Stanley, D., & Grider, C. (1995). An analysis of the traits and motivations of college students involved in service organizations. *Journal of College Student Development, 36*(1), 27–38.

Winship, A., II. (1984). *The quest for major gifts: A survey of 68 institutions.* Washington, DC: Council for Advancement and Support of Education.

Winston, G. (2000). *The positional arms race in higher education* (Discussion Paper No. 54). WPEHE discussion paper series/Williams College, Williams Project on the Economics of Higher Education.

Winterich, K. P., Mittal, V., & Ross, W. T., Jr. (2009). Donation behavior toward in-groups and out-groups: The role of gender and moral identity. *Journal of Consumer Research, 36*(2), 199–214.

W. K. Kellogg Foundation. (2012). *Cultures of giving: Energizing and expanding philanthropy by and for communities of color.* Battle Creek, MI: W. K. Kellogg Foundation.

Wollebaek, D., & Selle, P. (2002). Does participation in voluntary associations contribute to social capital? The impact of intensity, scope, and type. *Nonprofit and Voluntary Sector Quarterly, 31*(1), 32–61.

Wunnava, P. V., & Lauze, M. A. (2001). Alumni giving at a small liberal arts college: Evidence from consistent and occasional donors. *Economics of Education Review, 20*(6), 533–543.

Wuthnow, R. (1995). *Learning to care: Elementary kindness in an age of indifference.* New York: Oxford University Press.

Yates, M., & Youniss, J. (1996a). Community service and political-moral identity in adolescents. *Journal of Research on Adolescence (Lawrence Erlbaum), 6*(3), 271–284.

Yates, M., & Youniss, J. (1996b). A developmental perspective on community service in adolescence. *Social Development, 5*(1), 85–111.

Yates, M., & Youniss, J. (Eds.). (1999). *Roots of civic identity: International perspectives on community service and activism in youth.* Cambridge?and New York: Cambridge University Press.

Young, P. S., & Fischer, N. M. (1996). *Identifying undergraduate and post-college characteristics that may affect alumni giving.* Presented at the Annual Forum of the Association for Institutional Research, Albuquerque, NM.

Youniss, J., & Yates, M. (1997). *Community service and social responsibility in youth.* Chicago: University of Chicago Press.

Yukl, G. (1999). An evaluation of conceptual weaknesses in transformational and charismatic leadership theories. *The Leadership Quarterly, 10*(2), 285–305.

INDEX

National Negro Conference 98
National Pre-Alumni Council (NPAC) 86, 88
National Survey of Giving and Volunteering 4, 11
Nayman, R. L. 14, 87
Neumann, A. 66
New Directions in Philanthropic Fundraising 106, 108
New England's First Fruits 103
Nissan, L. 10, 11, 13
Nixon, J. xiii
nongovernmental organizations (NGOs) 3
Nonprofit and Voluntary Sector Quarterly xii
Nonprofit Management and Leadership xii
Nonprofit Organizations: Theory, Management, Policy xii
Norgård, J. D. 45, 46

O'Connell, D. J. 62
The Ohio State University 70
The Ohio State University Development Fund Association 38
O'Meara, K. 46
organizational citizenship 62–4
organizational culture 29, 61
organizational identification 7–9
Organizational Leadership Assessment 64
out-group 91
Oyserman, Daphna 94, 95

peer review publications 104–6
personal donorship 9
Peter, K. 85
Pfeffer, J. 42
philanthropic modeling 10–1; reinforcement 13–15
philanthropy xiv; future research 87; youth 85–7
Pirola-Merlo, 61, 69
Powell, W. W. 43, 44; *The Nonprofit Sector* xii
Prairie View A&M University 88–9
private-good model 3–5; identification model 3–5; impact philanthropy model 5
Proper, E. 39, 40, 50, 104, 106, 107
ProQuest Dissertations and Theses 107
prosocial behavior 9
psychological capital 61
public-good 2–3; selflessness 2
publishing 108–9; *see also* dissertation research; peer review publications
Putnam, R. D.: *Bowling Alone* 81

race in philanthropy 98, 99
racial uplift 98–9
Ramey, G. 8
rational utilitarianism theory 3
Reed, A. 96, 99
reciprocity theory 4, 23, 31
relationship marketing 5–6, 25–6; antecedents of relationship commitment 26; building and testing 27–9; outcomes of relationship commitment 26; theory 27–8
religious participation 4, 10, 11–12, 31, 61, 62, 64, 69, 77, 80

Rensselaer Polytechnic Institute 70
research: advancement 103–9; dissertation 106–8; future 15, 31, 50, 58–9, 87, 102, 109
resource dependency theory 42, 48–9, 50
resource theory 78, 80
Riesman, D. 46
Roberts, R. D. 2, 3, 5
Rockefeller Philanthropy Advisors 97
Rodin, S. 61
role of wealth in philanthropy 99
Rooney, P. M. 12, 85
Rose, G. M. 29
Rosenhan, D. L. 11
Ross, W. T., Jr. 100

Salancik, G. 42
Sargeant, A. 5, 27, 28, 30
Sarros, J. A. 61, 69
Sax, l. J. 85, 86
Schervish, P. G. 3, 4, 11
Schouten, J. W. 30
Schroeder, D. A. 83
Schwartz, Jonathan 16
Segal, L. M. 77
self-categorization theory 93, 94, 102
selflessness 2
Seligman, Joel 16
servant leadership 62–4
Servant Leadership Assessment Instrument 64
sexual orientation and gender identity 100–1
Shang, J. 96, 99, 100
shared leadership 60, 65–7, 69; team building 66
Sherkat, D. E. 12
Siddiq, K. 65
Simmel, G. 24
Smart, J. C.: *Higher Education: Handbook of Theory and Research* xii
Smith, D. H. 77; *Annual Review of Sociology* xi
Smith, J. Mize 101
Smith College 23
Snyder, M. 2, 83
Snydman, Stuart: *The Nonprofit Sector* xii
social capital theory 42, 43
social exchange theory 5, 6, 9, 24, 28, 29
social identity theory xiv–xv, 91–102; categorization stage 91, 92; future research 102; identity-based motivation model 94–6, 99, 102; individual mobility 93; in-group 91, 93, 100; interpersonal-intergroup continuum 92; multiple and intersecting identities 96–7; and organizational identification 7–9; out-group 91; positive distinctiveness 92–3; self-categorization theory 93, 94, 102; social comparison 91; social identity, self-categorization, and identity-based motivation theories 97–101
social integration theory 80–1
socialization theory 80–1, 83
social justice modeling 11
social psychological perspectives 5–10; justice motivation theory 9; modeling theories 10; personal donorship 9;